BETTER TOGETHER

Restoring the American Community

Robert D. Putnam
and
Lewis M. Feldstein

with Don Cohen

Simon & Schuster

NEW YORK LONDON TORONTO
SYDNEY SINGAPORE

SIMON & SCHUSTER
Rockefeller Center
1230 Avenue of the Americas
New York, NY 10020

For information regarding special discounts for bulk purchases,
please contact Simon & Schuster Special Sales at
1-800-456-6798 or business@simonandschuster.com

Manufactured in the United States of America

1   3   5   7   9   10   8   6   4   2

"Above All" by Paul Baloche and Lenny LeBlanc © 1999 Integrity's
Hosanna! Music/ASCAP and LenSongs Publishing/ASCAP

Library of Congress Cataloging-in-Publication Data
Putnam, Robert D.
Better together : restoring the American community / Robert D. Putnam and
Lewis M. Feldstein ; with Don Cohen.
p.   cm.
Includes index.
ISBN 0-7432-3546-0
1. United States—Social conditions—1945–   2. Social change—United States—
History—20th century.   I. Feldstein, Lewis M.   II. Cohen, Don, 1946–   III. Title.
HN65.P877   2003
306'.0973—dc21   2003054220

To Lara and Jonathan
To Sarah, Rushi, and Robert
Whose lives teach their fathers

Acknowledgments

Like its subject, this book is the product of many hands.

It was as part of the Saguaro Seminar on Civic Engagement in America that we first examined the promising efforts that built and applied social capital to extract the lessons on how to do this work. The Saguaro Seminar was a gathering of leading thinkers and activists from many fields who for three years collaborated to develop a national agenda to build social capital. The participants in that seminar are listed individually in the seminar's final report, "Better Together: Report of the Saguaro Seminar on Civic Engagement in America" (available at bettertogether.org). We are deeply grateful to them all for their invaluable contributions to our thinking about these issues and for their friendship. We are indebted as well to the many foundations that supported our work during this period, notably the Carnegie Corporation of New York, the Ford Foundation, the Lilly Endowment, Inc., the John D. and Catherine T. MacArthur Foundation, the Charles Stewart Mott Foundation, the Pew Charitable Trusts, the Bernard and Audre Rapoport Foundation, the Rockefeller Foundation, the Surdna Foundation, and the Lila Wallace–Reader's Digest Fund and to the thirty-five community foundations that underwrote and partnered with us on the Social Capital Community Benchmark Survey.

Robert D. Putnam's *Bowling Alone* reviewed the vast body of evidence of declining social capital in America, but as we turned to the task of civic renewal, we recognized the value of highlighting some of the exceptional cases in which creative social entrepreneurs were moving against the nationwide tide and creating vibrant new forms of social connectedness. We selected each case study in this book from scores of alternatives from across the United States. The difficulty that we faced in choosing a single case illustrated the richness and diversity of first-rate work in building social capital.

First and most important among our collaborators on this book is Don Cohen. Don did much of the field research and most of the actual writing of the case studies, and he played an important role at all stages in the book from identifying cases to checking facts to extracting broader lessons. Don's intelligence, sensitivity, and eye for telling detail are evident throughout the book. These cases are often complex stories with competing themes and a narrative thread that is not always easily identified. That each of the case studies is a good read, telling a compelling story while at the same time illustrating how social capital is built and applied in each setting, was Don's singular contribution. Don's accomplishment is all the more remarkable in that he was working under a challenging deadline.

Sara Hallman was our researcher extraordinaire. Sara functioned as the team's reconnaissance arm, identifying a large pool of possible cases in a given field such as faith-based social capital building, or the role of government, or youth-based programs and then, once we had distilled the list, profiling each of the competing cases, identifying other relevant research on the cases, and framing the choices for us on the significance to be derived from each case on how to build social capital. Sara produced a huge volume of work and research and showed great analytic ability in discerning the social-capital issues inherent in each of the cases.

Tom Sander, Executive Director of the Saguaro Seminar, was "of counsel" to us throughout the process. Tom sat in on virtually all of the planning meetings, read the drafts, and provided pointed, thoughtful commentary on the substantive issues and offered leads to further research and suggestions on possible cases and related readings. At many times during our work Tom's deep knowledge of the social-capital field, the literature, and the issues was critical. There are few people in the country who know the field as well as Tom, and the book benefited immensely by his counsel.

Lois Shea joined the project when it was already well under way. A former reporter for the *Boston Globe,* where she had done some of the best writing in the nation among daily reporters on social capital, Lois conducted supplemental interviews in certain cases—Saddleback, Dudley Street, and the Harvard Union of Clerical and Technical Workers—to bring a richer texture to the cases and help amplify the social-capital lessons.

Lara Putnam (for many years Robert Putnam's most constructively critical intellectual collaborator and now a serious scholar in her own right) made major contributions both to the framing and to the drafting of the conclusion. We are especially grateful to her for reminding us of the larger issues of context that had been left implicit in the individual cases.

In addition to the contributions of Don Cohen, Sara Hallman, and Tom Sander, many insights into the lessons to be drawn from the case studies came from Putnam's research assistants at Cambridge University (England)—Amy Bates, George Georgiadis, Pedro Ramos Pinto, Nir Tsuk, and Catherine Wreyford.

Louise Kennedy, Karena Cronin, and Arja Neukam provided the key administrative support that held all of the moving parts on this team together amid competing schedules and work pressures. Because they have worked so closely with us over the years on issues of social capital and civic renewal, we have also benefited from their substantive insights as they spotted unasked questions and unnoticed answers.

Bob Bender, our editor at Simon & Schuster, joined us at the very beginning of the project. He quickly grasped the key elements and the larger story. In providing us with steadying and corrective counsel throughout, Bob had the lovely ability never to surrender his opinion, even when it challenged our writing, but to frame his comments in such a way that we could hear them and take them in. For editorial and other help at Simon & Schuster, we are also grateful to Janet Fletcher.

Rafe Sagalyn, our talented literary agent, played an even more important role in this project: Both the basic conception of the book and its title were his ideas. We are deeply grateful to Rafe, not only for his professional and intellectual contributions, but also for his unflagging personal support.

Lew Feldstein had the great joy and benefit of writing this book nurtured by the experience, savvy, and thoughtfulness of his gifted New Hampshire Charitable Foundation colleagues, who every day do superb work building New Hampshire's communities. He was blessed by the wonderful encouragement throughout of Mary McGowan, who waited many a dinner and whose support never stayed her judgment and counsel.

Bob Putnam continues to marvel at the extraordinary support, wisdom, and friendship of Tom Sander and Karena Cronin of the Saguaro Seminar. On this book, as on our prior projects, they contributed ideas, energy, and good cheer. Rosemary Putnam, Bob's wife and best friend for forty years, endured absence and absent-mindedness and offered affection and good advice.

For eight years the two of us have worked together on a rich mix of projects—the Saguaro Seminar, the nationwide Social Capital Community Benchmark Survey, the Grassroots Civic Labs plan, and now this book. Our collaboration continues to be among the most rewarding of our lives. Each of us considers the other a *mensch.*

Beyond this immediate team has been a rich network of individuals across the country. These colleagues helped us to identify and evaluate cases, to understand and interpret the work going on, and to draw lessons from what we were seeing; and they challenged our analysis in some instances. The study of social capital is relatively new. The work that identifies the impact of social capital has advanced more rapidly than the understanding of how social capital is built. Although we have discussed here some of the lessons that we draw from the cases we covered and others considered but not fully developed in the text, there is less science and more judgment in our articulating the elements of successful efforts to build social capital. As the research continues and the field matures, observers will gain far greater skill in distinguishing the elements that make a difference. We will get far better at illuminating the elements within the black box that is the process of building social capital. At this juncture, though, it has been our judgment and that of the many colleagues and observers listed below that have guided our work. While we take full responsibility ourselves for our conclusions, we express our immense appreciation to the many below with whom we talked as we assembled this book. We apologize to any whom we have inadvertently omitted. There is a great army of committed, smart practitioners and thinkers who grasp the centrality of social capital and willingly gave their time and counsel to us in this work.

Leith Anderson, Robb and Julie Ball, John Barros, Bo Beaulieu, John Borstel, Xavier de Souza Briggs, Marco Briolini, Margot Burke, Hodding Carter, Greg Chaille, Teri Dari, Mary Dempsey, Judy Donovan, Ros Everdell, Newell Flather, Marc Freedman, Pat Frey, David Goldstein, Vaughn Grisham, Matthew Heyd, Jane Hirshberg, Shannon Johnson, Steve Johnson, Steven Reed Johnson, Linda Kaboolian, Liz Lerman, Margaret Levi, Robert Liberty, May Louie, Dan McMackin, Mark Moore, Michael Moore, Ziad Munson, Craig Newmark, Nancy Pearl, George Pennick, Anne Peterson, Forrest Reinhardt, Mike Roach, Kris Rondeau, Ethan Seltzer, Dennis Shirley, Rick Siefert, Brad Smith, John Sommerville, Bob Stacy, Anne Taylor, Robert Tietze, Sam Verhovek, Mark Warren, Anthony Welch, Don Wofford, David Wood, Lynn Youngbar, Arnold Zack.

Contents

BETTER TOGETHER

Introduction

In *Better Together*, we invite you to join us on a journey around the United States. You will visit big cities, suburbs, and small towns and meet people engaged in a wide variety of activities. You will see bustling branch libraries in Chicago and an evangelical church in southern California that attracts more than 45,000 members, a middle school in a small town in Wisconsin where sixth-graders develop and carry out local improvement projects and a neighborhood of Boston that has rescued itself from catastrophic decline, an arts project that expresses through dance the history and work of a naval shipyard in New Hampshire and an activist organization that represents 60,000 families in the Rio Grande Valley. What these and the other undertakings described in this book have in common is that they all involve making connections among people, establishing bonds of trust and understanding, building community. In other words, they all involve creating social capital: developing networks of relationships that weave individuals into groups and communities.

Interest in social capital and research on the subject have grown dramatically in recent years—from a handful of esoteric research articles in the early 1990s to hundreds of new publications each year a decade later. Scholars, government officials, leaders of nongovernmental organizations including the World Bank, the United Nations, and the Organization for Economic Cooperation and Development, and business practitioners have increasingly recognized the essential contribution of social capital to the economic and social health of countries, regions, cities, and towns, to the success of organizations, and to individual accomplishment and well-being. Many of the stories in this book show the positive effects of social capital, the ways that people in relationship can reach goals that would have been far beyond the grasp of individuals in isolation. At the same time, these people enjoy the intrinsic satisfactions of association, of being part of a community.

As used by social scientists, *social capital* refers to social networks, norms of reciprocity, mutual assistance, and trustworthiness. The central insight of this approach is that social networks have real value both for the people in those networks—hence, networking as a career strategy, for example—as well as for bystanders. Criminologists, for instance, have shown that the crime rate in a neighborhood is lowered when neighbors know one another well, benefiting even residents who are not themselves involved in neighborhood activities.

Just like physical capital (tools) and human capital (education), social capital comes in many different forms—a coffee klatch, a civic organization, a bowling league, a labor union, the Ku Klux Klan. As that last example illustrates, social capital can be put to morally repugnant purposes as well as admirable ones, just as biochemical training can be used to concoct a bioterror weapon or a life-saving drug. Social capital is a powerful tool, as our stories will illustrate, but whether it is put to good use or ill is a different issue.

Among the many different forms of social capital one distinction will be especially important for our purposes in this book. Some networks link people who are similar in crucial respects and tend to be inward-looking—bonding social capital. Others encompass different types of people and tend to be outward-looking—bridging social capital. Both bonding and bridging social networks have their uses. Bonding social capital is a kind of sociological Super Glue, whereas bridging social capital provides a sociological WD-40. If you get sick, the people who bring you chicken soup are likely to represent your bonding social capital. On the other hand, a society that has *only* bonding social capital will look like Belfast or Bosnia—segregated into mutually hostile camps. So a pluralist democracy requires lots of bridging social capital, not just the bonding variety.

The problem is that bridging social capital is harder to create than bonding social capital—after all, birds of a feather flock together. So the kind of social capital that is most essential for healthy public life in an increasingly diverse society like ours is precisely the kind that is hardest to build. For this reason, in our case studies we have paid special attention to the challenges of fostering social networks that bridge the various splits in contemporary American communities.

Community building sometimes has a warm and fuzzy feeling, a kind of "kumbaya" cuddliness about it. Some of our stories fit that image, but others allow us to see that building social capital is not free of conflict and controversy.

- First, some of our protagonists are building social capital precisely because it can empower disadvantaged groups (like Mexican Americans in the Rio Grande Valley or clerical workers at Harvard) in their struggle for greater influence. Social capital represents not a comfortable alternative to social conflict but a way of making controversy productive.
- Second, by organizing some people in and others out, social capital can sometimes have negative effects on "outsiders." We'll see evidence of this in the role of part-time workers at UPS and in the forced annexation of East Portland. (This is one reason why bridging social capital is especially important.)
- Third, even when the effects of community ties are wholly admirable, the means by which they work can be unsettling. Social capital relies on informal sanctions and gossip and even ostracism, not just on fellowship and emulation and altruism. The solidarity that enabled Boston's Dudley Street neighborhood to rebound rests in part on camaraderie and shared aspirations, but in part on fear of what the neighbors would say about those who did not do their part.

In short, the concept of social capital is not treacly sweet but has a certain tartness. Nevertheless, each of our stories illustrates the extraordinary power and subtlety of social networks to enable people to improve their lives.

Even as the value of social capital has been more and more widely acknowledged, evidence has mounted of a diminution of social capital in the United States. In *Bowling Alone,* one of us (Putnam) has shown that whereas during the first two thirds of the twentieth century Americans were becoming more and more connected with one another and with community affairs, the last third of the century witnessed a startling and dismaying reversal of that trend. Beginning, roughly speaking, in the late 1960s, Americans in massive numbers began to join less, trust less, give less, vote less, and schmooze less. At first people hardly noticed what was happening, but over the last three decades involvement in civic associations, participation in public affairs, membership in churches and social clubs and unions, time spent with family and friends and neighbors, philanthropic giving, even simple trust in other people—as well as participation in the eponymous bowling leagues—all have fallen by 25 to 50 percent. A variety of technological and economic and social changes—television, two-career families, urban sprawl, and so on—has rendered obsolete a good share of America's stock of social capital.

Bowling Alone presented a sweeping statistical overview of several decades of decline in sociability and civic participation across the United States, but it closed with the optimistic hope that social reformers might invent new forms of social capital to replace the dying forms. *Better Together* does not suggest that the downward trend has suddenly reversed itself. We do not yet see evidence of a general resurgence of social connection or involvement in the public life of the community. But hidden within that broad statistical truth of the erosion of social ties is a tremendous variety of particular experiences. A general decline does not mean decline everywhere, in every situation. We began this project on the assumption—based in part on the evidence of particular cases that came to our attention as we traveled the country, speaking about social connectedness with Americans from all walks of life—that new social capital was being created in interesting ways in many places and situations, even as overall levels of association and participation continued to fall.

To write this book we descended from the statistical heights of *Bowling Alone* to ground level, entering the living room of Catherine Flannery, a longtime resident of Roxbury, Massachusetts, who has seen her neighborhood unravel and then knit itself together; a classroom in North Philadelphia where an Experience Corps volunteer was helping a second-grader learn to read; a meeting room in a United Parcel Service hub in Greensboro, North Carolina, where package handlers discussed how to help new employees adjust to the job. We sat in the pews of a Los Angeles church that had undergone explosive growth and in the office of a coordinator of neighborhood associations in Portland, Oregon.

We focus on these social-capital success stories, hoping and believing that they may in fact be harbingers of a broader revival of social capital in this country. We hope and believe that they may perhaps guide and inspire others who are seeking ways to build social capital and to accomplish goals or solve problems that are as challenging as those faced by the groups described in *Better Together.*

Many readers of *Bowling Alone* and others who have understood the value of social capital have asked what can be done to build or rebuild community and social relationships. Indeed, as we have traveled the country in the past few years, speaking with tens of thousands of our fellow citizens, the toughest challenges have come not from scholarly critics but from ordinary Americans who have asked, "So, if you're right, what can I do? What are people out there doing to address this problem? Are there exceptions to the general collapse of community in America?" Despite the flood of recent academic research on social capital, these practical questions remain largely unexplored. We hope that the examples in this book can supply some answers to those important questions.

We want to emphasize that this is a book of stories about social capital, not a textbook of social-capital creation or a casebook designed to elucidate or test a particular theory of social-capital development. We mention this partly to caution readers not to look for the strict definitions, quantitative measures, or rigorous theoretical frameworks that might belong to a different kind of study but that we have not tried to develop here or impose on this material. *Bowling Alone* presented and tested a wide variety of hypotheses about the causes and consequences of social capital against evidence as rigorous as could be discovered. *Better Together* aims instead to illustrate some of the ways in which Americans in many diverse corners of our society are making progress on the perennial challenge of re-creating new forms of community, adapted to the conditions and needs of our time.

Our aim in telling these stories as stories is not to excuse ourselves from the rigor of social science, but to gain the positive advantages of storytelling. We believe that stories, with their specificity and ability to express the complex realities of particular people and places and their possibly unique ability to express thought and feeling simultaneously, are the appropriate medium for capturing a sense of how social-capital creation works in real life. It is no coincidence that the chapters that follow include numerous examples of people building social capital by sharing stories about their experiences. The rich mixture of events, values, feelings, and ideas that stories communicate has long made storytelling an important mechanism of social connection. Stories help us relate to one another. The U.S. Army uses the term "ground truth" to describe the real experience of soldiers in the field—the moment-by-moment truth of being in combat, as opposed to generalizations about combat or theories about how it should occur. In these stories, we have tried to capture some of the ground truth of social-capital creation—the ways it really happens rather than theories or frameworks describing how it might or should happen.

We should say a few words here about how we chose these particular twelve stories. We do not claim that they are the dozen best contemporary examples of social-capital building in the country (whatever "best" might mean in this context), nor do we claim that any of them is an unalloyed success. Indeed, we have sought in each case to explore some of the shortcomings and remaining challenges that are inevitable in practical efforts to build community. Nevertheless, we believe that all the cases make valuable and interesting contributions to the social-capital discussion.

We applied two main principles in choosing our cases. One, as we have already suggested, was to focus as much as possible on substantial cases of social-capital success. In our preliminary investigations of candidates for inclusion, we looked for evidence of longevity, scope, impact, and established reputation that would give us reasonable confidence that we had found genuine stories of social-capital development. (We also favored cases that exhibited some particularly creative or innovative approach.) Overall, we sought examples that are robust and successful enough to serve as convincing and potentially instructive models of social-capital creation. In about half of the cases, we were able to draw on the valuable work of other researchers to help confirm that the activities and organizations we had chosen had enough substance to stand up to scrutiny and to reward attention.

Our second basic principle in selection was to include as much variety as possible. The social-capital development described in this book takes place in the Northwest, the South, the Midwest, the Northeast, and southern California. It happens in big cities and small cities, in suburban communities, and in small towns. Some of these efforts are strictly local; others have ties to national or regional organizations. One is mainly youth led, one brings together children and senior citizens, and others focus on adults or a wide range of age groups. The organizations and examples we examine include a labor union, a pair of churches, an arts program, a community development corporation, a large business, a city library system, and the history of citizen participation in an entire metropolitan area. When faced with a choice between a story that differed from the others (in region, setting, participants, or purpose) and a story that might be "stronger" in terms of scope or success but resembled one we had already settled on, we opted for greater variety.[1]

Why this emphasis on variety? For one thing, we sought to illustrate the point that social capital can be created by different people in different situations for different purposes to avoid any implication that successful efforts belonged only to certain kinds of groups with certain aims in certain settings. We believed variety would make it more likely that readers interested in working to build social capital in their many situations would find inspiration and guidance in one or more of the stories. We also hoped that we might find some underlying similarities among the diverse cases and that—because the cases were diverse—those similarities might suggest useful general principles or techniques of social-capital development. We selected these twelve stories from a pool of more than one hundred examples that have come to our attention over years of traveling, speaking, and meeting people and groups interested in the subject of social capital and convinced of its importance.

Our aim has been to learn from these varied experiences rather than impose themes on them or use them to illustrate pre-existing pet ideas. In fact, when we began we did not know what, if anything, we would discover in the way of common themes or general lessons in these diverse settings and activities. We did bring some basic questions to our exploration of these stories, however. One is whether the success of the endeavor depended on the involvement of a charismatic leader or had a structure or some form of shared or distributed leadership that would enable it to survive leadership changes and especially the departure of a visionary founder. In other words, we asked whether these groups or programs were self-sustaining. A related question is whether the social capital–building techniques and structures we saw could be replicated in other settings (related because reliance on an individual charismatic leader argued against a program or group succeeding elsewhere without that unique leadership). We also asked what kind of social-capital creation was going on in these cases: whether it was primarily bonding or bridging social capital. And we tried to discover the mechanisms of social-capital creation in these different situations, looking not only for evidence of new and strengthened relationships but for insight into how these bonds were formed.

In the interest of telling these stories as stories, we do not ask and answer these questions directly in every case, but they shaped our investigations, and the answers are usually evident, if not always explicit. In our reflective concluding chapter, we deal more explicitly with those questions as part of our effort to draw some general themes and lessons from these dozen cases.

In fact, several themes have emerged from the stories. In our last chapter, we draw out those themes in some detail in an effort to derive some usable lessons about how and why social capital is created. One lesson is that creating robust social capital takes time and effort. For the most part, it develops through extensive and time-consuming face-to-face conversation between two individuals or among small groups of people. (See especially the chapters on Valley Interfaith, HUCTW, and Tupelo for examples, but other cases also demonstrate the point.) It takes person-to-person contact over time to build the trust and mutual understanding that characterize the relationships that are the basis of social capital. So we see no way that social capital can be created instantaneously or en masse.

A second conclusion, related to the first, is that social capital is necessarily a local phenomenon because it is defined by connections among people who know one another. Even when we talk about social capital in national or regional organizations (United Parcel Service or the Texas Industrial Area Foundations, for example), we are really talking about a network or accumulation of mainly local connections. The Internet and the World Wide Web, though much in the news as technology that would transform community and relationship, play a surprisingly small role in most of our stories. We do devote one chapter to craigslist, an online bulletin board/community, to try to understand some of the limitations and promises of this developing phenomenon, but our investigations strongly suggest (as we have indicated) that trust relationships and resilient communities generally form through local personal contact.

The concluding chapter also summarizes some of the dilemmas that face would-be social capitalists. Many of the cases illustrate, for example, that for creating bonds of trust and reciprocity smaller is often better, but for extending the power and reach of social networks bigger is often better. We believe that some of the cases also illustrate how this dilemma can be resolved, at least in part, by creating networks of networks, that is, by nesting smaller groups within larger, more encompassing ones. The cases also allow us to explore the challenge of reconciling cohesion (bonding) and heterogeneity (bridging), for many of the protagonists of our cases have discovered an impressive array of strategies for finding unifying themes in the presence of diversity. Storytelling itself turns out to be an unusually effective technique in this regard, as does the creation of common spaces, both physical and virtual.

The endeavors we have studied also suggest that social capital is usually developed in pursuit of a particular goal or set of goals and not for its own sake. For the most part, the people and groups we describe here seek better schools, neighborhood improvement, better contracts with their employers, economic advantage, or some other particular good, with social capital a means to those ends and an important fringe benefit but not in itself their main aim.

After its extensive marshaling of evidence of decades of deterioration of social capital in the United States, *Bowling Alone* found reason for optimism amid the doom and gloom by looking back a century to another era when a decades-long decline in social capital gave way to (and in some sense stimulated) a renaissance of social connection that, among other things, saw the creation of now familiar fraternal and social-service organizations. That book expressed a hope that the downward trend of the last three decades of the twentieth century might also end in a new era of social-capital growth, possibly with the creation, again, of new kinds of institutions and forms of association. If *Better Together* provides insight, unlocks new ways of thinking, and sparks enthusiasm that contributes in even the smallest way to such a revival, it will have more than justified our hopes and efforts.

CHAPTER 1

{ Rio Grande Valley, Texas }

Valley Interfaith
"The Most Dangerous Thing We Do Is Talk to Our Neighbors."

In the early 1990s, teachers and administrators at the Palmer Elementary School in Pharr, Texas, began working with Valley Interfaith, a coalition of church and school groups, to organize parents and other area residents to improve the school. Pharr is in the Rio Grande Valley, not far from the Mexican border. Many of Palmer's students came from "colonias" in the surrounding area—unincorporated communities of mainly Mexican Americans and Mexican immigrants, among the poorest localities in the poorest region in the United States at that time. Many colonias lacked even such basic residential services as electricity, sewers, and paved roads. The lack of adequate sewers forced the closing of the elementary school several days each year. Eighty-six percent of the students at Palmer were classified as economically disadvantaged; 58 percent had limited proficiency in English.[1]

Significantly, the teachers did not ask parents to come in to the school but made visits to students' homes, asking parents about their hopes and worries regarding the school and their children. For many parents, it was their first real connection with the school, the first time anyone had bothered to ask their opinions. For the teachers, it was a first glimpse of their students' lives outside school. In *Valley Interfaith and School Reform*, author Dennis Shirley quotes school principal Salvador Flores: "When we first started doing our home visits, some of the teachers would come back to the school crying when they saw the conditions that the children were living in."[2] These home visits, the face-to-face conversations between a teacher and a child's parent or parents, gradually built up a group of parents who believed enough in the possibility of improving the schools (and believed enough in the goodwill of the teachers) to meet together to take the next step in organizing and planning. These were the parents who came to the small- and medium-sized gatherings known as house meetings organized by Valley Interfaith with and for the school.

The heart of a house meeting is when participants break into small groups of six to ten so they will all have a chance to express their concerns and listen to stories about what has brought them there, why they care enough to act. Later, the groups will describe the issues they discussed to the meeting as a whole and all will vote for what they consider the most important ones—part of the process of developing an action agenda to address the problems that matter most to the people affected by them.

In a small group at one of the Palmer Elementary house meetings, an older man who seemed restless and distracted while others talked interrupted a parent and launched into a tirade against the school district: how the people who worked for the district cared only about their next promotion, how they didn't care if streets around the school were safe or if drug dealers prowled the neighborhood.[3] It wasn't the first time the man, Mr. Ortiz, had spoken out; he was raising his grandson and regularly launched into similar tirades at these meetings. The group leader tried to get him to talk more directly out of his and his grandson's experience, but he went on in the same loud, angry style and then crossed his arms and turned away from the group, mumbling angrily to himself while others talked.

After a while, the leader addressed him: "It's obvious that you're angry about things at this school. I'm angry, too, because I want my daughter in special ed to get the services she needs but the district is cutting back. That's why I'm here—to organize so we can make sure our kids succeed. Can you tell me a story about something that happened to make you so angry?"

For a moment, Mr. Ortiz stayed as he was, arms across his chest, body twisted in his chair. Then he dropped his arms and turned to face the group, his face softening. His voice, when he spoke, was different, too. This was a man speaking about the pain in his life. He told about his other grandson, the one who had been hit and killed by a car outside his elementary school five years earlier.

The group's frustration and impatience with Mr. Ortiz melted away. They could see him as a man who had suffered a terrible loss and had had no way to express that pain except through his rage. Another member of the group who had not yet spoken said, "I've never lost a kid, but I know what that kind of being powerless feels like." Then she told the story of her daughter, who had joined a gang. Mr. Ortiz looked at her and listened. He nodded when she said, "It's too late for my daughter, but damned if I'm not going to do something so that other parents don't have to go through that pain."

Father Alfonso Guevara, pastor of Christ the King Church in Brownsville, Texas, and a longtime leader in Valley Interfaith, says, "We make private pain public." The house meeting was part of the process, a step toward making the pain public in a local group to build the energy and commitment needed to bring that pain—and the actions needed to relieve it—to a wider public stage where officials would have to recognize it and respond.

Relational Organizing

It's called relational organizing. The Southwest Industrial Areas Foundation network, of which Valley Interfaith is a part, builds its membership through one-on-one conversations and at house meetings like the one Mr. Ortiz attended. Catalina Mendiola, a local organizer, says, "The heart of our work is one-on-one meetings with people. Organizing is all about building relationships. It's not about meetings. These are not counseling sessions. They are not an interview. It's a conversation. You're building a relationship here. Not extracting information. Not pushing an agenda. And the only way to do this is to leave yourself open to be changed by the conversation."[4] Unlike activist organizations that develop a public agenda first and then try to attract people who support it, the IAF encourages the emergence of local agendas from these conversations. Similarly, it allows each organization in the network to develop its state or regional agenda; it does not impose one from above. The IAF's power to make progress on the issues it takes up resides in the relationships. Although people come together because they have similar concerns, building relationships is the first priority, the foundation for defining and acting on public issues that represent an accumulation of personal and local concerns. The professional organizers who work for the IAF organizations see their primary job as finding and training the leaders in the community who will develop a following to devise and carry out the organization's agenda. The "Iron Rule" of the Industrial Areas Foundation is "Never do anything for anybody that they can do for themselves."

The Texas Industrial Areas Foundation originated in the Industrial Areas Foundation movement created in Chicago in 1940 by reformer Saul Alinsky. (The name, which survives in organizations that have few or no industrial workers as members, refers to the Chicago industrial areas where the work began.) Alinsky believed that reform could best be achieved when the citizens of poor and neglected communities organized and exerted power on their own behalf. He saw doing *for* others as less effective and as a kind of welfare colonialism. The inability of these citizens to accomplish much previously, he was convinced, stemmed from their isolation, not from any lack of intelligence, skill, or desire for a better life. Alinsky's idea shapes and motivates the Industrial Areas Foundation organizations of the twenty-first century.[5] At present, more than sixty IAF organizations representing more than one thousand institutions and a million families are active in the United States and the United Kingdom.[6]

Ernesto Cortés, Jr., brought the IAF concept to Texas, beginning with his native San Antonio. Cortés had had organizing experience with the United Farm Workers in the Rio Grande Valley when he went to Chicago for leadership training with IAF organizers there in 1971. After that training and a year of organizing with the IAF in several northern cities, he returned to San Antonio in 1974 to apply and adapt what he had learned. Through hundreds of one-on-one conversations with community figures from the mainly working-class Mexican-American West Side of San Antonio, he learned about local problems while establishing personal relationships with members of the community. Cortés worked closely with church congregations, rooting his organization in the networks and values of those institutions—an innovation that made it possible to tap into well-established ties of trust and mutual interest, as well as shared religious beliefs that supported justice and social action. Professional and lay leaders in the churches drew other members of their congregations into the conversation about local needs, forming groups large enough to get the attention of local politicians.

Those organizing efforts in parts of San Antonio that had largely been ignored by city government led to some early local successes: the installation of pollution controls to reduce the noxious fumes of a hide-processing plant, a footbridge over a drainage canal, traffic lights at some dangerous intersections. The neighborhood accomplishments and the continued work of Cortés and activist clergy led to the creation of Communities Organized for Public Service (COPS), a movement based on two dozen churches in San Antonio organized to respond to problems that affected the whole area—problems having to do with drainage, parks, and libraries, for example—that could not be addressed one parish at a time.[7] The first IAF organization in Texas, COPS is still thriving and effective more than twenty-five years later. In 1978, a second IAF group was founded in Houston, the Metropolitan Organization, a network of thirty-two churches. In 1982, Valley Interfaith came into existence.

Over the past twenty-five years, Texas IAF organizations, individually and as a statewide network, have improved underperforming schools and created effective job-training programs, helped direct hundreds of millions of state and federal dollars to infrastructure improvements in neglected parts of Texas cities and the small colonias in the Rio Grande

Valley, and helped pass living-wage laws and health-care regulations. The network now represents about half a million Texans.

In training programs, in conversation, and in his writings, Cortés emphasizes participation, relationships, and "relational power." He argues that we are social beings, defined by our relationships with other people—with "family and kin, but also with less familiar people with whom we engage in the day-to-day business of living our lives in a complicated society." Without organizations that connect people to political power and public participation, these broader social relations "disintegrate." "There is no time and energy for collaboration," he writes, "no reciprocity, no trust—in short, no social capital."[8] The IAF strives to rebuild or replace some of the lost networks of relationships—lost social capital—organizing in churches and schools "to reconnect these critical institutions around a vibrant culture of relational one-on-one and small-group conversations."[9]

Getting individuals to articulate their needs and the possibilities they see and creating relationships that knit individuals into powerful groups is the core of the IAF's work. Cortés lays out the principles underlying the organization's methods in his response to a college student who asked what "motivates people to support a cause with actions as well as words":

> When I hear your question, what I think you're really saying is, "How can I convince people to do what's good? How do I get them to do what's right? How do I get them to follow my agenda?" That's not organizing. What I mean by organizing is getting you to recognize what's in your best interest. Getting you to recognize that you have a child, that you have a career and a life to lead, and that there are some things that are obstacles to the quality of your life. I need to get you to see how you can affect those things through relationships with other people.[10]

If the people who live on the West Side of San Antonio or in the unincorporated colonias of the Rio Grande Valley see their first priority as getting paved streets and drainage, that becomes the primary action item on the local agenda. If the parents of schoolchildren in an elementary school in Austin worry most about the dangers their children face crossing busy streets near the school, then getting a stop sign installed or a traffic pattern changed will be their first goal. Other aims and actions may follow, once they experience their collective power. "Winning creates imagination," says Sister Judy Donovan, leading organizer of Valley Interfaith. "Once they see they can get a stop sign, they start thinking about what might be done in the school." Successful action gives people lessons in their own power.

Member after member of Valley Interfaith recalls the same two victories as moments when they truly understood what their collective efforts could accomplish, banishing their old feelings of powerlessness. One was the passage of a half-cent increase in sales tax that politicians had previously tried and failed to pass. Valley Interfaith agreed to work for passage in exchange for a commitment that roughly 30 percent of the tax revenue would go to support the organization's family-friendly agenda. "We went out and did house meetings," says Joe Hinosa. "We negotiated for weeks with the city to get agreement on where the money would go before we agreed to support it."[11] The other was the drive to change political representation in McAllen from at-large commissioners to single-district commissioners, a modification that would open the door for representatives who were not part of the all-white elite that had governed the city for many years. Those involved saw the victories not only as important in themselves but as revelations of what was possible.

The group had to overcome the charge that they were radicals. "We had this mayor for twenty years—Othal Brand—who used to throw us out of city council meetings. He said we were too radical, that we were communists, dangerous. . . . Yeah, the issue still comes up some, but he's gone now, and we have won single-district commissioners," says Hinosa. "The most dangerous thing we do is talk to our neighbors."[12]

There is nothing abstract about the issues they take on, or the events that motivate them. Father Bart Flaat, pastor of St. Joseph the Worker and a longtime Valley Interfaith leader, describes going to bless the house of a parishioner during his first months in McAllen, a city near the mid-point of the highway that crosses the Rio Grande Valley east to west and about ten miles from the Mexican border. After the short ceremony, the family asked him to visit a sick neighbor. Entering the house next door, he found a woman with a high fever and an injured leg that was obviously gangrenous. Why didn't she go to the doctor? he asked her. She could lose her leg or even her life if the leg wasn't treated soon. She told him that even a doctor in Mexico would cost forty dollars, money she did not have. Enraged at the idea of this woman losing her leg for lack of forty dollars, he gave her the money himself. The woman's plight was no isolated case. Finding people in his congregation concerned about the unavailability of health care, Father Bart began working with them and Valley Interfaith to get a free clinic built in the area. Four years later the clinic opened.

Relationship-building is a way of looking at the world, not just a strategy. The IAF Alliance Schools initiative has procured money for physical improvements in schools, for in-school clinics, and for changes in the school day (toward block classes rather than shorter class periods, for instance); but as in the case of Palmer Elementary, the core of its school-improvement efforts has been building relationships: between the school and the community; between students and teachers. Relationships are not just the engine of reform, they are one of the goals of reform. So, for instance, Houston's Metropolitan Organization worked with teachers and parents at Jefferson Davis High School to introduce block scheduling in the school, the longer classes meaning more effective teaching and more opportunities for teachers and students to get to know one another, to have genuine relationships. As Dennis Shirley points out, the IAF organizations see schools, and learning, as embedded in the community, not as isolated institutions that can be fixed by applying the latest philosophy of teaching.[13] Unsurprisingly, the document in which the Texas IAF describes its vision for public schools is subtitled "Communities of Learners."[14]

Two IAF job-training programs, Project QUEST (Quality Employment Through Skills Training) in San Antonio and VIDA (Valley Initiative for Development and Advancement) in the Rio Grande Valley, use relationship building to bring potential employers into the process. Before enrolling trainees, IAF leaders negotiate with employers to get their commitment to hire the individuals who successfully complete the program. The employer promises good jobs with good pay; QUEST and VIDA agree to deliver well-trained, productive workers. Thus the interests of both sides are served.

Similarly, the IAF maintains working relationships even with politicians who often disagree with its aims. The organization exerts public pressure on politicians, notably at "accountability sessions," highly ritualized performances in which each politician has a minute or two at most to tell a hallful of voters whether or not he or she supports the IAF agenda. The IAF plays hardball. But it also works to develop solutions, not just voice grievances. Through "research actions," members educate themselves in the political, legal, and budgetary details of their issues, in part to know where to exert pressure, but also to be able to offer officials practical plans. The accountability session is only one moment in an ongoing relationship. Public commitment by the politicians comes after long conversations with up to a dozen IAF leaders to hash out the issues. The relationship continues after the session, not only because the IAF keeps an eye on the politicians but because it works with them to turn verbal commitment into action. "No permanent allies, no permanent enemies" is a core principle. The organization neither endorses nor opposes candidates but works with whoever can help it achieve its goals. The IAF has built relationships not only *with* outside individuals and groups but *between* outside groups. In 1998, when the Texas Water Development Board withheld $100 million in funding because it judged that Hidalgo County was not complying with state subdivision rules, Valley Interfaith discovered that the officials and agencies involved had different understandings of the problem and were not communicating effectively with one another. Interfaith organized a meeting of all the parties during which each had a chance to explain its view. That conversation led to a joint understanding that freed up the money.[15]

The Valley and the Colonias

In 1999, 39 percent of the residents of the lower Rio Grande Valley in Texas lived below the poverty line, compared with 17 percent in Texas overall and 14 percent nationwide. Per capita income in the area was less than half the national average.[16] Forty percent of working-age adults lacked health insurance (compared with 28 percent in all of Texas and 15 percent nationwide).[17] Sixty percent of Valley adults lacked a high school diploma (compared with 28 percent in Texas and 24 percent nationwide). For a long time, agriculture had been a main source of jobs. Citrus groves and fields of sweet onion and aloe vera still employ some in the valley, but service work now dominates the economy.

The colonias are the extreme embodiment of the Valley's deep economic and social problems. Colonias are unincorporated settlements of residential property that, until recently, were mostly sold by developers with no services—only a promise of running water, sewers, electricity, and paved roads that was seldom kept.

As resident Idaleica Valdez told us, "I thought I was done with this forty years ago when I grew up in a colonia with no water or sewers. But it is still there. Look at this. Look at these roads. No curbs, filled with holes. When it rains these are streams of mud. Weeds all over. They allow them to build and sell houses that have cracks in the walls and holes in the floors. We don't have police here. No library. About to lose some of the limited bus pickup for our kids. At Benavides Elementary School the teachers have to wash the kids' clothes sometimes because their parents can't afford to buy water to do laundry. These people are so poor. They don't think they can do anything."[18]

Until 1995, the colonias appeared on no official map and in effect had no official existence. Thus there was no chance of their being included in plans for infrastructure improvement. The families that bought a plot of land in a colonia for $100 or $200 down and a small monthly payment often first lived on the land in a used trailer or small mobile home. When they had saved some money, they began building a house, one room or even one wall at a time. Driving through the colonias today, you see properties in all stages of development. Some still have only trailers, patched and rusting, or shacks made of tin roofing. In many cases, the old trailer sits behind a small cinder-block house—one or two rooms—and serves as a kitchen. Here and there you see more ambitious construction: a house of several rooms, a mobile home with an added carport or a small extension. IAF organizations across Texas worked together to craft, build support for, and pass (in 1995) a bill requiring that all new residential property be sold with water, sewage, and electrical service and a paved road. As of 2002, about 25 percent of colonias still lacked running water, a sewage system, drainage, and paved roads. More than two hundred thousand of the Valley's one million people live in colonias.

La Pradera colonia was built in 1998, after the new law came into effect, so its houses border a paved road and have electricity, running water, and septic tanks. Though it is one of the newest colonias, La Pradera looks old. The second- or third- or fourthhand trailers are battered; the unpainted walls of the houses look worn and dingy. The road that connects La Pradera to the rest of the Valley is unpaved. One rainy February day, a school bus slipped off the muddy surface into a ditch. The accident occurred before the driver had picked up students, but the residents could easily imagine the same thing happening with their children on the bus. Above all else, they wanted to see the road paved.

The Power of Stories

In one-on-one conversations and in house meetings, organizers and leaders elicit people's stories. Abstract ideas do not connect people, and social action, when it is not rooted in the heart of people's life experience, withers in the face of opposition and disappointment. At Palmer Elementary, real stories broke down the barriers between Mr. Ortiz and other members of his group. At a house meeting at the Nikki Rowe High School in McAllen, during an early stage of participation in Valley Interfaith in the spring of 2002, parents and students gathered in groups of half a dozen to express their concerns about the school and their hopes for it. One woman explained her commitment to her children's education: "I couldn't go to school. My dad died when I was young; I had to work for family survival." That simple statement had a more powerful effect than the long, generalized list of complaints another woman reeled off. To be effective, these conversations have to be face-to-face, so people can read each other's emotions, can express sympathy and work through disagreement together. (Later, Sister Judy Donovan, marveling at how earlier organizers had managed to stay in touch with members of the organization before the days of cell phones—she always has hers with her—goes on to say, "But the problem with a cell phone is that it makes you think you've had a conversation.")

Many of the women who have found their voices and vocation as Valley Interfaith leaders tell stories of watching their mothers silently tolerate their husbands' abuse. In contrast, Father Alfonso Guevara makes one of the sources of his dedication to action and education clear in a very different story about his father: "He was not an educated man himself, but he believed in education. When he went to the local Catholic school to enroll my sister, they told him there was no room, not even a desk for her to sit at. He said, 'If I build a desk, will you take her?' They agreed. He built a desk big enough for two students, and they admitted her and another girl."

Sister Judy Donovan has her own story to explain why she devotes her life to organizing. As a young nun, she lived in Brazil, engaged in the liberation theology movement, which used biblical stories of oppression and liberation to raise people's consciousness of the injustice of their situation and the need to take action. Late one night, a man from a nearby village where she and others had preached that message woke her up.

Emboldened by the activist clergy's teaching, the villagers had stood up to the landowner's agents and refused their demand for an even greater share of the income from their work. The agents had burned all the crops and put the villagers in jail. "And I was responsible," Sister Judy says. "That night I became an adult. We stirred people up without giving them the tools to do anything." It took six months for a coalition of churches, lawyers, and other groups to get the villagers out of jail, an effort that taught Sister Judy about the power of groups working together. She determined to become an organizer.

Whenever someone tells his or her story—in a colonia house meeting, at Palmer School, at Nikki Rowe—you feel the power of narrative. The listeners lean toward the speaker, their eyes on her face; their silence deepens, rich with attention and connection. Often, the stories are similar in ways that bind the tellers together and also different, individual, revealing the variety of human experience. Stories build relationships; they knit communities together. And IAF organizers work hard to help people interpret their stories in a wider context, inspiring action.

Developing New Leaders

The heart of the IAF's strength and the core of its work is developing new leaders. Ernie Cortés describes the job of organizers as "holding forty individual meetings each week and teaching leaders to hold these same kinds of meetings." He continues:

> Leaders and organizers are constantly seeking out new leaders that have some energy, the ability to reflect, a sense of humor, some anger and the ability to develop a following. It is only through these types of conversations that a community can develop a collective leadership that is able to claim their birthright through collective action.[19]

The Iron Rule of never doing anything for people that they can do themselves implies, ultimately, the kind of community of leaders that Cortés suggests here, an organization in which everyone's potential is discovered and nurtured and leadership is genuinely collective. He and others in the IAF emphasize active citizen engagement, as opposed to the idea of citizens as clients or consumers who expect to have things done for them or to them.

The Iron Rule may be unambiguous, but the temptation to step in and "lead" potential leaders when they hesitate or falter is strong. Sister Judy tells the story of a new organizer who proudly reported on a meeting that had resulted in an important commitment from a politician, the agreement clinched by the organizer's own impassioned intervention. Rather than praise him, she dressed him down: "You taught them that they cannot speak for themselves. Now they'll turn to you instead of doing it themselves."

The Nikki Rowe meeting demonstrates how hard it can be for organizers and leaders to remain in the background and let the meeting evolve. Toward the end, when people came together to discuss the issues that the small groups had identified, some students repeatedly brought up the planned dismissal of some favorite teachers. Apparently they had come to the meeting expecting that it would be about that one topic. Organizer Andres Ibarria lost his cool and not only said that their concern was not the subject of the meeting but started berating one of the most forceful students: a mistake, a violation of the principle of respecting individuals and their concerns. He later apologized, but the incident shows how tempting it can be to step in. His passion for action had made him impatient.

A brief evaluation among leaders after the small La Pradera house meeting includes related criticism: instead of letting the residents tell their stories and gradually articulate their concerns, the leaders had lectured them about the power of working together while the residents of the colonia listened in silence. Again, the leaders' own passion had caused them to talk too much and try to move too quickly, as they forgot for the moment that their job was to encourage people to speak and act for themselves.

The Iron Rule and the intensive leadership-development efforts that support it give the IAF organizations much of their strength and effectiveness. One consequence is that a remarkably small professional staff keeps Valley Interfaith going. That organization of forty-five churches and public schools representing sixty thousand families (with its ability to bring two thousand people to an accountability session and sign up seventy-five thousand voters) is supported by a paid staff of two organizers, a trainee, and a secretary. The organizers cite the biblical story of Moses and Jethro. When Moses is overwhelmed by the task of leading the Israelites in the desert, Jethro warns him that he will wear himself out and advises him to delegate authority to capable men who will share the burden and resolve disputes in groups of "thousands, hundreds, fifties, and tens."

The fact that Valley Interfaith's actions, like those of other IAF organizations, develop from the concerns of its member leaders, rather than a national agenda, gives the organization rootedness and resilience; people fight for what they care most deeply about, for their own causes. Perhaps most important, active participation—genuine engagement in leadership—makes community possible. When someone gives marching orders and others march, you are unlikely to find living relationships and real community. The trust relationships and norms of reciprocity that characterize social capital depend on a reasonable measure of equality and mutuality: "one-sided relationship" is an oxymoron.

A leader, says Ed Chambers, national IAF director, is someone capable of delivering a following.[20] Some of the best ones, Sister Judy Donovan thinks, do not seek leadership positions and may be skeptical about their abilities and about the whole enterprise. Many—especially but not exclusively women—have been quiet all their lives and are surprised at first to discover their hidden ability to speak out and lead. All the leaders show passion and courage, but it comes in different forms.

Though a powerfully effective force in Valley Interfaith for years, Father Alfonso Guevara seems at first glance an unlikely leader. He is short and soft-spoken, and obviously shy. He says that even learning to preach to his own congregation in his own church, Christ the King, was difficult.

His reliability and persistence are legendary, though. He says, "I don't move as fast as some people, but I outstay them, I wear them out." The actions he's been involved in include living-wage work, improvement in the colonias, helping eight hundred people obtain citizenship, and supporting a VIDA program to train six hundred men and women as welders and place them in well-paid jobs. Asked whether some people in the parish object to his and the church's involvement in all this political and social activism, he mildly answers, "People come to the church to be fed, but some people want to be fed baby food." Now, he believes, his most important work is "finding new leaders that find new leaders." One of his finds is Lupita Torres, a retired farmworker and longtime member of Christ the King.

Her power and presence are evident as soon as she speaks, but for a long time she was one of the skeptics. She says, "I expected everything in the U.S. to be perfect, but when I came to live here my barrio had no paved street, no streetlights. An abandoned area in the middle was filled with dead animals and old cars. It was dangerous, and unhealthy for the children." When she spoke to Father Alfonso about the problems, he urged her to meet individually with other concerned parishioners (applying the IAF model of one-on-one conversations). "But I didn't think I could do anything," she says, "and I didn't think the church should be involved in politics. My idea of politics was the politics of Mexico, where the politicians did whatever they wanted."

Ramon Duran, a Valley Interfaith organizer, was attending a neighborhood meeting on the subject of religious education when one of the other women said, "Lupita, are the chairs arranged right?" Alert for a potential new leader—someone that other people turned to—he said, "Who's Lupita?" and immediately asked to meet with her one-on-one. She refused, saying, "If this is about politics, I don't want to talk to you." But she started attending Valley Interfaith house meetings when she learned that people discussed scripture there. She was gradually drawn into Interfaith activities related to her neighborhood. She was part of a group that met with the mayor to discuss the problem of unpaved roads.

The mayor sympathized, but he informed them that there simply wasn't money in the budget to solve the problem. Discouraged, the group fell silent. Then Lupita spoke up: "You don't own the money, you administer it. We're here to make sure you administer it wisely."

Later, the group took the mayor and other officials on a tour, saying, "We're going to introduce you to your city." After the tour and further discussion, money for paving was found after all. The mayor's aide asked Lupita, "When do you want the road paved?"

"June first," she told him.

"What time?" he asked sarcastically, amused or annoyed by her definitive answer.

"Seven A.M.," she said simply.

On May 31, city workers knocked on her door and asked where she wanted them to start. She directed them to the other end of the street, so that people would know she had fought for all of them, not just herself.

Now the barrio has paved roads, street lighting, drainage, and fire hydrants. Lupita sees changes in the people of the neighborhood, too, as a result of their joint efforts: "We got to know each other. There used to be squabbles and jealousy, little groups that gossiped about each other. Now there's more friendship, and we know how to gather people to deal with problems."

Gathering people—and especially finding and developing the leaders who can gather people—is the foundation of IAF work. That was true in San Antonio in the 1970s, when many months of one-on-one conversation and house meetings created a commitment to work together for change among a group of people that was large enough to influence the officials who could allocate funds to neglected neighborhoods and, later, to what became the Alliance Schools. It was true in the late 1990s, when Ernie Cortés went to Los Angeles to invigorate an IAF organization that was not doing well. On his advice, the group ceased its public actions while a team of a dozen organizers led by Cortés did nothing but meet one-on-one with potential leaders in local communities for an entire year—a total of ten thousand conversations whose aim was to build the relationships that would build more relationships that would finally give the organization the strong community roots it needed to act effectively.[21] In the Valley, too, Valley Interfaith had essentially called a halt to actions in June 2001, to devote itself to developing new leaders.

But no simple dichotomy exists between action and leadership development. Yes, being embroiled in a long, difficult action can divert energy and attention from finding new leaders. The history of the IAF includes instances of organizations that focused too much and too long on action and weakened themselves. But people learn to lead by leading, not just through conversation and training. Their leadership skills are tested and sharpened in practice, and success teaches them that they have the power to motivate people—and what that power can accomplish. Actions can and should be about building the confidence and know-how of inexperienced leaders and identifying new leaders, as well as about winning. Tension necessarily exists between the two aims, and the balance between them must be struck consciously.

At the accountability session on March 3, 2002, in the Valley, winning mattered a lot. Organizers worked hard to get candidates for key political offices to attend the meeting. Both candidates for governor of Texas would be there, as would candidates for the U.S. Congress, candidates for lieutenant governor and attorney general, candidates for the Texas House and Senate, and county candidates. Getting their public commitment to the Texas Industrial Area Foundation's agenda of a living wage, health care, and investment in infrastructure would be essential. That is the point of an accountability session—to demand an unambiguous public commitment from candidates. This is the moment when the social capital of networks and trust painstakingly built in months and years of one-on-ones and house parties is most clearly translated into raw political power.

This empowerment has an individual as well as an organizational dimension. Valley Interfaith organizers and leaders chose to give major roles in the session to relatively inexperienced leaders, using veterans in minor roles or having them participate only as delegates. Such a session may not run as smoothly or powerfully as it might, but the only way someone can learn to speak to two thousand people (or forcefully tell a candidate for the U.S. Senate that his speaking time is up) is to do it.

The Accountability Session

The afternoon and evening before the March accountability session, Sister Judy Donovan's cell phone rings often. A congressman's aide calls to ask if the meeting is still on, claiming that the congressman has not received any materials about it, though Sister Judy knows the information has been sent more than once. She makes a call, arranging to have it faxed again. Leaders at member churches and schools call to check when buses will leave or to report a misunderstanding with the bus company or to raise last-minute issues about someone's part in the session. She clarifies times, offers reassurance, or tells callers whom to call with their problems. Sister Judy remains calm and even cheerful. "I learned a long time ago that anxiety is contagious," she says. Remarkably, there is little she actually has to do herself, given the logistical demands of readying the hall, transporting two thousand people spread over fifteen thousand square miles of southern Texas to the site of the session in Pharr, and keeping track of the politicians and media representatives who will attend. The grassroots leaders, rather than the organizers, are handling most of the work.

At 9:00 A.M. Sunday, Valley Interfaith members start setting up chairs for the 2:30 P.M. meeting: two thousand folding chairs, forty rows of fifty filling the Pharr International Civic Center—formerly a bingo hall—the second-largest meeting space in the Valley and the largest available.

More than two hours before the meeting, Interfaith leaders are on the stage, practicing a script developed over months of weekly meetings. Half an hour before the start of the meeting, the room begins to fill as busloads of people arrive from member institutions and sit together under signs naming their affiliations, like groups of delegates at political conventions: Christ the King, Brownsville; Our Lady of Guadalupe, Raymondville; Nikki Rowe High School, St. Joseph the Worker, and Sam Houston Elementary School, all from McAllen; Holy Spirit; and the McAllen Taxi Drivers Association. There are small groups from other organizations in the IAF network: Dallas Area Interfaith, Austin Interfaith, the Border Organization, and the Metropolitan Organization. Ernie Cortés is there. Medium height and roundish, wearing a gray suit, he looks professorial and deceptively mild. He shakes hands with some of the leaders, hugs some he has known for a long time. He has no official role; he is present as a supporter, observer, and mentor. The organizer who supervises IAF projects in Texas and Lousiana, Sister Christine Stephens, sits next to him, also lending her support and evaluating the proceedings but not publicly involved, except as one of the two thousand members holding the politicians to account.

By the time the meeting begins, the hall is jammed; every seat is taken, people are standing at the back. Led by the trumpets and strummed guitars of a mariachi band in white suits, the Valley Interfaith Escort Team guides the politicians down the center aisle to their seats on the stage. This is not just a courtesy but a deliberate tactic to prevent politicians from "working the crowd" and to keep control of the session in the hands of the IAF. In emphatic Spanish and English, Rosalie Tristan and Father Alfonso Guevara of Valley Interfaith declaim the opening focus statement: "We are here to do our work as citizens. . . . One quarter of the colonias still have no water and sewer services." Without naming names, Tristan refers to a couple of candidates who turned down the invitation to attend the session because, she quotes them as saying, "Sunday is a family day." "We have a family-friendly agenda," she says. "Was Governor [Rick] Perry thinking of families when he vetoed the living-wage bill on a Sunday, on Father's Day? We want a living wage so fathers can be with their families and not have to go north to earn enough money."

Leaders present the Valley Interfaith agenda: living wages and job training; education; infrastructure and colonias; health care for all. One by one, the candidates pledge their support. Carmen Anaya, a small, elderly woman but a powerful presence at the microphone, a legendary leader, says, "We're watching you." The words are backed up by Valley Interfaith's pledge to sign up seventy-five thousand voters committed to the agenda, their contribution to the five hundred thousand committed voters that the Texas IAF network has undertaken to mobilize statewide through its "Sign Up and Take Charge" initiative. Those numbers explain why so many candidates are here, many of them having flown in from other parts of the state to speak for their allotted minute or two. One IAF speaker says, "There are two sources of power, organized money and organized people. We don't have organized money, but we have the people."

The representatives of other IAF organizations in the Texas network, all sitting in the first few rows of the meeting hall, are a visible reminder of just how many organized people stand behind Valley Interfaith. The seventy-five thousand voters Interfaith believes it can sign up to support the agenda is an impressive and influential number, but half a million voters is a force that cannot possibly be brushed aside or fobbed off with half measures. Looking out at the crowd of two thousand filling the hall makes it possible to picture the gathering of ten thousand IAF members who are to meet in Austin in September. The combined power of the organizations in the network has made state and local actions successful. Cortés says, "Valley Interfaith couldn't do what you see it doing without the network. They couldn't have gotten action on the colonias." Most impressive, perhaps, has been the ability of Texas IAF organizations to function effectively as a network while maintaining strong local roots and continuing to develop issues and leaders locally. Asked about tension between local organizations and the network, Cortés says with his characteristic bluntness, "Sure, there's tension. There's always tension, but we recognize it and we deal with it."

After the session, organizers and grassroots leaders crowd into a small upstairs room for a brief meeting, part celebration, part evaluation. Sister Judy goes down the list of objectives. "Turnout? Fantastic. You delivered two thousand people. Public business? One hundred percent commitment by the largest gathering of powerful officials in the state in this election. If this were a hunting trip, Sister Maria would get the big-game trophy." When she gets to "tension and drama," Donovan has some criticism: at one point the meeting was running twenty-two minutes late, a real lapse in a session designed to derive some of its power from speed. (Cortés later comments, "I kept waiting for her to intervene. Sometimes you have to break the Iron Rule." Although he himself did not break it to give her that advice during the session, no doubt he had much to say to her in private later. Self-critical evaluation is an IAF key to leadership development.) Sister Judy softens her criticism by noting that half of that time was made up by the end. She concludes, "This is the fruit of the decision nine months ago to stop other action and dig in to develop new leaders." Sister Christine delivers the same message: "We judge an action not just by the candidates but by the number of new leaders." People are talking, for instance, about the forcefulness of Joanna Alvarado, a slight, dark-haired college student and a second-generation Valley Interfaith leader, and the way she looked the politicians in the eye when she asked, "Will you support the Valley Interfaith agenda?" Talking later about the session as leadership development, Sister Judy says, "It's great to have two thousand people here, but we want to know who are the two hundred people who brought those two thousand."

Valley Interfaith and its sister organizations in the Texas Industrial Areas Foundation provide the premier example of grassroots organizing for progressive causes in America. These efforts are not without challenges and difficulties. TIAF has worked hard at transcending cleavages of race and religion, for example, and has had more success than many other civic organizations in America, but it continues to struggle to build bridges among Hispanic Catholics, black Protestants, suburban Jews, and so on. Moreover, sociologist Marshall Ganz has argued, IAF selection of its leaders through "cooptation" by professional organizers, not through election from below, means that its procedures cannot be said to be entirely democratic. On the other hand, the empowerment that Valley Interfaith has brought to its constituents is hard to match in other impoverished places in America. Valley Interfaith well illustrates that hardnosed political power can come from taking community building seriously.[22]

CHAPTER 2

{ *Chicago, Illinois* }

Branch Libraries
The Heartbeat of the Community

Among the predictions made in the mid-1990s about the influence that the Internet was likely to have on society was the idea that public libraries would lose their importance and might even disappear altogether. With limitless information available online, including the texts of books, why would people bother going to libraries, and why would government continue to fund them? A well-documented long-term decline in reading was already having an effect on libraries. In Chicago, circulation fell and budgets were cut all through the 1970s and 1980s. Staffing was reduced and hours of operation were shortened. In the late 1980s, the temporary home of the central library was torn down and the collection divided among other temporary sites. It seemed the growth of the Internet would be the final blow. In a 1998 *American Prospect* article called "Will Libraries Survive?" linguist Geoffrey Nunberg presented the doomsayers' case:

> A 1998 Commerce Department study found that 62 million people are using the Internet, and other estimates put the figure still higher. Most of these . . . are people who already use the public library less often than their parents did for purposes of obtaining recreational and instructive reading. Now they no longer need to rely on the library even for the sorts of information they can't easily get on National Public Radio or at Barnes & Noble. . . . They may still want to have a library around as an information

source of last resort, but they have a number of more convenient options
to exhaust before they are driven to use it.[1]

The library should be dead or dying, but that is not what is happening,
at least in Chicago. In little more than a decade, Chicago has built thirty-
two neighborhood branch libraries and renovated nine others. The
downtown Harold Washington Library Center, opened in 1991, is one of
the largest public library buildings in the world. Its green metal roof with
huge gargoyle-like owls, their wings extravagantly unfurled, makes it an
unmistakable landmark. Fourteen more new branches are scheduled to
open by 2005. More to the point, the libraries are humming with activity.
As of spring 2002, circulation was up 17 percent over the previous year,
which had seen an increase over the year before that. Go into almost any
branch after school or on a Saturday and you find crowds of students
doing their homework; adults scanning the shelves, studying, and participating in book discussion groups (in one of four languages), in writers'
groups, or in classes; and all of the branch's computers in use.

What is going on here? This surprising success reflects a big investment in facilities and staff. Now a separate line item in the city's budget
and funded by property tax revenues, the Chicago Public Library is
somewhat shielded from the economic ups and downs that affect many
government services. But money alone is not the answer. The CPL
thrives today because it embodies a new idea of how a library functions.
No longer a passive repository of books and information or an outpost of
culture, quiet, and decorum in a noisy world, the new library is an active
and responsive part of the community and an agent of change. In addition, the Internet, which seemed to threaten its reason for being, turns
out to be one of the things that bring people to the library.

The Near North Branch: Bridging Communities

The Near North Branch Library, which opened in 1997, represents the
new style of neighborhood library in Chicago. A freestanding tan stone

building with plantings of shrubs and flowers along two sides and a good-sized parking lot, it is several times bigger than typical old storefront neighborhood branches. Like all the other new libraries in the system, it has meeting rooms available for classes, discussions, and neighborhood groups. Like other branches, it incorporates artwork by local artists—in this case, a mural of dancers in the entryway and portraits by Illinois artists. As in other branches, its collections and services reflect the needs and interests of the community it serves, and they change as that community changes.

The Near North Branch sits between two very different neighborhoods. The Gold Coast, along the shore of Lake Michigan, is wealthy and mainly white, an area of expensive apartments, town houses, and condominiums. The mostly African-American Cabrini Green to the west has been known especially for its grim, high-rise public housing, for empty lots, gang violence, and run-down schools. Members of both communities use the library and, some of the time at least, meet one another through its programs and activities.

On weekday afternoons, as many as seventy schoolchildren, most of them from Cabrini Green, fill the children's section. Some of them work with the volunteers in the Homework Help program, most of whom are Gold Coast residents, retirees looking for satisfying and interesting ways to stay connected with the world. Claire, an energetic older woman from the Gold Coast, is one of the most active volunteers. She is at the library many afternoons when the kids arrive, and they know her as someone ready to sit down and help them with their assignments. She also attends the branch's adult book club meetings, where conversations about books draw personal stories from participants. "You hear astounding things from other adults," she says, and adds, "I have two homes. This is my other home." The meeting rooms at Near North are used for book discussions, condo association meetings, meetings of the Negro Women's League, finance workshops, job skills classes, teachers' in-service training, and other activities. Any group in the community can reserve a room. The computers that provide Internet access at the branch are used by people of all ages. High school and college-age "cybernavigators" teach basic computer and Web-search techniques.

Some adults who come to Near North have been using public libraries all their lives; others get their first library card here. A woman who lives at a nearby mental health residence often spends hours in the library. Sometimes street people snooze at one of the tables, as welcome as anyone. On a Friday afternoon in late May, a young woman coming from a graduation event stands in front of shelves of books while her father takes a picture of her in her lavender dress.

Millie, a forty-eight-year-old African-American woman, watches her five children as they spread out to various sections of the library, pursuing their own interests. While her three sons and two daughters explore Near North, Millie talks about the opening of the library and its meaning for her and her children. "I never had my own library card before they built this library," she says. She calls her children over; each proudly displays his or her own library card. "Putting this library here was more than just adding a building. It was about changing a perception. Before, I thought no one cared about people around Cabrini. And so we didn't care. Now I feel like someone is watching, trying to make things better. So I am trying to better myself and my children."

Children's librarian Anne Ayres greets children and adults as they come in. She knows all the regulars by name. "Libraries have changed," she says, and admits that a few people do not like the changes. "You don't get perfect quiet," she explains. "Some older people have trouble with the noise and activity." For most, though, this new style of library is more comfortable and useful than the old one, a place to be known and get to know others, a source of services as well as of books and information. "Now people say, 'I'll meet you at the library,'" Ayres says. "It's a safe place. It reminds me of the old neighborhood grocery store, where the grocer knew everyone and everyone saw their neighbors."

Near North's success at being a resource and meeting place for these two neighborhoods is no accident. The location of the branch, the design of the building, the collections, artwork, and staffing all reflect an explicit determination to make the library attractive to the whole range of potential users. It is meant, too, to be a social force in the neighborhood, a "community anchor," in the words of Mayor Richard M. Daley, and a catalyst for change.[2] Daley refers to the neighborhood library as the "heartbeat" of the community.

The library and the mayor hoped that locating Near North on the border between Cabrini Green and the Gold Coast would accomplish two things: encourage other improvements in Cabrini and bring together residents of two neighborhoods who had virtually no contact with one another. Assistant Commissioner for Neighborhood Services Charlotte Kim says that Gold Coast and Cabrini Green residents had long been requesting their own new branches. Winning the support of the aldermen in those communities for a single, shared branch took years of conversation—to communicate the vision of a library that would bridge the neighborhoods, as well as the practical and persuasive point that the Chicago Public Library would not fund two branches in the area. Once the decision to build the branch was made, Chicago Public Library Commissioner Mary Dempsey and her staff faced the challenge of building a library that would attract patrons from both communities.

Choosing exactly the right location was critical. Dempsey says she was offered two sites on Division Street, one just west of the El (the elevated rapid transit line) that runs north and south along Orleans Street, one just to the east of it. She chose the eastern site, believing that Gold Coast residents would not patronize a library farther west (and farther into Cabrini Green) and that the El itself created a physical and psychological barrier. The site chosen was still in Cabrini, in a run-down neighborhood and adjacent to a liquor store that attracted a lot of daytime drinkers. She hoped, though, that it would be close enough to the Gold Coast to "feel" accessible. The decision to build a good-sized parking lot was based explicitly on a desire to draw patrons who might be uneasy about walking into a neighborhood they perceived as dangerous.

At least as important as these considerations was the choice of a branch manager. Dempsey's search for the best candidate, for someone, she says, "who could speak quietly to both communities," led her outside the library system to Craig Davis, who was working in the private sector. Davis served as Near North Branch manager for its first five years. (He moved to a job at the Harold Washington Library Center in the spring of 2002.) His basic principle, he says, was "No matter who walked in, we treated them as equal to anyone else. They received whatever services they needed." Though he is pleased with his new position, you hear in his voice a hint of regret at no longer being in the thick of things at Near North, figuring out how to serve and bring together the diverse population of the area. During his first year or so as branch manager, he says, the library received frequent calls from Gold Coast residents, asking if the neighborhood was safe. The calls gradually decreased and then ended: experience, word of mouth, and changes in the neighborhood (more about the changes later) put the fears to rest. Anne, an attorney who lives in an impressive Gold Coast condominium with a view of Lake Michigan, brings her eleven-year-old daughter, Savannah, to Near North to check out books for her science project. "When I first moved to this area, I honestly could not have imagined coming this far west on Division. The library has won us over," she remarks, and her daughter nods. "There is a feeling of safety here, and I really enjoy coming to a place where such a diverse group interacts positively."

At Near North, as at other branches, the staff actively connect with the community. The old idea of the librarian behind her wall of books, passively waiting for patrons to arrive, is gone. Anne Ayres says that children's librarians reach out to all the schools in the neighborhood. (Commissioner Dempsey says unequivocally, "The library has an obligation to connect with every school principal in Chicago.") Before Near North opened, Ayres met all of the school principals and took photographs of the schools. On Dedication Day, when Near North opened its doors for the first time, children found a map of the area surrounded by photographs of the schools, including their own (plus a picture of Hogwarts to give young readers the thrill of imagining that Harry Potter's school might be hidden somewhere in Cabrini Green). Ayres regularly makes the rounds of the elementary schools to read stories. She describes how children's faces light up when they come to the library for the first time and recognize her—"Hey, you came to my school!"—and begin to think of the library as theirs, too. Davis says that the schools were "our inroad into the Cabrini community." One young mother noted the influence of the librarian's visit on her son's desire to go to the library: "One day, someone from here, maybe the librarian, visited my son Antonio's school. He came home and wouldn't stop talking about a library card and having his own books." She paused, smiling and shaking her head. "He took me, I didn't take him."

Davis used a Polk Brothers Foundation grant to fund workshops and programs that addressed the needs and interests of residents—often predominantly from one neighborhood or the other, but sometimes from both. A series of workshops on résumé writing, interviewing techniques, and how to enter a GED (General Equivalency Diploma) program attracted mainly Cabrini residents; seminars on financial planning drew more participants from the Gold Coast. Poetry readings and book discussions draw mixed crowds, though Davis laments what seems to be a decline in participation by Cabrini adults. Many who were actively involved in planning for the branch and were among its first patrons seem to have drifted away. The well-attended discussion of Harper Lee's *To Kill a Mockingbird*, the first book in the "One Book, One Chicago" program designed to encourage city residents to read the same book at the same time, was the biggest recent success at bringing in people from both neighborhoods and an opportunity to hear some of the "astounding things" about people's lives that Claire mentions. The summer children's reading program is popular with all children. In the summer of 2001, more than thirty thousand children participated in the program throughout the city, collectively reading more than 415,000 books.

Before he left Near North, Craig Davis oversaw new acquisitions for the branch's African-American history collection, one that has a particular focus on local history. "The library should be a custodian of knowledge of the neighborhood," he says. And in fact the localness of this and other branches is one of the first things that strike a visitor used to the idea of the library as a refuge from the world outside and a repository of a higher culture the neighborhood may aspire to but cannot reach. The local art, the pictures of schools, the meetings of neighborhood groups, and the collections that reflect the languages and interests of patrons make the library a place where people see a reflection of their own culture even as they get access to a wider one.

In the six years since the Near North Branch opened, the area around it has changed. As with most instances of urban improvement, the changes tell a complex story. The liquor store is gone, purchased by the Chicago Public Library and replaced by a garden. A nearby park has been renovated. A new high school opened nearby in 2000 and a new police station in 2001. Condominiums are going up on what had been empty lots, and a new Dominick's supermarket across the street from the library draws customers from both neighborhoods. The streets that, in Dempsey's words, "you wouldn't want to go down a few years ago" are much safer. Most of the Chicago Housing Authority high-rises have been torn down. Eliminating those failed experiments in urban renewal and public housing makes sense but comes at a cost: the mixed-income housing built to replace them cannot accommodate all the former tenants. So neighborhood improvement here means displacement for some, as it often does. The decline in the number of adult patrons from Cabrini Green may reflect the disappearance of some of those people from the neighborhood. In effect, then, the Gold Coast has crept farther west and the library, though still on the border, sits in a neighborhood that is becoming more middle class.

To what extent is the library responsible for these changes? Mary Dempsey believes that renewal (and some gentrification) was going to happen in this part of the city with or without the library. But the Near North Branch has been a source as well as a sign of change, the first substantial investment in a neighborhood that had been declining for a long time. With a laugh, Dempsey says, "We've been called the Marines, because we are the first to go in." Their going in has symbolic as well as practical value, as Millie's comments suggest. "A five- to seven-million-dollar investment tells people in a neighborhood they're valued," she says. In a community like Cabrini Green, starting with a library sends a very different and much more positive message than starting with a police station. Unquestionably, the Near North Branch has been a boon to Cabrini residents, attentive to their needs, respectful of their backgrounds and cultures. At the same time, it cannot escape the irony of helping to make a neighborhood too expensive for some of its longtime residents by making it attractive to people with more money. Some Cabrini Green residents complain that they are being forced out just when the area is becoming a safer place to live, with more amenities. An elderly African-American woman, a lifelong resident of Cabrini Green, speaks of how she no longer lives in the area but is just visiting her daughter, because she can no longer find a place to live: "My building closed and was knocked down. I wanted to stay here, close to my family. But how can I afford that? The new places are expensive." Her daughter adds, "As soon as it gets nice, we all have to go."

This is one of the ironies of investing in social capital that we will see in some other stories, too: improvements that help bring members of a community together sometimes also disrupt or sever old ties.

The area around the Harold Washington Library Center in the Loop has changed from an unappealing and somewhat unsafe area into a lively residential community that new people are moving into, many of them couples coming back from the suburbs after their children have grown. In response to finding itself in what is now a residential neighborhood, the library has opened "CPL Express" on the ground floor—in effect a neighborhood branch within the central library. In 2002, following the lead of many bookstores, it also opened a café, creating a new meeting place for area residents.

Mayor Daley believes that improving neighborhoods should be an explicit aim of the library. Speaking at an Urban Libraries Council conference in 2000, he said, "Unless you are out there changing neighborhoods, you are not completing the work you are to do."[3] Commissioner

Dempsey clearly believes that she serves the city, not just the library. Riding with her from the Harold Washington Library Center on South State Street to the Near North Branch on West Division, you get a sense of how engaged she is with the dynamics of a changing city and the way the library will affect and be affected by the changes. She knows which new businesses are moving into particular locations, which businesses are closing, which buildings will be renovated and which demolished, and what will replace them.

Other Neighborhood Branches

The outreach and responsiveness of Near North—the extent to which its neighborhood shapes its collections and activities—are typical of branches throughout the system. All reach out to local schools; all tailor their collections and programs to the character of the neighborhood, sometimes in surprising and subtle ways. The Humboldt Park Branch, in an area with a large Latino population, maintains an extensive collection of Spanish-language books, magazines, and newspapers. Branch manager Tom Stark chose to combine the youth and adult nonfiction sections, since he was sensitive to the fact that adults with a wide range of reading abilities patronized the library; the blended collection would allow readers to find easy-to-read books without the humiliation they might feel searching for books in the children's section. And because nearby Humboldt Park has lakes stocked with fish, the library keeps a rack of fishing rods near the circulation desk, lending them to anyone who has a library card, with or without books on how to fish.

Stark, who is married to Anne Ayres, lives a few blocks from the library, so he is part of the community and participates in local organizations to understand neighborhood issues and learn what residents want from the library. He says that the Friends of the Library, who were deeply involved in getting the branch built, have their fingers on the pulse of the community and help keep the library connected.

Meeting local needs and connecting with the community also shape the Teacher in the Library program. Erma Marks and Kelly Bodkin are teachers at nearby schools who spend after-school hours at the Humboldt Park Branch. Marks says, "Children come to you, but sometimes their parents come to learn how to help their children with schoolwork, and some adults working on their GEDs ask for help for themselves. We're available to anyone who wants help." Kelly, who, like Tom Stark, lives and works in the neighborhood, says she never imagined she would want to work with children at the library after a full day at school with them, but her hours at the library make her a more effective teacher and connect her more closely with the neighborhood. "Being here makes the teacher part of the community," she says. "I see some of the kids I teach at school here, and they come to think of a teacher as someone who listens to them. And I'm always preaching the library at school."

On a Thursday evening in late May, seven or eight people from the neighborhood meet to discuss Amy Wilentz's *Martyrs' Crossing* in a book discussion group at the Humboldt Park Branch. One of the women in the group leads the discussion. Tom Stark takes part, though he is careful to let others shape the conversation. The group is much smaller than the one that gathered a month earlier to discuss Elie Wiesel's *Night*, the second book in the "One Book, One Chicago" program. Most of them express dissatisfaction with Wilentz's book, something of a letdown after Wiesel's powerful short novel. But the diverse group of women and men, Hispanic, African-American, and white (including one transplanted Briton) use the novel as a jumping-off place to share stories of their own lives. One man talks about growing up in a violent Chicago neighborhood and so understanding how violence affects the lives of the Palestinians and Israelis who populate the book. Another man describes dropping out of school as a youth and discovering his intellectual capacity and love of reading later on. Impressed by the beauty of the writing, he likes the book best of anyone in the group. At the end of the session, they consider what to discuss at their June meeting: maybe some poetry next time. Stark promises to track down some possibilities and be in touch with them so they can choose.

The Bezazian Branch in Uptown is smaller than those in Near North and Humboldt Park but built on the same model, a freestanding building with a row of windows on the street letting in plenty of natural light, a large public meeting room, Internet-access computers, and collections and decorations that reflect the surrounding community. Uptown has a large Southeast Asian population, so the library has books in Vietnamese, Cambodian, and Chinese, along with English-language books and smaller collections in Russian and other languages. The area is extremely diverse, says branch manager Mary Clark. Children come to the local elementary school with thirty-two different native languages, and the school offers bilingual education in seven of them. Sometimes the groups that sign up for courses in ESL (English as a second language) are mostly Vietnamese, sometimes Bosnian; sometimes the members are elderly Russians. In the spring of 2002, green shoots of bamboo sprouting leaves sit in glasses of water on the circulation desk, in display cabinets, and in Clark's office—growing the shoots is a spring custom of many of the library's patrons.

Clark says that the first public act of many newcomers in the city is to get a library card. It is the first official document that connects them to their new home, that makes them part of the place. They can get one even if they do not speak English, and they do not have to prove anything except that they live in Chicago. Mary Dempsey describes the library as "the least threatening public institution." Its absence of barriers to members, its determination to welcome everyone, proves the point. So the library frequently functions as a point of entry into the society for new immigrants, a safe and easy first step to participation in community and public life. "I learn English here," a middle-aged Vietnamese man says, pointing to a sign on the wall for ESL classes. He smiles at the seven- or eight-year-old girl beside him and adds, "My daughter, she teaches me, also."

On a Saturday afternoon in late May at the Bezazian Branch, members of the Neighborhood Writing Alliance gather in the meeting room—about twenty people, African-American, Hispanic, Asian, Latino. Most are here to read from their work, a few are just looking for a place to sit for an hour or so and maybe hear something interesting. A woman who identifies herself as Patty reads excerpts from her harrowing, matter-of-fact account of her five months of homelessness in the neighborhood. Anton, who says he edits a newsletter for people in his building, reads a piece called "New Beginnings," which includes these lines: "In life there are choices and chances. Make a choice, take a chance, reap the rewards." Chuck reads a love poem, "Electric Touch." Anifa maneuvers her battery-powered wheelchair to the front of the room and reads a long, critical letter to Oprah Winfrey about how women should and shouldn't be portrayed on her show. Everyone is applauded. Many of the people taking part in the Saturday reading meet at the library every Tuesday afternoon, so they know one another and one another's work well.

There are few children in the library this afternoon. Clark says sixty or more show up after school, some to work with Homework Help volunteers from the neighborhood. But the computer terminals are in constant use and adults of various ages and races occupy every seat in the place. Their concentrated attention to the books and papers in front of them suggests that most are engaged in serious work or study.

Clark, who has managed the Bezazian Branch for two years, talks about how the role of the librarian has changed and is now more active and engaged. She recalls the young woman who recently asked for a book on zoning regulations because she wanted to open a nail-care salon. "In the past, I would have just handed over the book," Clark says. "But she was really asking a small-business question, and I worked with her to get the answer." Similarly, library staff helped a woman who needed to fill out a financial aid form for her grandson—a form available only online. Having never used a computer before, much less gone on the Internet, she could not have found the form or completed it without their help.

Though Clark has been a librarian for a long time, the enthusiasm she feels for Bezazian is evident. Staff throughout the system appear energetic and proud of their work. Adequate funding, the active support of the mayor, and an effective library commissioner no doubt contribute to morale. But as Mary Clark, Anne Ayres, Tom Stark, and others talk about their jobs, you sense their excitement at doing something new and valuable, being in on the creation of a new, more active role for the librarian.

Bridging the Digital Divide

That elderly woman's struggle with the online financial aid form exemplifies two main elements of the problem of what is called the digital divide. One is that many people still do not have computers, computer skills, or access to the Internet. The other is that institutions increasingly assume that "everybody" uses computers. So the computer have-nots, who often lack other advantages, too, are left behind by the information revolution, locked out of opportunities to improve their situation. Case in point: the grandparents and parents who do not live near a library where the staff will help them fill out a form on the computer to get financial aid for their children or to seek critical services and information.

The rooms full of computers on several floors of the Harold Washington Library Center, the five hundred new Internet-access computers added in 2000 alone at the Chicago Public Library, the computer classes, and the paid "cybernavigators" support what the library considers one of its critical roles: to bridge the digital divide, at least to some extent, by making computers and the Internet available to people who have no private access to them. So the computer and Internet developments that some believed would kill public libraries actually provide new reasons for going to them. (Buried in the death-of-the-library prediction is that false assumption that "everybody" has a computer at home, along with, probably, a parallel assumption that "everybody" can afford to buy books.) "I cannot imagine how I could have ever learned computers without the library's help," a Hispanic man states as he searches for information on how to apply for a mortgage online. "I am forty-five years old and wasn't born in this country. My English is very good. But I have no computer. I can come here, use a computer, and get help."

The prediction that the World Wide Web would kill libraries ignores another essential role of the public library in the Internet age. The almost inconceivable variety of information available online is a mixed blessing, as even casual Internet users quickly discover. Finding a few needles of useful, reliable information in vast haystacks of junk calls for precisely the skills that librarians have always had. In the past, people counted on them to locate and evaluate printed information; now they look to librarians for help in making sense of what they find on the Internet, and for distinguishing good information from bad. The reference librarians whose job it is to answer every question phoned in to the library report that they get as many questions as ever, but the questions have gotten more sophisticated as Internet use has increased. Many people find answers on the Internet to questions they used to ask librarians—phone numbers and addresses of institutions, sources of quotations, basic facts of science and geography. Now they ask the questions that arise after they get answers to the simple ones, along with asking which electronic sources of information are reliable and which are not. The techno-utopian belief that access to unlimited information automatically translates into understanding and knowledge has proved to be false. Trained guides are more important than ever, and libraries provide them.

In serving as a gateway to the Internet, the Chicago Public Library finds itself in the middle of the current societal debate about how to deal with the openness of that new medium for all types of human expression, including pornography and every imaginable prejudice and hatred. On the same weekend that members of the Neighborhood Writing Alliance read their work at the Bezazian Branch, CPL press secretary Margot Burke was fielding calls from reporters looking for the library's reaction to a group of South Side clergy who were protesting the library's Internet policy and demanding that filters be installed on computers to shield children from pornography and other inappropriate material. Consistent with the views of the American Library Association, the Chicago Public Library opposes filtering. In addition to pointing out that critics usually overestimate the extent of the problem—patrons rarely access pornography sites in the library—Burke presents the reasons for the CPL's position: that filtering software (most of it based on keywords) works poorly, locking viewers out of sites offering, for instance, medical information, as well as pornographic ones; that the public library is in the business of providing, not limiting, access to information; and that blocking full Internet access at the public library offends against the founding democratic principle of that institution in the United States—that all residents, not only those who can afford to buy books, computers, and Internet connections, deserve equal access to information.

The New Third Place

As our glimpses of the branches in Chicago show, the new neighborhood library functions as a kind of community center, a place where people get to know one another, where communities find themselves. The book discussions, readings, and classes, the homework help after school, the nods and hellos people exchange when they see each other at the library for the second or fifth or twentieth time, the librarians greeting people by name, and even the artwork that reflects the talents and interests of the neighborhood all contribute to the connections that bind people in community. Death-of-the-library scenarios define libraries as information repositories. If they were no more than that, then their eventual displacement by more convenient electronic repositories would make persuasive sense. But the library is a gathering place, too, like an old town square or the corner grocer Anne Ayres remembers. People may go to the library looking mainly for information, but they find each other there. Although the World Wide Web holds out the promise of online communities and cyberspace main streets (a subject we look at a bit in Chapter 11), those electronic "places" do not—or not yet—give people the ability to meet face-to-face or to connect with others in the community merely by being there, part of the scene, even when they do not actively participate.

In *The Great Good Place*, Ray Oldenburg describes what he calls the "third place," a place that is neither work nor home where people can spend time together.[4] The café, the pub, the neighborhood tavern, the old-fashioned drugstore-with-soda-fountain are some of the examples he uses. A good third place makes few demands on the people who gather there, beyond requiring them to abide by some basic local rules (for instance, that individuals and especially newcomers will not dominate the conversation). A third place is a neutral ground where people from different walks of life in the community can meet and get to know one another, having in common perhaps only their desire to frequent this particular place.

Oldenburg laments the disappearance of many third places in America. Prohibition and a lingering association between alcohol and dissipation undermined the old beer gardens and many of the taverns that used to be community meeting places. The replacement of local shops by chain stores and single-use zoning that puts housing, workplaces, and retail establishments in different areas have eliminated the corner drugstores and the coffee shops where people met one another and found out what was happening in the neighborhood. (Starbucks and other café chains represent a partial countertrend.) Television keeps people at home in the evening, when in the past they would have sought one another's company in a third place.

The crowds at cafés—even at some uninviting corporate café chains—attest to the continuing need people feel for third places. The Chicago libraries help meet that need. Although Oldenburg does not include it in his catalogue of third places, the branch library shares many third-place characteristics. It welcomes everyone who abides by its basic rules of appropriate behavior. It recognizes as "regulars" people who come, say, more than a couple of times a month. It provides opportunities for meeting and conversation. It is a place where you can discover what is happening in the neighborhood. Granted, the library is not as purely a social place as the coffee shop or tavern—it may be more purposeful than the ideal third place. But the CPL has made its neighborhood branches meeting places for the community. Keeping quiet with your eyes on a book no longer represents what happens in the library. And, like other third places, these neighborhood branches mirror their communities, showing residents who they are collectively.

One Chicago, One Library, Many Branches

Nancy Pearl, executive director of the Washington Center for the Book, came up with the idea of mobilizing the residents of a city to read the same book at the same time. Seattle did it first, where the program was known as "If All of Seattle Read the Same Book." Rochester, New York, and then dozens of other cities followed suit. New York City made news for rejecting the idea, the letters and columns of its newspapers full of indignation at the thought of diverse individuals being "forced" to read the same book and of literature being made to serve a social purpose. But Chicago embraced the idea.

Chicago's 2001 choice, *To Kill a Mockingbird*, was checked out of branch libraries more than eight thousand times over the course of a couple of months. Bookstores sold thousands more copies—*To Kill a Mockingbird* was on the Barnes & Noble top ten list for two months. The library published a study guide, handed out "Are you reading *Mockingbird?*" buttons, scheduled book discussions and showings of the movie version of the story, and organized a mock trial to match the trial in the book (the trial advertised on paper fans with wooden handles, like those people might have used in a southern courthouse years ago). Tens of thousands of people read the book. The library collected stories of read-aloud sessions between parents and their adolescent children, of classroom discussions about prejudice, of strangers striking up conversations when they saw one another with the book. The library's deputy commissioner, Kathy Biel, reports having a conversation for the first time with people she had seen for years on her commuter train when they noticed her *Mockingbird* button and started talking to her about the book. A Chicago high school junior named Neil recalled, "I was reading the book for school and my mom decided to read it with me. We had very different views of the book, and so we joined a book group at the library to see who was right." Who *was* right? "We both were," he said with a smile. "And neither of us was."

For its second book, the Library chose *Night*, Elie Wiesel's fictional account of a boy's experience of the Holocaust. That program in the spring of 2002 included a talk by Wiesel, discussions in classrooms and libraries (some of the latter attended by Holocaust survivors with their own memories to share), related stories in the newspapers and on public radio, and simultaneous book discussions in Starbucks cafés throughout the city.

In most cities that have tried the one book, one city idea, libraries see the program mainly as a strategy for encouraging reading. The Chicago version shares that aim but has a larger one, too, consistent with the library's role as a force for social connection and social improvement. Mary Dempsey talks about the program's moving reading into the "public domain" and giving a "public voice" to what is usually considered a private activity. (Note the similarity to the Texas IAF's strategy of "making private pain public.") Library staffers delight in telling stories of conversations between people drawn together by the book, and of book discussion groups where people who have known one another casually or not at all exchange stories from their lives. "One Book, One Chicago" expresses the goal: to discover or build unity in a diverse city.

Why does a program that cannot get off the ground in New York City thrive in Chicago? One senior CPL staff member describes Chicago as "New York without the attitude" (a distinction that we suspect many New Yorkers would proudly acknowledge). It may be truer and more useful to say that Chicago feels like a very large and very diverse midwestern town, with a small-town friendliness and civic pride, and a small-town sense of joint ownership of public institutions. Commissioner Dempsey says, "People choose to live in this city because of its free institutions: the parks, the libraries, the lakefront." Though Chicago has its competing constituencies and serious tensions over racial and economic differences, it feels like a place where people still have a common, democratic stake in the life of the city.

It feels like a small town, too, in the closeness of its networks of relationships. Dempsey says, "In Chicago, there are two degrees of separation, not six." Those networks have helped the library develop partnerships with public and private institutions. In addition to maintaining close ties with schools, the library works with the police and the Housing Authority to address neighborhood problems. It develops joint programs with the zoo and museums, and it worked with the Department of Sewers to create a "Down the Drain" program that would teach citizens about the history and workings of the sewer system. It offers free passes to the Art Institute of Chicago and each summer distributes more than thirty thousand lawn tickets to the jazz and classical concerts at the Ravinia Festival, while helping to develop music education programs to spur children's interest in serious music. Dempsey explains that Ravinia (the summer home of the Chicago Symphony) entered into partnership with the library because it feared the festival was becoming too elitist. She says, "We can reach people in the steel mills and the barrios that they can't. They are one place; we are seventy-eight buildings."

In the lower-level rotunda of the central library, these words of Chicago's late mayor Harold Washington are worked into a circular design in the marble floor:

> Chicago . . . has brought together black and white, Asian and Hispanic, male and female, the young, the old, the disabled, gays and lesbians, Moslems, Christians and Jews, business leaders and neighborhood activists, bankers and trade unionists—all have come together to mix and contend, to argue and to reason, to confront our problems and not merely to contain them.

Yes, these are the words of a politician, but one not afraid to raise potentially controversial issues—for instance, to include gays and lesbians in his list of diverse citizens and to invite argument and contention, not merely the kind of tolerance that ignores differences and avoids contact with people of other races, classes, religions, or sexual orientation. These particular words are embedded in the design of the central library because they express one of the Chicago Public Library's core missions: to reflect and serve the diversity of the city's residents while helping those residents discover the sympathies and interests that unite them.

CHAPTER 3

{ Portsmouth, New Hampshire }

The Shipyard Project
Building Bridges with Dance

Portsmouth, New Hampshire, is a picturesque port city of just over twenty-five thousand people on the southern bank of the Piscataqua River. Historic mansions and eighteenth- and nineteenth-century brick warehouses (now housing restaurants and shops) line its downtown streets. The spires of old New England churches rise above the two- and three-story buildings. Portsmouth is a destination for tourists, who visit the Strawbery Banke Museum, which preserves homes, taverns, and shops dating back to the first half of the seventeenth century. It is an artists' town, with galleries and theaters and annual festivals of music and drama. Though no longer the thriving port it was in past centuries, Portsmouth remains fairly prosperous, attracting retirees and young high-tech workers with its unusual combination of small size and sophistication.

On an island directly across the river from downtown Portsmouth is the Portsmouth Naval Shipyard. From the green lawns of Prescott Park in Portsmouth or from the riverside deck of one of the downtown restaurants, you can see the orange and slate-blue girders of half a dozen cranes rising above the shipyard's metal-sided buildings and storage sheds. Often you can spot the rounded, matte-black hull of a nuclear submarine lying in the water, or the nose cone of a sub, pointing skyward, on the dock. The massive stone building at the eastern end of the shipyard, now empty, was a naval prison until the mid-1970s.

Established in 1800, the shipyard has been part of the life of Portsmouth and nearby towns in New Hampshire and Maine for more than two centuries. During World War II, when it produced a new submarine every nine months, it employed more than twenty thousand people—a workforce almost equal to the population of present-day Portsmouth. In recent years, its smaller workforce of just over three thousand has repaired and refitted nuclear submarines built elsewhere.

Despite this long history and the fact that shipyard workers and some submariners and their families live in the Portsmouth area now, as they have for generations, by the 1990s many residents of Portsmouth with no personal connection to the shipyard saw in it an odd and ugly contrast to what the city had become: on one side of the river, restaurants, theaters, bookstores, and shops selling work by local artisans; on the other, heavy machinery and nuclear submarines. Some people were openly hostile to the pollution caused by shipyard work or to the whole idea of submarines designed to carry weapons of mass destruction. Most, hostile or not, had no clear idea of who worked at the shipyard or precisely what the workers did.

That gap in knowledge and sympathy between much of Portsmouth and the naval installation a few hundred yards across the Piscataqua led Christine Dwyer to conceive the idea of an arts project about the Portsmouth Naval Shipyard, one that would reveal and explain it to the city and maybe bring the two communities closer together. Dwyer was president of the board of trustees of the Music Hall, an organization in Portsmouth that presents "live and cinematic arts." Early in 1994, she decided that the Music Hall should propose a shipyard arts project to the Lila Wallace–Reader's Digest Arts Partners Program, which was offering grants for feasibility studies on projects that would jointly involve arts organizations and other community organizations.

Building Bridges

Dwyer asked Jane Hirshberg, director of development and education at the Music Hall, to write a grant proposal for a shipyard arts project feasibility study. Hirshberg was skeptical about linking the arts and the military in general and about the shipyard in particular.[1] Like many political liberals, she had qualms about military power—the dangers it posed, the political views she believed it represented. Before writing the proposal, she interviewed people connected with the shipyard to see whether they had any interest in participating in an arts project, judging that the first requirement of a meaningful project would be the willing participation of former and current shipyard personnel. Her conversations with shipyard people, including Portsmouth's mayor, Eileen Foley, a former worker there, began to humanize the Yard for her and broaden her view of the military installation. She found shipyard workers to be like other people—they cared about their families and took pride in their work, and, contrary to her expectations (or prejudices) about the military, they expressed a wide range of political and social opinions. So the first beneficiary of the project's bridge-building aim was Hirshberg herself, as she gained a sympathetic understanding of the Yard. From the beginning, she heard compelling human stories that fired her enthusiasm for the proposal.

Hirshberg soon decided that Liz Lerman, founder and artistic director of the Liz Lerman Dance Exchange of Takoma Park, Maryland, was the one artist she could imagine successfully taking on the project. In 1992, Lerman had conducted a series of dance workshops in Portsmouth for students, seniors, health-care providers, and even some shipyard workers. That work was grounded in Lerman's almost two decades of experience creating dances about and with people of all ages and backgrounds who did not think of themselves as dancers, and it demonstrated Lerman's talent for connecting with people and tapping into their enthusiasm and creativity. More to the point, Lerman had a reputation for a spirit of open inquiry, discovering and respecting people's varied points of view rather than imposing her own or listening only to the voices that echoed hers. A successful arts project about a naval shipyard demanded that kind of openness. Hirshberg asked Lerman if she was interested.

As adaptable as she was, Lerman had, not surprisingly, never thought of doing anything remotely like creating a dance about the people who repaired nuclear submarines. The subject seemed hard to reconcile with her own liberal political views, but the idea intrigued her for several reasons. Projects that "come out of left field" are the best, she says, because "they make you go somewhere new." Seen from that perspective, the apparent lack of a fit between Lerman's beliefs and her subject was an incentive, not a drawback. The "somewhere new" in this case included moving away from art that tended to express a liberal social agenda when it dealt with political or social issues at all. Also, Lerman firmly believed that everyone has a right to tell his or her story, and the stories of the shipyard workers had never been told publicly, never told in art. She believed, too, in the importance of talking across boundaries, and here was an opportunity to do just that. The gulf of silence and misunderstanding between the shipyard and the rest of the community was what had sparked Dwyer's initial interest. For all these reasons, Lerman agreed to take on the project.

Hirshberg contacted 125 current or former shipyard workers, a list of names that began with suggestions from Mayor Foley and grew as the people she spoke with suggested others, who suggested others in turn. This process of following branches of connection—tracing the pathways of social networks—continued throughout the project, bringing in new people and their stories. Twenty-five of those 125 agreed to come to a meeting in October 1994 to explore the possibility of working with Lerman, who came up from Maryland with a couple of dancers from her company. During that first meeting, she asked people about the shipyard: the work they did or had done there, the images that came to mind when they thought about it. The conversation marked the beginning of a relationship between the artist and the shipyard and the beginning of the dance: the discovery of gestures that, two years later, would express the life of the Yard in movement. A rigger talked about his job, his hands moving to show what he did, gestures that long years of doing the work had made graceful and economical. Some of those movements found their way into the dance. Everyone who talked about the image of the Yard mentioned the cranes that rise above the surrounding buildings and dry docks. Lerman asked, "If you were going to make a picture of a crane with your body, what would it look like?" Immediately, everyone's arm went up, stretched out at an angle, wrist bent, crane-like, and another of the dance's gestures had been discovered. At the end of the evening, Lerman led people in a brief dance of shipyard gestures they could do sitting in their chairs. Connecting with people, learning from them, and making art from their experience happened simultaneously. That first, exploratory meeting proved that dancing the shipyard story would be possible because that, in embryo, is what people did that evening.

Origins of a Different Way of Making Dances

How did Lerman arrive at the idea of democratic, participatory dance, and why has it defined her career for more than a quarter of a century? She believes that the *why* is a legacy of her parents. She says that the most important things in her father's life were human rights and civil liberties and that he challenged her every day to be aware of and involved in those issues. Her mother had a passionate interest in art. She was an elitist, Lerman says, not in the sense of having a snobbish preference for so-called high art over popular art but caring deeply about quality. She was the one who made sure that her daughter studied with the best dance teachers. Lerman sums up the values she learned from her parents as a blend of "nurture and rigor."

But nurture was hard to find in the professional dance world of the early 1970s, when she began her career. "It was cold, distant, and boring," she says. "The only people who came to performances were other dancers. The more professional I became, the further I felt from what drove me to dance in the first place."

Her mother's death from cancer set her on a new path. (So her mother was part of the *how* as well as the *why* of her career.) She felt compelled to create a dance for and about her mother and knew it could be realized only by "old bodies." "I had no choice," Lerman says. "I had to find those old people." She went to the Roosevelt Hotel for Senior Citizens in Washington, D.C., to find them and began teaching dance Thursday evenings for five dollars a week. The experience taught her that elderly people dance with special energy and conviction when their movements come out of real stories and situations, so she began to mix storytelling and dance. She brought her dance students from George Washington University to the class and discovered that both elders and young dancers gained from working together. After five months of classes, she told her senior citizen students about wanting to create a dance for her mother. Six volunteered. They, along with some professional dancers from the community and dancers from the university, formed the company that would perform the dance that Lerman describes as "spirits welcoming my mother."

The audience's emotional reaction to the first performances of that dance and the senior dancers' desire to do more led eventually to the creation of Dancers of the Third Age, a program of classes, rehearsals, and performances involving older adults. Lerman does not see creating that first dance as especially daring because, she says, she had "no choice." But she does call her conscious decision to continue working with older, nonprofessional dancers "an act of courage." It meant turning her back on how professional dance defined and judged itself. Some of her former colleagues accused her of becoming a social worker, that is, of abandoning her art.

But she did not give up on artistry, the rigor that her mother valued. She did reject the idea of a hierarchy of art, with the most abstruse and forbidding professional work at the top, followed by lesser and more popular styles of performance and so on down the scale to amateur and community efforts. She has talked about "hiking the horizontal," turning that rigid scale on its side so that nothing is categorically above anything else, recognizing that good—or bad—art can happen anywhere on the continuum. Assuming that the best is always the most rarified and serious professional work is the wrong kind of elitism. Then and later, she demanded a lot of her dancers. She does not condescend toward "amateur" dancers of any age by assuming that they are not capable of much. Enthusiasm and sincerity alone do not make good art. The dancers respond to the challenge, working toward the discipline and expressiveness that make good dance, improving over time. Lerman describes one of the older dancers in the piece she created for her mother coming to her after they had been performing for four months and saying, "I finally feel like a spirit welcoming your mother."

"What were you doing before?" Lerman asked.

"Counting beats," the woman told her.

Lerman has a gift for encouraging her dancers to work hard at improving without feeling pressured or criticized. Participants in the Shipyard Project talk about how much fun rehearsals were and how, as one put it, "everyone was smiling."

By the time she began the project in Portsmouth, Lerman had also learned how to shape the stories and gestures of the people she worked with into art that expressed her own vision as well as their experience. The process of learning about her subject—of entering into the lives of the people she works with—is completely open and inclusive. But, she says, "There is a difference between the all-accepting creative process and art making. I'm listening for what interests me." She describes the process of art making as "reversing the funnel," that is, moving from gathering as much material as possible to selecting and refining the elements that strike her as most expressive, finding the juxtapositions that add meaning, the patterns of moving bodies and sounds that turn people's stories and gestures into a dance. This is where the rigor comes in; it is how she makes something that genuinely speaks to the audience and the performers. In a way, the process is not so different from what any artist does—observing the world around her, selecting and interpreting—but the collaboration is closer, less in the artist's own head. Lerman opens the "funnel" wider at the beginning to see more of the art in everyday movement. (In 2002, the MacArthur Foundation recognized Lerman's unique contribution to art and community by choosing her for one of its "genius grants.")

Creating Connections, Creating Dances

The process of connecting with the shipyard and discovering dance elements in the stories of people who talked about it continued for many months after the October 1994 meeting. Jane Hirshberg says that many of the ideas for the dance, including its content, were developed by the committee of twelve Portsmouth people who met every month for two and a half years to work on the project. The group included Jane herself, some local dancers, a historian, and current and retired shipyard workers. They identified most of the sites in Portsmouth and at the shipyard that would be effective venues for the dance; they developed the idea of a multiday, multitheme performance. Most of all, says Hirshberg, the members of the group got to know one another, sharing their personal histories as they met month after month. "When we got into the meeting agenda," she adds, "the storytelling just got more interesting." The shipyard stories that the performance eventually expressed, stories they told one another and gathered from others, had much of the character of intimacy and trust that they had established among themselves.

During their visits to Portsmouth, Lerman and other Dance Exchange members talked with workers at the Yard; they invited anyone who had experiences with the shipyard or impressions of it to tell about them; they held workshops where people could begin to learn some of the dance movements that were gradually coming together. Lerman's enthusiasm and sympathy persuaded people who had never imagined dancing in public to join the project.

Charlie Lawrence, a thirty-six-year veteran of Portsmouth Naval Shipyard work who became a dancer and storyteller, signed on after Lerman's first visit to the Yard. He was impressed, he says, by "the way she heard people's stories and told the stories back to them." That quality of attention and understanding convinced him that she could help tell the real story of what it is like to work in a submarine. Another shipyard employee, surprised to find himself willingly involved in a modern dance project, remarked, "Liz could talk a hound dog off a truckload of meat bones."[2]

Peter Bowman, who had been commander of the shipyard until his retirement in 1990 after thirty years in the Navy, describes being drawn in when Lerman interviewed him. Wary at the start, prepared to decline to answer questions that touched on sensitive military issues or certain aspects of the Yard's pollution problems, he was disarmed by what he calls Lerman's "skill, softness, and compassion." The anticipated confrontation never happened. At the end of the interview, she asked if he would serve on the project advisory committee, and he agreed. She said, "I should tell you that advisory committee members need to dance in a couple of things."

Bowman responded, "You don't understand. I can't dance."

She told him, "Peter, you don't understand. Everyone can dance."

And he did. "The Shipyard Project transformed me from a passive participant in the arts to an active one," he says. "Liz makes you seem capable of more than you ever thought you could be." After the project ended, Bowman became a member of the Music Hall's board of trustees and then president of the board for two years, the direction of his life changed by the experience and his circle of acquaintances enlarged to take in the arts community he had begun to work with.

The process of building a relationship with the shipyard was not a simple progression of ever-increasing trust and cooperation. The decision makers at the Yard were cautious, concerned about how their story would be presented. They also had other things on their minds, including the possibility that the base would be closed in the next round of cutbacks.

In June 1995, having been involved with the project for more than a year, Hirshberg agreed to testify on behalf of the shipyard at a hearing in Boston that would help determine which military facilities would close. Twice before, in 1991 and 1993, the shipyard had been listed among the installations being considered for closing. It had survived both rounds of cuts, but now it was on the list again. Not an enthusiastic supporter of military spending, Hirshberg had mixed feelings about her role in testifying. She certainly knew she had nothing to contribute about the Yard's military importance. Instead, she spoke for the shipyard in terms of its importance to the community and described the work in process to develop a dance about it. She does not pretend that her testimony was an important factor in the decision to keep operating the shipyard, but her participation demonstrated goodwill to shipyard personnel and opened the doors to cooperation with the project a little wider.

Some months later, it seemed the doors were closing again. Lerman was given a five-minute meeting with the current commander, Carl Strawbridge, to convince him to continue to work with the project. He said, "People don't understand the shipyard. They don't understand what we do or why we do it."

She asked, "Are you talking about the shipyard or modern dance?" and added, "This is a literacy project about the Yard and about art." He was convinced and he supported the project from then on.

That exchange exemplifies one key to bridging communities and cultures: finding common ground, a meeting place, while recognizing and respecting differences. Lerman is good at it. When she asked a shipyard worker to explain his work and his hands started drawing graceful arcs in the air as he described what he did, she told him, "This is where you and I are going to cross paths, in the physical nature of your work."[3]

Over time, deeper and more powerful stories of the shipyard began to emerge. Lerman and a few other members of the Dance Exchange team met with six or seven wives of submariners, who described what being a Navy wife was like, especially the months of managing home and family while their husbands were at sea. Gestures that accompanied their stories became part of the dances, too. This one, for instance: a woman's hands held at the small of her back, thumbs and forefingers pressed gently together, as if grasping some small object. Her hands circle forward at the level of her belly, thumbs and forefingers touching in front of her. It is a thoughtful gesture, and somehow both enclosing and reaching out, generous.

It came from a woman who told about her husband leaving on a nine-month tour of duty soon after she became pregnant for the first time. She explained how week after week she had measured her growing belly with a piece of string (and here her hands illustrated what she had done) and put the longer and longer strings in her letters to him. He hung them in his locker aboard the submarine, short to long, like harp strings. When a shipmate asked about them, he said, "That's my baby."

Then there was the story of the *Thresher*, the worst moment in the Portsmouth Naval Shipyard's history. One of the early atomic submarines, the USS *Thresher* was serviced in Portsmouth before it went out on maneuvers in 1963. On April 10, during a test dive 220 miles east of Boston, something went wrong—exactly what has never been determined—and the *Thresher* sank, its hull crushed by water pressure as it fell toward the ocean floor 8,500 feet down. All 129 people aboard died—sailors and 17 civilian technicians. More than thirty years later, engineers who had worked on the *Thresher* still felt the burden of guilt and sorrow; family members of lost submariners who still lived in the Portsmouth area continued to blame the shipyard and its workers. Some of those people met and heard one another's stories for the first time at Shipyard Project rehearsals. One engineer gave the now adult daughter of one of the lost men a picture of her father, a gesture of reconciliation that marked the beginning of a friendship between them.

Lerman brought as many parts of the community as possible into the Shipyard Project. Middle school children, elders, and members of the Officers' Wives Club danced along with shipyard workers themselves and members of the Dance Exchange; the Dover and York high school bands performed music written by composer Wayne Horvitz, and their color guards performed flag routines. Musicians, singers, artists, and clergy from the area took part. The one community group that refused to participate was the environmentalists, who believed that the shipyard was not doing enough to clean up the pollution it had caused. Lerman regrets not being able to draw them into the project.

The long, intricate, collaborative process of creating the dances brought people and their stories together. The heart of the project was the almost two years of preparation, rather than the week of performance, as satisfying as that proved to be. People working together over time is what built connections and understanding. It took time to let the stories come out, to shape stories and gestures into art, to establish trust and understanding. It takes time for arts projects to grow out of the life of a community, but, Lerman comments, financial support from sources such as the Lila Wallace–Reader's Digest Fund for lengthy residencies is rare. "Time is everything, but nobody wants to pay for the time it takes to do something like this," she says.

Performance

Because the history of the Portsmouth Naval Shipyard and its relationship to the seacoast area was so long and complex, the committee and Lerman decided to create a series of dances to be performed over the course of a week, with different days featuring different sets of themes. Monday would focus on history and personal stories; Tuesday would explore battleground and common ground, including environmental issues, the *Thresher* disaster, and a border dispute between Maine and New Hampshire over which state the Yard belonged to; Wednesday would deal especially with technology and teamwork and much of the choreography of shipyard work. On Thursday, there would be songs, stories, and a Yard "fashion show," with a grand finale on Saturday, September 21. The performances would take place all over the city and the shipyard: in the Music Hall, the largest formal performance space in Portsmouth, but also in Prescott Park across the river from the Yard, in St. John's Episcopal Church, atop the USS *Squalus* submarine memorial at the shipyard, on the lanes of a bowling alley (the dancers wearing rented bowling shoes so as not to damage the wooden surface), and on Memorial Bridge, which spans the Piscataqua River, connecting Portsmouth with Kittery, Maine, near the entrance to the Yard. No one but Lerman knew how all the pieces would fit together, and she probably did not fully know what the dances would look like or what effect they would have until they happened.

The performances begin in the afternoon of Sunday, September 15,

1996, twenty-three months after Lerman and people from the shipyard met for the first time to talk about the Yard and create a little dance together. On Four Tree Island, adjacent to Portsmouth's Prescott Park, dancers in white move among the trees; the high school color guards wave white flags, semaphore-like. Dancers standing by the water's edge, with the shipyard across the river at their backs, teach a few movements to the audience—150 to 200 people at this first performance—and invite them to join the dance. In an open area near the river, an oblong of a dozen interlocked dancers moves across the grass. In the middle of the group, a woman sits on a man's shoulders, raised above the rest. The dancers embody the image of a submarine, she the conning tower. As they begin to crouch, still moving, they are a submarine beginning its dive. They crouch lower; the woman is lifted forward and down and the whole structure of bodies subsides. Then individuals peel off, somersaulting left and right, like waves curling out from a moving vessel, and the shape dissolves, leaving behind the idea of a submarine moving unseen below the surface.

The performance in the bowling alley is both funny and serious. That is where the shipyard "fashion show" takes place: dancers dressed in work clothes and safety equipment—gloves and masks, white protective suits designed to shield workers from chemical and radioactive contamination. Stylized fashion-show gestures clash comically with the bulky gear, but the costumes evoke the pollution issue even as they pay tribute to difficult, dangerous work. A woman dancer's outsize costume recalls the stories of the first women who took these dangerous jobs and had to wear men's work clothing because no outfits for women had yet been ordered. There is a performance in a rest room, and there are performances on the grassy mall of the shipyard, where workers come for lunch.

Outdoors at the shipyard, six or eight dancers, heads bowed, move to elegiac music, recalling the *Thresher* disaster. They lean on one another; one dancer carries another's prone body. The postures suggest both sorrow and mutual support. On the stage of the Music Hall, the Navy wife's measuring gesture is repeated during a dance performed while personal stories are narrated. On the deck of the *Squalus*, Charlie Lawrence recites a text about the Yard—"the lives that ride on the quality of your work"—while dancers swirl slowly around him.

All through the week, gestures discovered during conversations and rehearsals play out in dance: the grasping, pulling, and gathering motions of work; the fluttering, sweeping, and diving motions of hands and arms that suggest the sea and the submarines; the raised-arm imitation of shipyard cranes. The gestures are not mime. That is, they are not meant to create the illusion of real work with invisible objects. These are not people pretending to do things. Stylized and repeated, the gestures communicate something *about* the human elements of the work, the concentration, strength, and precision it requires, the grace and dignity of purposeful physical skill. And the dances freely mix these work-based gestures with more abstract expressions of exuberance or grief.

Then the finale. Once Lerman thought of it, the idea must have been irresistible: that the culmination of a week of performances designed to bring Portsmouth and the shipyard together should take place on Memorial Bridge, which joins the two. There was, though, the question of getting permission to use the bridge for a dance, closing U.S. Route 1, a heavily traveled connection between two states (though not the only one: Interstate 95 crosses the river by way of the high-arching Piscataqua Bridge half a mile upstream). Memorial Bridge is a vertical-lift drawbridge: the center section of roadway rises straight up between two towers to let ships pass underneath. Lerman first asked officials if she could put dancers on that center section and have it lifted—a striking idea but not really what she wanted. Not surprisingly, the answer was no. But that request may have paved the way for the approval of a more reasonable one: that the bridge be shut down briefly so the project could use it as a performance space. Lerman's success in getting the bridge closed impressed some people more than the expressive power of the dances. It was tangible proof of the power of art.

A fortuitous bit of history helped shape the finale and give it another layer of meaning. In 1923, five-year-old Eileen Dondero cut the ceremonial ribbon to mark the official opening of the bridge. Now, seventy-three years later, Eileen Dondero was Eileen Foley, mayor of Portsmouth. Lerman asked her to tie halves of a ribbon together at the center of the bridge to symbolize the connection, or reconnection, of Portsmouth and the shipyard. To make a ribbon that would stretch from bank to bank, from New Hampshire to Maine, project leaders invited people to write stories of the town and the shipyard on lengths of fabric. Those pieces became the ribbon that united the city and the shipyard, a physical ribbon of stories that represented the connections made by telling, dancing, and witnessing the shipyard stories.

So on Saturday, September 21, at 2:00 P.M., color guards marched from either end of the bridge toward the center, leading dancers who held the ribbon aloft, along with marching bands, and public officials and members of the audience, who followed them onto the bridge, becoming performers themselves, part of the final dance. They met in the middle; Mayor Foley tied the ribbon. The bands played and the crowd of participants sang "America the Beautiful." Then everyone raised one arm in the air, elbow bent, and pulled down. The shipyard steam whistle blasted its note out over the river. It was, for the moment at least, city joined with shipyard, past joined with present, the art of dance joined with the military. A thousand people filled the park and streamed onto the bridge at the closing.

The project did not—could not—eliminate all the tensions, disagreement, and misunderstanding between town and shipyard or knit the two into a seamless community. But the week of performances and, more than that, the many months of conversation, negotiation, and rehearsal did connect the two and at least contribute to healing the pain of the *Thresher* disaster and the deep division that the Vietnam War had opened up between the American military and many citizens. In part, at least, it fulfilled Lerman's aim of creating wholeness: bringing mind and body together in dance and bringing parts of the community together as they participated in and watched the dances. The project affected the audience, but it affected the participants more. They were the ones who discovered new interests and skills and who met people they had not known were their neighbors. Many of them took part in the later community arts efforts inspired by the Shipyard Project and shaped by its goals of inclusion and connection.

The Legacy of the Shipyard Project

The effect of the performances on the community as a whole is hard to gauge: who knows what the audience members took away from the experience? (Who knows what members of any audience take away from the performance they attend?) Peter Bowman thinks that the direct effect on the community as a whole was limited, partly because the number of people who saw the performances was fairly small. At some performances early in the week, he says, dancers sometimes outnumbered their audience. Attendance grew as the days went by, reaching a thousand at the final event. Bowman attributed the small audiences to the fact that no one—except possibly Lerman—had any idea how good the dances would be. Most people have low expectations of a community dance project; it seems the kind of thing to attend only if you know someone in the cast, like going to the junior high school concert because your daughter is in the band. By the time word got around that this was something special—that the old hierarchy of good professional art and bad community art was wrong—the performances were over.

Had the audiences been two or three or ten times as large, the Shipyard Project would still have had its profoundest effect on the participants themselves. In some cases, it transformed lives. Jane Hirshberg says that it changed her response to art: "Working for a presenting organization like the Music Hall, you see a lot of art. After the Shipyard Project, I couldn't get excited about dance performances that don't 'speak' authentically. Your definition of quality changes. I'm not interested in just seeing pretty bodies fly across the stage."

It also led her to change careers. She left the Music Hall and now works for the Dance Exchange as producer of the Hallelujah Project, another community-based dance experience. Hirshberg says, "I ran away to join the circus." Paula Rais, another Music Hall employee, left to work on other community arts projects. School psychologist Nancy Hill now works as an arts grant administrator. Peter Bowman joined the Music Hall board. Charlie Lawrence, still working at the shipyard, has performed in community theater events. These people and other Shipyard Project participants have worked on a variety of community arts efforts inspired by the project.

Soon after the week of dances ended, participants met to discuss the effects the experience had on them. Many described it as a "spiritual high." Lerman urged them "to take the spirit that was alive in us and keep it alive." Sometime later, a smaller group began meeting to see what they could do to keep the spirit alive. Nancy Hill recalls, "We discovered we all loved the experience and wanted it—or something like it—to happen again." The group met every month for a year to discuss possible new projects that would build on the experience of the Shipyard Project. Lerman helped spur the group to action when she attended their August 1998 meeting and assured them that they did not need to get everyone's agreement on everything; they could choose a project and start to work on it.

The group named itself Lullabies and Reveilles when it decided to develop arts projects to celebrate the millennium in Portsmouth that would, in Hill's words, "sing the old millennium to sleep and wake up the new one." Their principal project involved gathering oral histories from Portsmouth residents and presenting them in performance. They asked Genevieve Aichele, artistic director of the New Hampshire Theatre Project, to weave the stories into a drama. That work adopted many of the features and values of the Shipyard Project. It drew on the experiences and emotions of local citizens. It brought together many different people and talents (the interviewers and interviewees; a cast of forty with an age span of seventy years, from seven to seventy-seven; a small band; and singers), and it included musical settings by a local composer of poems on the subject of home by participants in a writing project at the Methodist church. The drama, *Neighborhoods*, was designed to teach Portsmouth about itself, to build or rebuild bridges between people ignorant of one another's history. Like the Shipyard Project, it uncovered some old wounds in hopes of beginning to heal them.

The most painful injury formed the dramatic climax of the play, when performers articulated the bitter memories of onetime residents of a mainly Italian North End neighborhood that had been destroyed by a so-called urban renewal project in the early 1960s. Despite protests and petitions, the homes of residents of this vibrant community had been taken by eminent domain and bulldozed. In that era, many urban planners and government official considered high-density housing undesirable by definition. More money was available for knocking down neighborhoods than fixing them up. The fact that nothing was built on the site for ten years compounded the displaced residents' anger. Today, a Sheraton hotel and the offices of the *Portsmouth Herald* occupy the site, but it is uninviting and still feels relatively barren. The large brick buildings surrounded by parking lots and empty lawn seem lifeless and inhospitable compared with the busy variety of the nearby downtown streets.

Neighborhoods has been performed three times. Each time, like all good storytelling, it has evoked the stories of people in the audience.

Nancy Hill says that the most important lesson she learned from the Shipyard Project experience and especially from watching Liz Lerman work was that "when you're organizing something, you don't need to know what the end product will be when you begin." (Lerman herself says that the willingness to trust in an unknown outcome is "an incredible life skill," not just an artistic strategy.) That understanding gave Hill the courage to launch ambitious projects with no certainty of success or clear sense of where they would lead, and the patience to let them develop. Paula Rais, who has worked with Hill, adds, "You need time to meet, to get to know each other and trust each other, to let common issues bubble to the surface." That insight, too, reflects the experience of the Shipyard Project.

Some learned the basic lesson that ambitious local arts projects are possible. Inspired by Lerman's work, the chair of the arts department at Portsmouth High School commissioned a local composer to set the work of area poets to music. The new piece was performed in 2000 by four hundred singers drawn from ten community choruses.

After the *Neighborhoods* project ended, Genevieve Aichele engaged in negotiations with the Portsmouth Naval Shipyard command to make one of her performance groups the resident company of the Yard's five-hundred-seat theater. By the end of the summer of 2001, they had come to an agreement that promised to form a new and lasting connection between the facility and the rest of the community. But the September 11 attacks in New York and Washington, D.C., meant tighter security at the shipyard. For now it is off limits to the public; the theater project has been put on hold but not abandoned.

Before the Shipyard Project, Hill says, the city government demonstrated little interest in the arts and offered little support. Genevieve Aichele adds that the arts were viewed as separate from most of the Portsmouth community. Both have seen a change. Aichele says that the project awakened an understanding of the arts as part of the fabric of community life. *Neighborhoods* was one manifestation of that connection. The Poet Laureate Project established by Hill is another, and also an example of government recognition of the arts.

In the last five years, Portsmouth has named three poet laureates, local poets who receive a stipend and whose status is officially announced by the city government. Each of them has engaged in projects to bring poetry to the community: a CD featuring readings by area poets and music performed by a local group; poetry installations in public places; and, most recently, a book of poems by local poets about the Portsmouth area and its history. One of the poets also established a monthly "Poetry Hoot," which combines readings by established poets with open-mike readings and draws forty or more people to each session. Poets from high school age to over ninety read their work. Hill says that poet laureate activities have built a community of poets and an audience for poetry over the years. More than 120 people attended a recent talk on poetry, more than a similar event would be likely to draw in a much larger city. And the audience is more varied than most poetry audiences, she believes, because of how the Shipyard Project brought together people from different parts of the community; some of them continue to attend one another's events, some have discovered that they care more about the arts than they thought they did. In May 2002, a publication party for a book of local poetry drew, says Nancy Hill, "two hundred people from every corner of the community, youngsters, older people, rich and poor." One idea from the Shipyard Project that has guided these later activities is the conviction that good art does not have to be rarified and distant, the province of a few geniuses. It can be created by and for the people of the community, and take as its subject what they see every day.

In some ways, Portsmouth seems an ideal place for an arts project designed to unify the community. It is relatively small and compact; it has a long, vivid history; it already had an active artistic life. Those conditions helped make the Shipyard Project as successful as it was and have supported other community arts activities since. It would be an exaggeration to say that the Shipyard Project brought the community together in a thorough or lasting way. Bridging social gulfs as wide as those between artsy young professionals and hard-hat welders is exceptionally difficult in contemporary America. The Shipyard Project has created some bridges that still stand and networks that continue to grow, though. Hill remarks that before the Lerman project she did not even know Jane Hirshberg, Paula Rais, or Genevieve Aichele—women who are now among her closest friends and collaborators. Paula Rais says, "You meet people in shops or in a class and you recognize them from the Shipyard Project. Working on that project, you got to know people you never would have met. And the circle keeps spiraling out to involve others."

CHAPTER 4

{ Boston, Massachusetts }

The Dudley Street Neighborhood Initiative
Grass Roots in the City

Julio and Sandra Henriquez moved to the corner of Dean and Judson Streets in Roxbury, a residential district of Boston, Massachusetts, on a cold night in December 1973.[1] The price of the two-family house was right. Their sons, eight and four years old, had their own bedrooms and a big yard to play in. But their new neighborhood did not look much like the American dream. A cul-de-sac behind the house had become an automobile graveyard. At night, Julio and Sandra heard the crash of metal and glass as more cars were dumped; in the morning they would survey the growing tangle of wreckage from their back window. Teetering refrigerators, rusty old stoves, and worn tires littered empty lots across the street. Contractors working on housing and renovation projects in the city would dispose of loads of debris here, including asbestos and lead-paint-coated molding.

The Henriquez family moved to the neighborhood known as Dudley Street the week before Christmas. They woke up on the morning of Christmas Eve to find that their Mazda station wagon had been stolen from the driveway.

In the 1970s and early 1980s, the Dudley Street neighborhood was disintegrating. Only a couple of miles from Boston's Symphony Hall, it was a wasteland of burned-out buildings and vacant lots filled with weeds and rubbish. By 1984, more than 30 percent of the land was vacant. Illegal dumping and trash transfer stations bred rats and filled the air with noxious odors. Drugs were sold openly on the streets. Arson was so common, says Elizabeth Centeio, who grew up in the area, that children considered the fires entertainment. "Every evening we went outside to watch the flames and smoke," she remembers. But the spectacle had unhappy consequences even for children not directly affected. Many of the burned buildings had been occupied by renters who had no other place to stay in the area; a fire at night often meant friends gone from school the next day and never seen again.

John Barros and his friends also would hear the sirens and look outside for the smoke. Watching house fires became about as routine as watching television. Kids played in abandoned houses, and Barros walked home each day past what he calls a "drug gang house" on the corner. He looked up to the older youths who made good money selling drugs. When the police chased them down Clarence Street, his street, he rooted for the local heroes to get away.

Bob Holmes, one of three trustees of the Boston-based Mabel Louise Riley Foundation, toured the neighborhood in 1984. He says, "We were astonished that a city could let a neighborhood get that bad. The vacant lots were strewn with burned-out cars and animal offal from slaughterhouses. We were outraged. And we couldn't find any plan anywhere to improve things."[2]

Not only was there no plan for improvement; forces were dragging the neighborhood down. Banks had redlined the area, refusing mortgages to people willing to build or improve houses there. As Charles Finn explained in a study of mortgage lending written for the Boston Redevelopment Authority, "Mortgage and construction lending decisions are often made based upon expectations about neighborhood growth or decline. . . . Banks' expectations . . . often become reality—a 'self-fulfilling prophecy.' "[3] In Dudley, as in many redlined neighborhoods throughout the country, that economic decision had an implicit racial component. Decades of "white flight" to the suburbs had reduced the white population (including whites of Hispanic origin) from 95 percent in 1950 to 16 percent in 1980.[4] Banks, planners, and government officials saw neighborhoods with increasing nonwhite populations as being in decline almost by definition. Shrinking property values made arson attractive to property owners; insurance money was the one sure way to get a return on their investment. Lax arson investigation by police in the area made the crime almost risk free—hence the nightly fires that Centeio and Barros remember. Antidumping regulations were not enforced.

Egidio "Gino" Teixeira opened the Ideal Sub Shop on Dudley Street in 1986, scraping together resources when banks refused to lend him money. "There was no such thing as loans for this neighborhood," says Teixeira. "We all had a good job and we couldn't get a forty-thousand-dollar loan from any bank at all."

He managed to open anyway, the sandwich shop an oasis amid the wreckage of the neighborhood, but he had trouble drawing customers. "There was trash all over the place," he explains. "Abandoned cars, refrigerators, washing machines, you name it. And the drug dealers used to sell drugs right in front of the store, across the street, all over the place." People on these streets averted their eyes. "People used to be afraid to talk with each other," says Teixeira.

So, looking at the Dudley Street neighborhood in the early 1980s, what you saw was low income, high crime, poor schools, burned-out buildings, acres of vacant lots used as dumping grounds, abandoned cars, and the night lit by fires. The smell of smoke hung in the air, mixed with the stench of rotting trash.

Decades earlier Dudley Street had been a very different place. Catherine Flannery was four years old when she first saw the spires of St. Paul's Church. "I thought it was heaven," she says. "And I still do, in a way." While hundreds of her neighbors were packing and migrating to the suburbs after World War II, Flannery stayed. "I love the neighborhood," she says. "I never wanted to be anyplace else." But as she watched apartment buildings and businesses burn down around her, she started to lose hope that the neighborhood could come back. "Fifteen years ago, I didn't think any of this was possible," she says of Dudley Street today. "I thought it was gone."

But the neighborhood has come back. The spacious semidetached two-family homes of Winthrop Estates and their fenced lawns and gardens occupy what had been dismal vacant land. In fact, almost half the thirteen hundred lots that were vacant in the 1980s have had permanent improvements, including 144 units of new housing, about half of them owner-occupied. Since the neighborhood's low point in the 1980s, more than 260 new units of affordable housing have been built, the great majority of them owner-occupied. A quarter century after their first grim Christmas here, the Henriquez family still lives at the corner of Dean and Judson. But the car dump is now a community farm where sunflowers, eggplant, peppers, and broccoli grow. Across the street, earthmovers prepare land for a new playground. The Henriquez children are grown now, and two still live in the neighborhood. After decades of decline, the number of businesses in the area has increased, from 425 in 1992 to 643 in 1999. Crime is down. Between 1990 and 2000, calls for police assistance dropped 21 percent (compared to 7 percent for all of Boston). Calls related to drugs dropped 61 percent (18 percent in Boston).

According to the 2000 census, the Dudley Street neighborhood remains disadvantaged compared to Boston as a whole—unemployment is higher, income and education levels, lower. The non-English-speaking population in the neighborhood is proportionately higher and rising—in 2000, 41 percent of people in the neighborhood spoke a language other than English at home, compared to 36 percent in the area in 1990 and 33 percent in Boston as a whole. This is not (yet?) a gentrified part of the city. On the other hand, in the last decade educational levels in the Dudley Street neighborhood have risen, the high school dropout rate has declined by a third, and home ownership is up a bit.[5]

But statistics don't tell the whole story of the Dudley Street renaissance. The smell of burning and trash is gone; the abandoned cars have disappeared. Egidio Teixeira's Ideal Sub is bustling. "This place is always full," he says. "People aren't afraid to come in anymore." Two sites near where Dudley Street and Blue Hill Avenue meet, once wasteland, have been turned into a two-section urban town common. The south common has a broad stage area where concerts are held in summer and a farmers' market sets up twice a week; Santa Claus greets local kids here in December. The five horizontal black bars of a length of fence that sets off the area look like the lines of a musical staff, and in fact they support the notes of a jazz tune, "Black Nairobi Nights," written by a local composer. Two columns with a large clock face between them are decorated with metal silhouettes, in various colors, of people from the neighborhood. Locals can tell you who the man with the trumpet to his lips is, the name of the woman holding a child's hand, the names of the children, and what they are doing now that they have grown up. The fence in the north common site is decorated with plaques recounting the history of the area from its days as a colonial village through its time as a wealthy suburb, to its decline and renewal. Mosaic tiles in a low curved wall spell out a "Declaration of Community Rights" that begins, "We, the residents of the Dudley area, have the right to participate in all planning, programs, and policies affecting our lives." There is a small fountain for kids to splash in near the center of the common, and behind it a map of the world, formed out of metal continents on a metal mesh. A world map is part of the Emerson school playground, too.

As with the branch libraries in Chicago and the Shipyard Project in Portsmouth, local art shows the community to itself. The metal silhouettes of residents, a "Nubian Roots" mural of locals on the walls of a grocery and auto repair shop, the mosaic Declaration of Community Rights, and the jazz phrase worked into the fence at the commons communicate a cluster of messages: that the people who walk these streets matter enough to be portrayed in painting and sculpture; that talented artists live and work here; that these people we know and these things we care about make us a community. John Barros worked on the mural with other kids from the neighborhood. It was painted at a time when graffiti covered sidewalks, signs, buses, and buildings in the city, but the mural was left alone. "Everything else was getting 'tagged,'" says Barros, "but that [didn't] get touched."

The maps have meaning, too, both because they situate the Dudley neighborhood in the wider world and because they honor the various countries of origin of Dudley residents (though some have complained that they are not detailed enough to show the islands that many come from). The Dudley Street area is unusually diverse for Boston or for any American city. In the 2000 census the population of the wider Dudley area was 56 percent African-American, 24 percent Latino, 5 percent Cape Verdean, 4 percent white, and 11 percent other.

For almost two decades, members of all of these ethnic groups have worked together through the Dudley Street Neighborhood Initiative, or DSNI, to save and revitalize their neighborhood. Members of DSNI got the wrecks and the refuse cleared away, the broken streetlights repaired, and new houses built. Teixeira believes that they also did something less tangible and more valuable. DSNI staff and volunteers banged on doors and introduced themselves to their neighbors. At countless community meetings, at the multicultural festival, through hard side-by-side labor, they helped people in this place connect and reconnect. "Now," says Teixeira, "most people know each other, and they talk to each other. And it feels more like a family than a neighborhood." The story of the Dudley Street Neighborhood Initiative is a story of people connecting to build the neighborhood they want for their families. Catherine Flannery calls this neighborhood's turnaround "a miracle," but Dudley Street rose from the ashes through the tireless labor, endless organizing, and tenacious spirit of the people who live here.

Creation of a Neighborhood Initiative

It started with a worn-out carpet in the Dudley Street office of La Alianza Hispana, a social services agency for Latinos. In 1984, Nelson Merced, executive director of La Alianza, asked the Riley Foundation for a grant to replace the tattered carpet. The foundation distributed about $2 million a year, mostly small grants in the area, many of them to agencies and activities that benefited children and youth. Bob Holmes, one of the Riley trustees who visited La Alianza in response to Merced's appeal, says that giving money for new carpet "didn't turn us on." But the short drive to Dudley Street (not more than three miles from the foundation's downtown office) had shown the trustees a part of the city, unknown to them, that had much deeper problems than worn office carpeting. They asked Merced if he would convene a meeting of leaders of other agencies in the area to try to put together a broader plan for neighborhood improvement. "What was the point of fixing up Alianza when the neighborhood was falling apart?" Holmes asked. Given the overwhelming problems of the area, the trustees decided not only that Riley should go beyond Merced's request but that it should change its own strategy of scattering small grants throughout the city. They believed the foundation could do more good by focusing many of its resources on this single neighborhood. Said Holmes, "How could Riley consider itself a leadership foundation if there was a community like Dudley?"[6]

Merced brought together twenty or so agency leaders who, with the Riley trustees, formed the Dudley Advisory Group. Holmes says that people were suspicious at first, wondering what Riley's agenda was, and at the same time looked for promises about how much money the foundation would contribute before there was any program to put money into. But their suspicions were gradually put to rest and they began to work together to define the shape of a new organization. Holmes remembers giving hundreds of hours to the project: "I took off my trustee's hat to act as a lawyer to help them hammer out a plan: the target area, bylaws, who would have the votes, etc."[7] The group officially chose the name Dudley Street Neighborhood Initiative in January 1985 and organized a community meeting to present and explain the new organization to the neighborhood it would serve.

A meeting at St. Patrick's Church on February 23, 1985, defined the Dudley Street Neighborhood Initiative. The community's unexpected hostility to the plan presented that evening by the Dudley Advisory Group and the advisory group's response to that attack underlie the success and durability of DSNI. About two hundred Dudley area residents attended. At the start of the meeting, Merced explained the background and the aims of the proposed initiative. Someone else in the planning group described the board structure. Then, in the words of Bill Slotnik, cochair of the meeting, "All hell broke loose."[8] People did not know what Riley was or what the foundation wanted; they feared being displaced by the kind of urban renewal that had razed whole neighborhoods in Boston's West End—the same "clean slate" approach that destroyed vibrant neighborhoods in Portsmouth, New Hampshire; Portland, Oregon; and many other U.S. cities. Local resident Ché Madyun, later president of the DSNI board, asked how many of the group seated at the front of the church lived in the neighborhood. Perhaps one person raised a hand. Tito Fuster, who worked at Alianza and was part of the advisory group, remembers how eloquently the residents argued that the so-called neighborhood initiative would be under the control of outside agencies, not the neighborhood, and said, "We want to be sitting at the table." Faced with this unexpected opposition, the advisory group excused itself from the meeting and held a brief caucus. That could easily have been the end of the story.

Remarkably, though, when the advisory group reconvened, they told the audience that they agreed with the criticisms and announced that they would scrap their laboriously crafted plan. They promised to hold open meetings to discuss a new governance structure, one that would give a controlling majority of board seats to residents. This response was unusual and surprising for several reasons. Defensive stubbornness seems a more likely reaction to hostile public criticism—certainly a more common one. Besides, most of the people who admitted error were highly educated lawyers and social workers who had put a lot of effort into the initiative; they could easily have resented the suspicion and "ingratitude" of the people they were trying to help. Also, resident control of a neighborhood improvement program was unorthodox—and especially so for a devastated neighborhood like Dudley. Holmes describes the incredulity in the world of professional planners and grant makers when word of the new organization spread: "People said, 'What is Riley doing now? Three lawyers going down to Dudley Street making grants to residents? Where are the consultants and advisors?' " But, then as now, Holmes was convinced that DSNI was on the right path. "If you want to know what a neighborhood needs, ask the residents, not some guy from Weston [a wealthy Boston suburb] who writes a paper." He said the advisory group members at the meeting had no pride of authorship and, when they caucused, quickly decided to throw away the plan. Tito Fuster also remembers that the criticisms did not spark animosity in the organizers. "There was basically no opposition," he says. "We were all willing to hand the project to the community."[9]

Within days, public discussions began that led to the formation of an expanded governance committee and a new plan: instead of the originally proposed twenty-three-member board with four community seats, the DSNI board would have thirty-one members with a minimum of sixteen from the community.[10] The group also decided that twelve of those community seats would be divided equally among the four major ethnic groups in the neighborhood: African-American, Latino, Cape Verdean, and white residents. A determination to prevent the organization from favoring or seeming to favor one ethnic group lay behind the decision to specify equal representation, rather than representation proportional to population.

That choice has stood the organization in good stead, though people have been quick to suspect favoritism to one group or another from time to time throughout the history of the initiative. At the beginning, some residents feared that DSNI would benefit mainly Latinos, since it developed out of conversations between La Alianza Hispana and the Riley Foundation, and Nelson Merced of La Alianza was elected first board president. Later, when Ché Madyun, an African American, became president, some expected DSNI to favor the African-American community. In 1999, a Cape Verdean, John Barros (the same John Barros who had watched the police chase youths down Clarence Street years before, and who, at seventeen, was elected the first youth member of the DSNI board), became executive director of the organization. After almost three years on the job, he says that he has to deal with the perception among some that "the Cape Verdeans are taking over," and he describes the difficulties of balancing fairness and the appearance of fairness—that it is important not to underserve Cape Verdean residents out of fear that some will see favoritism in any actions that help them specifically.

Neighborhood leadership and control have guided DSNI ever since. Those first public meetings established the principle. Holmes describes the call he got from officials in Los Angeles after the 1992 riots that followed the acquittal of the police officers who had been videotaped beating Rodney King. Having heard of Riley's work with the Dudley Street Neighborhood Initiative, they asked if they could visit to learn some lessons of successful neighborhood renewal. "Of course," said Holmes. He asked how many residents of the area would be part of the group. "None," he was told. He withdrew the invitation.

Early Success

The first board election took place in the spring of 1985, with more than a hundred area residents voting. The Riley Foundation made its first grant, of seventy thousand dollars, the following fall, and DSNI hired Andrea Nagel as its first professional community organizer in the spring of 1986.[11]

She and Executive Director Peter Medoff employed the same strategy Industrial Areas Foundation groups use to understand local issues, build relationships of trust, and identify local leaders: they knocked on doors and listened to people's stories. Nagel says, "I spent a lot of time at the beginning visiting people in their homes. There was so much history and a lot of people had been struggling in this neighborhood for so long. . . . Their stories would go on and on and on."[12]

These conversations gave DSNI its first action issue. Residents had a variety of grievances, but nearly everyone complained about the garbage piled in vacant lots and the cars abandoned on the streets, visible (and unhealthy) signs of a neighborhood in decline. The "Don't Dump on Us"

campaign that developed from that common concern would first organize residents to clean up the trash-strewn lots and then pressure the city
to remove abandoned cars and close down the illegal trash transfer stations that polluted the neighborhood. A community meeting to launch
the campaign drew more than a hundred residents, along with a few city
officials. The turnout and the passionate, unified expressions of purpose
took the officials by surprise. One called then-mayor Ray Flynn, who
showed up before the meeting ended and pledged his support. The city
promised to prosecute illegal dumpers and set up a hot line for citizens to
report them; it provided equipment for a community cleanup later in the
spring.

This gathering refuted the common myth that the residents of the
Dudley area and places like it do not really care about their neighborhood (and the implication that their indifference and neglect created
the local problems in the first place). From the first public meetings
about the proposed Dudley Street initiative, when two hundred people
showed up, through the meetings that followed and the election for seats
on the board, residents demonstrated their concern about their community and their conviction that they *were* a community. Longtime resident
Ayeesha Lane remembers the community spirit that already existed for
DSNI to draw on and says, "There was a lot of hope in that neighborhood." The "Don't Dump on Us" meeting also showed the residents
what they could do when they worked together. As an organized group of
a hundred or more, they got the attention of the media and the city. As
with the early victories of the Industrial Areas Foundation groups in
Texas, this first success showed residents that they could make things
happen by working together and laid the foundation for more ambitious
efforts. Looking back over the history of DSNI, Riley trustee Bob Holmes
sees that kind of collective action as DSNI's great accomplishment and
the heart of its success: "It's about getting people together who could
speak as a group. That gave them enormous political power. That was
more important than the cash." [13]

Relationships continue to be an important part of progress in the neighborhood and a foundation of the quality of life people now find there. Recently, Joe Susi of neighboring Dorchester stepped out of a truck in front of Julio Henriquez's house. A neighbor whose son knows Susi asked if the Susi excavating company would level the playground land—for free. "Yeah," said Susi. "We're in the community, too."

As they spoke, a DSNI worker went house to house in the neighborhood, talking to everyone who answered the doorbell. She carried yellow flyers, headlined "Calling All Residents of Julian, Judson, Gayland and Dean Streets," that announced a community meeting about the playground and asked for help with planning, other volunteer work, and organizing a grand opening.

The close relationships have benefits beyond getting work done. When Julio Henriquez had surgery, cards and food and good wishes came from all over the neighborhood. "That thought alone strengthens the idea that if you live in a neighborhood where people care about each other, you can recover from anything," he says.

Catherine Flannery, who met Henriquez through DSNI, remembers his birthday every year with a card. And when she needs the snow cleared from her walk, Julio Henriquez sends over the DSNI "land-trust crew" of young workers. "As soon as you need a snowblower, they'll be here for you," he assures her. Before he goes, she chides him for not coming to tea more often. Flannery took part in some early outreach efforts, climbing porch steps and knocking on doors. "We wanted to get to know all of the neighbors," she says. "You can't do very much without people, and we were just trying to get to know them and hoped we might get them involved."

Many residents say they feel safer now, and Barros credits that increased sense of safety to a renewed sense of community. "You know more people in the neighborhood, so that makes it safer," he says. "You know who's who and who's doing what."

Eminent Domain

When DSNI was founded, it divided the one and a half square miles of the Dudley neighborhood into a "core" area, where improvement was most critically needed, and a "secondary" area that was part of the neighborhood but less desperately troubled. The "triangle," a central part of the core bounded by Dudley Street, Blue Hill Avenue, and Brookford Street, was the worst, with half of its sixty acres vacant land. Half of that acreage was owned by the city and half by 181 different individuals—the whole a patchwork of small city-owned and privately held lots that made organized redevelopment almost impossibly complex.

The surprising solution to the problem and a striking example of local control was the city's turning over the power of eminent domain to the community—specifically to Dudley Neighbors, Incorporated, or DNI, a nonprofit land trust formed by DSNI to acquire vacant triangle land for affordable housing and other uses that would serve the community. The eminent-domain idea faced initial skepticism in the neighborhood itself, because people associated the practice with the forced destruction of vibrant neighborhoods and the displacement of homeowners and renters. A "Take a Stand, Own the Land" campaign that described the goal of developing unused land *for* residents gradually won support for the idea. Some in the city government vehemently opposed the idea of giving up power to a group of residents, but Mayor Ray Flynn's firm support carried the day (and led to the resignation of some members of the Boston Redevelopment Authority). In *Streets of Hope,* Peter Medoff and Holly Sklar cite the mayor's view:

> Sometimes there is this elitist attitude that only the professional planners know how to get anything done. . . . I've seen professional planners screw up more things than you could shake a stick at, and I've seen a lot of projects that have been unsuccessful because they were jammed down people's throats in the neighborhoods. This is a very different kind of project. This is bottom-up.[14]

A multimillion-dollar low-interest loan from the Ford Foundation gave the DNI the resources it needed to compensate owners for the land it would take. The land trust would own the land and offer homeowners long-term leases that included some conditions, such as limits on the resale prices of a home, to preserve the affordability of homeownership in the area. "Development without Displacement" was the plan's stated goal. DSNI and DNI wanted to improve the neighborhood for its current residents, not for wealthier newcomers likely to be attracted to a revitalized area so close to downtown Boston. The Winthrop Estates homes, completed in 1994, were the first new homes built on land-trust land; they were followed by Stafford Heights and Brook Avenue cooperative housing (each with its own community center) and Woodward Park homes. Other reclaimed land is being turned into parks and gardens, a community greenhouse, and improvements in a local shopping area—all in the once devastated triangle.

Building an Urban Village

The concept of a semiautonomous urban village guides development of the triangle and the five-hundred-acre core area of which it is a part. The "urban village" idea grew out of a series of meetings in which residents were invited to imagine the neighborhood they wanted to live in in the future. (Ironically, the term *urban village* had acquired currency from a classic study by sociologist Herbert Gans that described the tragic demise of a once vibrant Boston neighborhood gentrified out of existence in the heyday of government-sponsored "urban renewal" of the 1950s.)[15] The Dudley Street residents' desires included many of the features of a traditional village. They described a cluster of homes, shops, religious institutions, schools, and public spaces compact enough that people could walk wherever they needed to go and offering most of the resources people need to live their daily lives. John Barros says that the Dudley area strives for (and achieves, to a significant degree) another aspect of village life: it is a place where people are in relationship with one another and everyone has a role in the community, including the elders who carry its history and much of its wisdom. He also notes that "village" translates into the languages and cultural experience of the various places Dudley residents have come from more readily than "town," "city," or other, less universal, concepts.

"We're re-creating our neighborhood into the kind of village we want it to be," says Julio Henriquez, a DSNI board member. "There's still some pieces missing, but we're working on that." Henriquez sees similarities here now, he says, with the town where he grew up in Panama. Both are small communities with one main parish church, where people know their neighbors. A girl walks toward Henriquez. "Good afternoon," he says. She makes eye contact, and smiles and says hello. "When I first moved to this neighborhood," Henriquez says, "everybody was a stranger. Nobody said good morning to each other."

The emphasis on finding a concept that resonates with different parts of the community is one example of the attention to language and the culture it embodies that has been part of DSNI's inclusivist strategy from the beginning. Newsletters and most meeting announcements are trilingual: in English, Spanish, and Cape Verdean. Simultaneous translation into each of those languages is available at the annual meeting. Directors develop slogans that will sound right in all three and will communicate a shared understanding. Along with the proportional representation on the DSNI board and the annual multicultural festival in September, the concern for language reflects efforts to create a unity out of diversity in the neighborhood.

One element of Dudley's urban-village development is quite literally a return to the area's roots. Centuries ago, orchards and farms flourished here. The Roxbury Russet apple was developed nearby. What is known in the United States as the Bartlett pear was first grown here by Enoch Bartlett on property owned by Thomas Brewer. Now the Food Project, which donates organic vegetables to shelters for the homeless and sells its produce at urban farmers' markets, grows tomatoes, peppers, beans, eggplants, and other vegetables on two-plus acres in the Dudley neighborhood. Some residents have turned their land into vegetable gardens and sell what they don't need at the local farmers' market. A community greenhouse is being built on the site of an old garage.

At first, says Henriquez, it was hard to help local kids understand that the gardens were theirs and that they should take care not to harm them. So the Food Project got some of the kids to work in these urban fields. "Now," Henriquez smiles, "you have them invested. In the evenings, I can sit on my porch and listen to the older kids say to the younger ones, 'Listen, get a move on. We've gotta clean up here. I'm responsible for this.' "

In a way, the urban village taking shape in the Dudley area, with its farmland and its focus on local identity, local resources, and local businesses, has more in common with the neighborhood's colonial past than with its recent existence as a more-or-less suburban residential area. In those early days, too, the town grew much of its own food, took care of its own needs, and saw itself as a close-knit community. But the urban-village vision and the steps being taken to create it are no exercise in nostalgia. The new homes in Dudley are serviceable contemporary buildings. The intermingling of homes and businesses here reflects the area's existing urban character. The diversity of this community—unlike both traditional villages and most new urban developments—gives the Dudley area a character that has no obvious counterpart in the past. And this urban village is developing out of the existing assets of the area and the values of the people who live in it, not from a desire to re-create an imagined idyllic past.

The DSNI Board at Work

The first Wednesday evening in June 2002, DSNI board members gather for their regular meeting. Resident members from all of Dudley's ethnic groups are there, along with DSNI staff members and representatives from area social-service agencies. Elizabeth Centeio, who used to watch the fires in the neighborhood when she was a little girl, is one of the Cape Verdean board members. Her five siblings are also involved in DSNI work. "It's a family thing," she says. Both she and John Barros have college degrees—Barros graduated from Dartmouth; Centeio from the University of Massachusetts. Barros says that most of the people who grew up here are back in the neighborhood, as he is. He left a good job in New York to become executive director. Barros counts the fact of returning young adults as an important sign of successful community development. "They come back because of good relationships and opportunities," he says. That is what he did, of course. After graduation, he went to work for the Chubb Group of Answan Company, was transferred to New York, and was, he says, "on track." Then he heard that DSNI needed an interim executive director. He left the big city and the big salary and came home. He took the job and bought the house he'd grown up in.

Ruth Grant, who now represents St. Patrick's Church on the DSNI board, is pleased that the executive director grew up in the neighborhood. She remembers when DSNI first worked to find a permanent director. She says that they read through "all these fancy résumés" that came "from people who really didn't know, who hadn't felt the pain of living here."

The evening's varied agenda reflects the ongoing tasks and challenges of the organization. The group votes to ratify the recommendations of the Sustainable Development Committee on requests for new uses of land-trust land. Citing potential benefits or disadvantages for the community as a whole, the committee supports half a dozen requests, opposes one, and suggests deferring another. Barros talks about budget issues, including some misunderstandings and internal politics that seem to be holding up a check expected from one of the foundations that support DSNI. There is an update from the Resident Development Institute, which provides leadership training for people in the community.

More than a decade of improvements in the core area means that it has caught up to and in some ways surpassed the once healthier surrounding area. The board votes to propose a new emphasis on the problems of that area at the upcoming annual meeting. If the wider focus is approved, it will likely mean a change in the board structure: the board also votes to recommend adding one resident each from the four ethnic groups to represent the secondary area. So the board as a whole would go from twenty-nine seats, with sixteen area residents, to thirty-three seats, with twenty area residents. The discussion is matter-of-fact, the vote nearly unanimous, but the change would constitute a major milestone, recognizing how much had been accomplished in fifteen years and accepting a broader challenge.

Later, Najwa Abdul-Tawwab, the board president, reminds people that they need to mobilize residents to attend DSNI's annual meeting: "How is it going to happen? Magic? No. We have to work to get this done. There's door knocking, phone banking, church outreach. You can't leave tonight until you sign up for something."

The meeting ends as people promise to see one another again on Saturday at the dedication of a new community center, the culmination of six years of effort to revitalize a building that had stood unused for ten years.

Vine Street Community Center

On Saturday morning, an arch of red, yellow, and blue balloons frames the door of the ninety-year-old building that, as of today, will be the Vine Street Community Center. A lectern has been set up for speeches at the ribbon-cutting ceremony. A crowd of people of all ages, black, white, brown, chats and laughs. People tell one another, "All your hard work paid off." One elderly man with a cane says to a young woman, "You're in community development and you don't know me? This used to be my program in this building."

Boston mayor Thomas M. Menino arrives and speaks—"It's finally over. I thought this building was going to kill me." Others involved in the work give brief speeches, including resident Deborah Wilson, who says, "I'd like to thank DSNI for bringing out the activist in me. I didn't know I had it in me." Then the ribbon is cut and people stream in to tour the center: facilities for day care and an after-school program, a youth room, a fitness room, a computer lab, a large gym that occupies the whole top floor.

Pat Riddick, hired by DSNI as community center coordinator shortly after the mayor committed money to the project, recalls the almost six years of work that lay behind the celebration and the community center's impressive facilities. The first challenge was to convince the city that residents should participate in the planning process. Riddick says, "In the beginning, the city's attitude was 'We know how to develop community centers; we'll let you know what we decide.' " The residents sent letters to the mayor and other officials demanding a role. Eventually they convinced the city that it made sense to work with the community, although they periodically had to remind officials what full participation by residents meant. "Why would you want to be in on hiring the architect?" officials asked when the residents' group insisted that it take part in all planning and decision making.[16]

Riddick also faced tensions within the Dudley community. The first public meeting about the proposed center drew two hundred residents and revealed conflict among different cultural groups, each of which argued that the project should be developed to meet its particular needs. Cape Verdeans contended that the center should be theirs since it had been a Cape Verdean community house in the late 1980s; African Americans had their own reasons for laying claim to the building. To deal with the divisions, Riddick invited everyone to a "unity meeting" the following week. Along one wall she posted a time line that ran from 1915, when the building first opened, housing a library, gymnasium, and bathhouse, to the present. She asked everyone at the meeting to write an explanation of their involvement with the building on the timeline. "People saw that they all had a stake," she says. "They had an opportunity to tell the stories of their relationships with the building. By the end of the meeting, they began to understand that they could work together." As in other settings we have looked at, getting people together to tell their own stories in their own words seemed to create the mutual understanding and sympathy that made collective action possible. Two or three other unity meetings led to the formation of the Vine Street Advisory Committee, which has been engaged with the project ever since and now, as a twenty-one-member council, has responsibility for governing the center.

Some of the usual problems that afflict municipal building projects extended a planned two-year process into an almost six-year one: a legal challenge to the city's choice of contractor; an especially complex and costly asbestos-removal effort. Riddick finds some benefits even in the frustrating, exhausting delays. "Working together for five years gave people the opportunity to become strong friends," she explains. "And the committee members took heat from the community for the delays and learned to take it gracefully." As an organizer, she sees her task as finding a way to move from getting a particular job done to developing leadership skills among the residents. As the work progressed, she left more and more in the hands of the committee. The current chair has told her, "I felt you stepping back and I resented it; I wasn't sure we were ready. Now I see why you did it."

The First Two Decades and After

The Dudley Street Neighborhood Initiative is almost two decades old. As of 2002, thirty-seven hundred area residents were voting members of DSNI. The organization's accomplishments are visible all along the streets of the area: in the new homes, the commons, the improved playgrounds, the vegetable gardens, the new businesses, the gatherings of residents for meetings, for the multicultural festival, for the opening of the new community center. A 1996 survey of Dudley area residents found that nearly 50 percent thought their neighborhood had improved over the past couple of years and more than 50 percent expected it to continue to improve (compared to about 10 percent who believed it would stay the same or decline). Respondents who said they wanted to stay in the community for many more years outnumbered by four to one those who wanted to move soon.[17]

Major challenges persist. The continuing scourge of gun violence in American cities challenges even the most dedicated neighborhood initiative. In 2002 newspaper stories highlighted violent crimes in the area and the controversial use of deadly force by police—stories that seem to echo the troubled past—but the overall decrease in crime holds true. The new playground across the street from the Henriquez home was dedicated to Trina Persad, a ten-year-old Roxbury girl who was shot to death in 2002. It was a gang member's bullet—intended for another target—that killed her. Henriquez and other community members have vowed to do all they can to keep this new playground safe.

State and city budget problems caused by a general economic decline may threaten some of the advances made in the quality of local public schools, and the decline itself could slow the painfully won economic advances. DSNI also must find a way to turn its attention to the larger (secondary) Dudley area without losing the effectiveness of the intense focus it brought to problems in the core and especially the triangle. It remains to be seen whether that shift will create new, competing demands and new tensions. DSNI must maintain the delicate process of continuing to improve the neighborhood without losing it to wealthier newcomers. So far, development without displacement has worked. Restrictions on the resale prices of homes and cooperatives on land-trust property keep housing prices within reach of neighborhood people, but creeping gentrification is always a risk.

Preserving unity among the ethnic groups of the area and maintaining both the perception and the reality of fairness may be DSNI's greatest ongoing challenge. Ayeesha Lane is not a direct participant in DSNI, but she admires its work and talks about how exciting it has been "to watch everyday people be in these incredibly powerful positions and evolve into community leaders." Lane works with the Development Leadership Network, a national association of individuals engaged in community economic development and fighting racism. She thinks DSNI needs to acknowledge tensions around race more openly than it has in the past. "If you don't acknowledge that tension, it becomes the elephant in the room no one talks about," she says. Lane believes that some area residents think of DSNI now as mainly a Cape Verdean organization. "Even a flyer announcing a meeting in only English and Cape Verdean sends a message," she says. "If that happens twice, people feel they're not welcome and pull out." The fact that DSNI has recently formed a committee to address a decrease in Latino participation and a corresponding sense among some Latinos of being neglected—its first committee that has focused on a single ethnic group—may suggest that it is acknowledging the elephant in the room. The key to maintaining the unusual degree of cooperation among racial and ethnic groups that has characterized DSNI is not only fairness but efforts to keep in contact, to keep encouraging people to share their stories, to maintain and build relationships. Barros says, "The success of this neighborhood has got to be about the relationships we build, because there are going to be conflicts." But sustaining trust and cooperation among diverse groups is no easy task.

DSNI must also deal with the consequences of its success and must keep alive the community spirit fueled by the terrible conditions that it has helped eliminate or improve. As with other organizations that exist for a long time, and especially those that change the conditions that brought them into existence, longtime participants have to keep telling the story of the community and the organizations to help newcomers understand and enter into the spirit of the place. In Dudley, notes Bob Holmes, institutional memory fades. For instance, new homeowners often do not understand the resale restrictions. Holmes says, "You have to go to them and say, 'This is what the restrictions are all about,' tell them the history."

Asked whether DSNI had a final goal in mind, one whose achievement would mean the organization should disband, its aims accomplished, John Barros said, "The role might change, but I can't think of any neighborhood that wouldn't be richer for having a DSNI. We should push for this in every neighborhood; it is the actualization of block-by-block democracy." [18]

CHAPTER 5

{ *Tupelo, Mississippi* }

The Tupelo Model
Building Community First

In 1940, Lee County was one of the poorest counties in America. Family income averaged $750 a year, one quarter of the national average. Many adults were functionally illiterate. Located in the southern reaches of the Appalachian mountains, Lee County (69 percent white) was less African-American than most of Mississippi. Nearly 80 percent of the population was engaged in agriculture, with cotton the principal crop, but the cotton market had been declining for forty years and showed no sign of reviving. To make matters worse, Tupelo, the county seat, had been devastated by a tornado in 1936, with 230 people killed and much of the town flattened. A two-week strike by textile workers in 1937 created deep bitterness in Tupelo between the workers and the owners and other business leaders. When it ended, the workers saw no increase in their ten-dollar-a-week salaries; the strike leader was dragged out of town and badly beaten. The town and the county were in tough shape when George McLean, owner of the local paper, went up and down Main Street, telling Tupelo's business leaders and bankers how they could make more money for themselves by investing in the farmers of the country.

McLean seemed the last person the town's leaders would listen to, much less agree with. He had been born in Winona, Mississippi, more than a hundred miles from Tupelo, and had hoped to become a Presbyterian minister, but he had been told that his radical social views—in favor of integration and support for laborers and poor farmers—would

98

not be accepted by any church in the denomination. After studying sociology, psychology, and philosophy, he taught briefly at Southwestern College in Memphis—until his efforts on behalf of laborers and tenant farmers got him in trouble and he lost his job. In June 1934, he bought the bankrupt *Tupelo Journal* and before long was ruffling feathers there, too. When McLean supported the workers in the textile strike, the town's leaders boycotted the paper; their hatred of the man intensified. The boycott "almost put him under," recounted Tom Pittman, who later worked for McLean. McLean learned that "you need to do the right thing, but you can't lead without people following you."[1]

Vaughn Grisham, Jr., is a University of Mississippi sociology professor who knew McLean and has devoted his career to telling the story of Tupelo's surprising revival, leading a one-man crusade to inspire other struggling communities to follow its example. Grisham describes one of McLean's encounters with Main Street businessmen in 1940, recounted to him by the owner of a hardware store that still stands at 114 West Main Street. (Some years later, Elvis Presley—born about a mile away—bought his first guitar there.)

When McLean walked into the store and introduced himself, Grisham says, the owner interrupted him: "I know who you are. You're a troublemaker. I don't put ads in your paper, and I don't subscribe to it."

McLean told him he wasn't selling ads or subscriptions. The businessman didn't care why he was there. Well over six feet tall, he began pushing the relatively slight McLean backward toward the door. McLean looked up at him and asked, "How much did you gross last year?"

The man told Grisham, "That made me madder than him being a communist."

As he was being propelled toward the street, McLean said, "You probably grossed two thousand dollars." Insulted by that paltry figure, the owner took the bait.

"I grossed eight thousand dollars!" he said.

"What if I could show you how to gross ten thousand dollars more in two or three years?" McLean asked. He pointed out that the average Lee

County family made $750 a year. "These are your customers," he said. "The only way you can make more money is for your customers to make more money."

"I can't help a man farm."

"Yes, you can," McLean insisted.

"I work eighty hours a week here," the hardware store owner said. But he was interested in making more money, and he let McLean talk, the two of them standing out on Main Street. McLean described the long, slow decline of cotton and the untapped potential of the area's small dairy industry. He had done some research into the new and relatively little known technique of artificial insemination, and he talked about that. He proposed that the store owner and the town's other prominent businessmen invest in a prize stud bull and in the expertise and facilities an artificial insemination program would require to bring the county's modest dairy industry to life. This would be no small investment. A prize bull cost about $50,000—the equivalent of more than $600,000 today.

The hardware store owner was one of seventeen Tupelo business leaders who invested in the plan, many of them mortgaging their businesses to come up with the cash. Most did not like McLean any better now than they had before, but his idea made sense to them. During the 1937 textile workers' strike, McLean had railed at the mill owners, "How can you do that to your fellowman?" He was hated for suggesting that their behavior fell short of their religious ideals, and his views were rejected. Now he appealed to the town leaders' self-interest, convincing them that area farmers and shop owners were in the same boat and would sink or swim together. They listened and agreed. Their gamble paid off. The first year that cows sired by the prize bull gave milk, they generated $1 million in income, a figure that rose to $10 million as the dairy industry grew. In the 1950s, Lee County surpassed many Wisconsin counties in dairy production, and the industry received awards for innovation five times. The business leaders got their money back many times over through increased sales that reflected the simple fact that people finally had money to spend.

Now, more than sixty years after McLean's plan was adopted, Tupelo and northeastern Mississippi are bustling. Tupelo is not an especially pretty town; it lacks the charm of sleepier places, but it is prosperous. The corner of Main Street and Bloster is the busiest intersection in all of Mississippi. The region is home to 203 furniture factories large and small, producing more upholstered furniture than any other place in the world. Interestingly, 186 of these companies are owned by men who learned the craft at the first furniture company in the region, Morris Futorian Company, or from others who had worked there. The Tupelo Furniture Mart is second only to the one in High Point, North Carolina. Twice a year, twenty thousand buyers from all over the world come to shop here, for two weeks filling every hotel room for fifty miles. In all, 202 firms have facilities in Lee County, including 17 Fortune 500 companies and more than 40 international corporations. In 1967, Lee County produced more new jobs than the other eighty-one Mississippi counties combined. Throughout the 1990s, the area consistently generated a thousand manufacturing jobs a year. Today, fifty-eight thousand people are employed in the area (only 2 percent of them in agriculture). Tupelo has a ten-thousand-seat coliseum and a new Advanced Education Center (a collaboration of the University of Mississippi, Itawamba Community College, and Mississippi University for Women). The North Mississippi Medical Center, located on a hilly 130-acre campus near the southeast edge of Tupelo, is the largest nonurban medical center in the country and the single biggest employer in the area, with five thousand employees. The current presidents of the American Medical Association and the American Bankers Association live and work in Lee County. In 1998, the poverty rate in Lee County was approximately one half of the national average.

After a half century of hard collaborative work, impoverished Lee County has been dramatically transformed. Tupelo's success in sustained community development is widely heralded. In 1994 *The Wall Street Journal* reported that "Tupelo's proven track record [in attracting new firms] without handing over the keys to the city and leaning on local tax payers has made it the envy of corporate recruiters across the U.S." Stuart A. Rosenfeld, a specialist familiar with regional and community development efforts across the country, rates Tupelo among the top five success stories nationwide. Sheila Tschinkel, an economist with the Federal Reserve Bank of Atlanta, adds, "Tupelo is what we always come back to in economic development circles."[2]

There is more to this transformation than the purchase of a prize bull in the early 1940s. That investment was one manifestation of a broad principle—that treating town and region as an interdependent community would be more productive than focusing on narrower interests, that community development is the sturdiest foundation for economic development. That is the idea that Vaughn Grisham emphasizes again and again in his presentations to struggling communities around the country. In Tupelo, it found expression in a series of innovations in the 1940s and after, most of them instigated by George McLean.

One of the earliest and most important innovations was the formation of the Rural Community Development Councils. McLean laid the groundwork for these groups, which brought together the residents of rural communities—to make them more genuinely communities— through one-on-one conversations with leaders in the rural areas surrounding Tupelo. Thanks to that intense personal effort—another example of the importance of the direct person-to-person connection that so many of our stories illustrate—the concept of community councils was already understood and supported by many when McLean distributed a leaflet about the councils to every citizen in the county. The RCDCs were to be conduits for technical assistance from the Doane Agricultural Service, the nation's largest private agricultural service, and other sources, but also, and probably more important, they would strengthen community and foster local leadership. In words strikingly similar to Texas Industrial Areas Foundation principles articulated by Ernie Cortés, McLean wrote in his leaflet: "Each Community must develop a Leaven of Leadership from Within the Community and Seek to Strengthen It in every possible manner. . . . [T]here is no Santa Claus at the State Capital, State College, or Washington. If you want the job done, you will have to do it yourself."[3]

Hodding Carter, Jr., famed southern journalist who won a Pulitzer Prize for his crusade for civil rights, in describing Tupelo's transformation in *The Saturday Evening Post* of February 17, 1951, cited McLean's community-based strategy: " 'The Rural Community Development idea is simple enough,' McLean says. 'We organize the farmers by communities and offer community, not individual, prizes for such things as improved farm practices, new crops, increased efficiency in dairying, chicken raising, and such. We hold community get-togethers every summer.' " In Tupelo, Carter reported, "There is an earnest concentration upon self-improvement. In a city and countryside of overwhelmingly Protestant faith, the churches and secondly the schools far outrank the pretty hillside country club as centers of recreation and community entertainment. If anything, Tupelo is overorganized—there appears to be a club of some kind, civic or religious, for every ten Tupeloans, and the eatin' meetin's dominate the social life."[4]

Like Texas IAF organizations, the RCDCs built on these existing networks of social ties and trust relationships. Their boards of directors included "local ministers, school administrators, vocational education teachers, farmers, and officers from women's home demonstration clubs."[5] McLean modeled the RCDCs after the New England town meeting, with all citizens expected to be full participants. Board members organized neighborhood groups of ten to twelve families, drawing virtually the whole community into the councils. Monthly meetings blended discussions of farming techniques and plans for local improvement with sociable meals and group singing. In addition to sharing knowledge to improve farm productivity, members joined in projects to fix up their communities, painting churches and schools and cleaning up public spaces. Here, as elsewhere, grassroots decision making could be frustrating for organizers who would have decided differently. In *Hand in Hand: Community and Economic Development in Tupelo*, Grisham and Rob Gurwitt recount McLean's occasional frustration when "some community elected to spend time and money fixing up, say, its cemeteries" when what people really needed was jobs. But he kept his criticism to himself, knowing that the key to community development (and ultimately economic development) was to allow people to do whatever evoked their collective passion and energy. McLean insisted that each RCDC be paired with a Tupelo civic club, to underscore the interdependence of city and rural areas.[6]

The Rural Community Development Councils were also instrumental in bringing about another innovation: the dissolution of the Tupelo Chamber of Commerce in favor of a new association, the Community Development Foundation. Like many other chambers of commerce, the Tupelo organization was seen as the agent of downtown merchants, not primarily concerned with the interests of the community as a whole and certainly not those of farmers in the surrounding countryside. The Community Development Foundation, as its name suggests, focused first on community, with the expectation that successful commerce would follow. Aware of the interdependence of town and country, it looked beyond the boundaries of Tupelo and saw the whole county as a community, or a community of communities. In its first year, the CDF attracted 151 members and had a budget three times as large as the chamber of commerce's had ever been. It was and still is an organization that tries to look at the whole picture, coordinating government, business, and educational entities that need to work together to foster community and economic development. The fledgling CDF learned the importance of community involvement the hard way. In 1948, its leaders developed plans to increase farm income by growing berries, sweet potatoes, and other crops, and contributed $30,000 to set up a marketing association for the new products. They neglected to involve the farmers themselves in the planning, however, and the project failed.[7]

Education and training are an essential part of the Tupelo success story, especially in terms of the region's agile shift from mainly agricultural to mainly industrial jobs and, more recently, to a service economy. One of the CDF's first actions was to build child-care centers to give rural adults the opportunity to go to classes and learn to read. Tupelo began investing in leadership training in 1949. "Education before industrial parks" became a local motto. In the 1960s, the CDF led the effort to create a community college that would focus especially on vocational training. At the start of the 1970s, the *Tupelo Journal* made the importance of public education the subject of an intensive editorial campaign that helped generate support for a bond issue to build a new vocational education building. A few years later, George McLean and his wife, Anna, pledged $150,000 a year for ten years to support a program to put a reading aide in every classroom from first to third grade in the county. When the program started, the county's students ranked in the twenty-third percentile for reading nationwide. Five years later they reached the sixty-eighth percentile, and in the mid-1980s they approached the ninetieth percentile.[8]

Today members of the CDF continue to talk about the long-term value of luring employers with a reliable, well-trained workforce, rather than a promise of cheap labor—the low-paying jobs that do little for the community and are most likely to be moved offshore, inevitable casualties of the competition for cheap labor. One leader says, "We're not smart enough to know what the future is. We have to put more and more into education and skill training; then [workers] can adapt and prepare for whatever opportunities [may] come."[9]

Until his death in 1983, McLean himself remained vigilant for thinkers and ideas that could benefit the region. Every morning from six to nine, before going to the newspaper office, he scanned newspapers, magazines, and books for valuable ideas. From W. Edwards Deming he learned the importance of measurement, and Tupelo institutions still put tremendous emphasis on measuring their progress. He brought Peter Drucker to Tupelo to talk about the distinctions between leadership and management. (The practice of outside speakers continues. In 2000, Harvard Business School professor Michael Porter was in Tupelo to talk with business leaders about competing in the world economy.) McLean had few books at home, remarks Grisham, because he was always giving them away, telling other people they should read them. McLean's wife guessed that he may have started more libraries than anyone else in the history of Mississippi.

As in the case of his editorial in support of education, McLean used his newspaper to help keep the community development vision alive through the years. He endowed the CREATE Foundation to collect funds for community projects. He also willed his newspaper to the foundation, so it would never be taken over by a chain and lose its local roots. (Grisham reports McLean saying, "I'd pour gasoline on the floor of this place and burn it down before I'd let a chain come in here and buy this newspaper.") The foundation, funded almost entirely by the newspaper, generates more than $400,000 a year, which is put into community projects. Beginning in 2003, CREATE will aggressively build its endowment though gifts from others in the community in order to provide more support for local projects.[10]

But Grisham thinks McLean gets too much credit for Tupelo's turnaround. He didn't make it happen, and he didn't invent the ideas that cohered into the "Tupelo model." His great skill, according to Grisham, was in bringing people together and introducing them to ideas that he borrowed elsewhere. He was mainly a catalyst; he unlocked other people's power. "He used the networks around him," Grisham says. "He tied in with people who trusted each other." And if most people in Tupelo came, grudgingly, to trust that McLean was true to his word and genuinely sought the community's success more than his own, there were many who never liked him much or found him easy to get along with. Grisham mentions the Tupelo business leader Jack Reed, Sr., who says he spent half his time "defending George McLean." Grisham describes an experience he himself had in 1975. As part of his research, Grisham conducted a random survey of Tupelo residents that year, knocking on doors throughout the town. The old man who came to the door at one house interrupted his explanation of why he was there: "I know who you are. Wait here."

A moment later, the old man was back with a shotgun. He pressed the barrel's mouth against Grisham's chest and said, "You're a friend of that communist George McLean, who sided with the workers in the textile strike." Thirty-seven years after the fact, living in the town that owed its prosperity at least in part to George McLean, this man was still furious at McLean.

Telling the Tupelo Story

On a weekday morning in March 2002, Vaughn Grisham presides over introductions among the fifty people gathered in a meeting room of the Presbyterian church in Oxford, Mississippi. About two thirds of them are from Conway County, Arkansas: owners of businesses, farmers, the president of the community college, high school students. Five years earlier, Barry McKuin, an accountant in Morrilton, the largest town in the county, heard Grisham speak and decided that the Tupelo story might have important lessons for Conway County, which had lost four of its five largest manufacturing plants. McKuin brought others to listen to Grisham. Together they helped launched Conway County's own community development effort, "Vision 2020." Some of the people who traveled from Arkansas for the meeting had been to similar sessions and were looking for renewed energy and inspiration for their efforts. Some were hearing the story for the first time.

Most of the others were from Columbus County, North Carolina. Like Conway County, and like Tupelo half a century earlier, Columbus County faced a difficult economic situation. Declining agriculture and a withering textile industry had eliminated five thousand jobs in five years—equivalent to the population of Whiteville, the county seat and largest municipality. The North Carolinians were here to find out if the Tupelo model could help solve their problems and also to learn from Morrilton's more recent efforts. Over the years, similar teams from three hundred communities in sixty-three countries have visited to learn from Tupelo.[11]

For most of the morning, representatives of the two groups described their communities to each other. The visitors from Morrilton contrasted their ineffectual and mainly defeatist reaction to the loss of a major employer in the 1980s with their more positive and community-oriented response to plant closings in the 1990s, after they learned about Tupelo's success with community development. They described the job fairs and free financial advice organized for people who had lost their jobs, the square footage of new construction, the efforts to beautify downtown Morrilton with new brick sidewalks and other repairs and improvements. They talked, too, about the disadvantages of not having an interstate highway running through or near the town, how that increases the difficulty of attracting businesses and residents. Most of all, they talked about a new sense of community and cooperation in an area once known for corrupt, divisive politics and a habit of not following through with plans. One of them told the story of the crusty sixty-year-old retired man, a longtime cynic and naysayer, who saw changes in the town and decided, "I have to change." He appointed himself the unpaid supervisor of downtown renovations and badgered the contractor into firing some incompetent workers and hiring better ones (still crusty, in other words, but now for the sake of the community).

In the afternoon, some Oxford public employees and businesspeople discussed local projects: the redevelopment of the town square, efforts to attract retirees to the town, an arts festival, a software business that had grown from a single employee to 220 in just a few years.

Attention is beginning to flag near the end of the long day when Grisham stands up to tell the Tupelo story: George McLean convincing the town leaders to buy that bull, the Rural Community Development Councils, the Community Development Foundation, the role of the *Tupelo Journal*. Grisham's complete command of the details of the story and his skillful delivery are the only indications that he has told it hundreds of times over the past twenty years. The story seems fresh and immediate. Appearing fully engaged in events that have occupied him for more than a quarter of a century, Grisham speaks with a dignified, warm energy that suggests generous enthusiasm more than showmanship and shows respect for his audience. You can feel people perking up, their attention captured by a story of insight, persistence, and prosperity that offers hope for their communities: If Tupelo could do it, so can we.

Grisham believes that the Tupelo model can be learned and replicated, despite what he sees as obstacles caused by people's negative stereotypes about Mississippi, their inclination to dismiss him as an academic, their tendency to say that "this won't work here—our town is different," and their focus on the resources they don't have. That is why he has traveled around the country for two decades describing it again and again to the leaders of other economically distressed towns and areas. "It began with an individual," he says, referring of course to McLean. "It always begins with an individual, but there is no way of predicting who that person will be." And Grisham argues that the leaders—or catalysts—of post-Tupelo community-development movements need not be charismatic, politically savvy, or exceptionally creative. He points to Barry McKuin, the accountant who brought the Tupelo story to Morrilton five years earlier and has been one of the community leaders there ever since. Shy and low-key, McKuin seems an unlikely crusader. His wife still remembers how his excitement surprised her when he came home and told her about hearing Grisham for the first time. "It was striking," she says, because "he never gets excited about anything." Nevertheless, he has been able to draw others to the vision of community development in Morrilton. "He has no charisma," Grisham says, "but everyone trusts him." He adds, "I can teach everything except trust. I tell people, if you don't trust 'em, don't send 'em."

Coach and cheerleader, Grisham applauds the Morrilton contingent for their energy and persistence. He talks to them about the importance of achieving a critical mass of people committed to the same vision of community development, how not much seems to happen until that critical mass is reached but how, when it is, change can come quickly. In *The Tipping Point: How Little Things Can Make a Big Difference*, published in 2000, Malcolm Gladwell makes the same argument, explaining that a small variation in how quickly and widely a new behavior, say, spreads at a critical point can make the difference between a phenomenon that explodes into cultural change and one that flickers on the edge of people's attention for a while and then fizzles out. Grisham tells the Conway County group that it has "a solid core of people who won't quit." Certainly they have not yet begun to see anything like the results Tupelo has achieved, but Tupelo has been at this for half a century and probably did not have very much to show for its efforts in the first five years. Persistence is key, as is continuing to focus on the community-development idea. Grisham says, "There's a myth that the tornado of '36 brought Tupelo together and started the turnaround. It didn't happen that way. That kind of crisis can pull people together for a short time, but they don't sustain the connection." Because Tupelo attracts so many resources, and because its citizens brag so much about its success, some people in neighboring counties say, "If Tupelo could suck as hard as it blows, the Gulf of Mexico would be lapping Main Street." But Jack Reed, chairman of Reed Department Store and Reed Manufacturing Company of Tupelo, has responded, "Our overestimating ourselves doesn't give you the right to underestimate us."

"If Tupelo is different from other places," Grisham says, "the story is no good; you couldn't replicate it." How much of Tupelo's extraordinary success depends on particular circumstances of time, place, and culture, and on particular personalities? Even granting that McLean was a catalyst more than a creator, the ability to bring people together is not easy to find. Grisham himself is aware of ways in which Tupelo suffers from McLean's absence. He mentions Route 6, the four-lane highway that runs east toward the town but stops ten miles short. Plans to bring it the rest of the way are being held up by disagreement about which part of town it should enter: the area that gets the road will see higher land values and increased economic activity. "If McLean were alive," he says, "he would get all the players in the same room and say, 'I don't care where the highway ends as long as it's decided. We'll all gain.' He would get them moving, but it's not happening."

The visitors from Arkansas and North Carolina pile into a caravan of rental cars, vans, and a bus. They turn north where Route 6 ends abruptly in the middle of nowhere—evidence of that unresolved dispute—and make their way to Main Street past furniture factories and industrial parks. Main Street is new construction, the multistory glitter of the BankcorpSouth national headquarters, the Community Development Foundation building (formerly a courthouse) at the corner of Main and Broadway, the Coliseum, surrounded by acres of parking. Just south and east is the Advanced Education Center, big and new, like so much in Tupelo. It is the first stop in a day devoted to listening to Tupelo leaders of the Advanced Education Center, the Community Development Foundation, the North Mississippi Medical Center, and the newspaper talk about their work in relation to the concept of community development.

Charles Harrison, executive director of the Advanced Education Center, tells his story of cooperation and community focus. Harrison says, "We are linked to the needs of Tupelo and northeast Mississippi." The Center works with the public schools to develop a regional education plan; its retraining programs include not only courses to prepare workers for existing jobs but others, based on the CDF's ten-year plan, to train them for future opportunities. (The foundation believes the furniture industry will eventually decline and will probably be replaced by "mid-tech" jobs, especially information management for small companies.) Harrison talks about making education accessible to working adults: not only by scheduling most classes at night but by making paperwork and parking as easy as possible. Cooperation among organizations extends to looking out for one another's particular interests. For instance, the Advanced Education Center offers no freshman or sophomore classes, so as not to compete with the community college.

The visitors from Arkansas and North Carolina ask question after question, hungry for strategies they can take home. Some address broad issues of education and community building; others are nuts-and-bolts specific: Who pays for workforce development programs? How much do they cost? What training should we give *our* people? After the last question, people cluster in buzzing groups. Ed Martsolf, another of the Morrilton leaders, who has been here before, leads Beverlee Nance of the Southeast Community College in Columbus County over to Harrison, saying, "I have to get you people introduced."

Most of the day is a showcase of Tupelo's accomplishments and variations on the theme of taking a coordinated approach to community development and the interdependence of education, public policy, and economic health. In the boardroom of the Community Development Foundation, Barbara Smith, vice president of the Chamber of Commerce division of the CDF, notes that almost all the furnishings of the room—the dark wood tables, the upholstered chairs, the carpet and wallpaper, even the lights—were made in Lee County factories, a visible embodiment of their success in attracting industry. The foundation now has more than nine hundred members and a million-dollar budget. Senior staff members talk about cooperation between the public and private sectors, about the importance of getting the participation of a wide group of business leaders, politicians, educators, and other citizens. They talk about looking ahead and attracting high-paying industries with highly skilled workers.

The North Mississippi Medical Center is another vivid embodiment of the area's success. The large, modern main building is being expanded; the 130-acre campus has centers for cancer care and for neurology, a women's services center, a wellness center, dozens of other buildings, a helipad for medevac flights. *U.S. News & World Report* named it one of four models for medical centers in the United States in 1996. It seems an unimaginably long way from the Tupelo of 1940. COO Gerald Wages adds to the now familiar story of community connection—in fact, of being owned by and embedded in the community. He explains that the school nurses in the Tupelo area are employees of the medical center, since this is one way to influence community health and catch health problems before they turn serious. The medical center partners with particular industries to make sure their health-care needs are being met. It shares its five-year staffing plan with the community college so the college will know what jobs to train students for and can assure students that the jobs will be there when they graduate. Wages describes the medical center board, one third physicians and two thirds citizens of the area, and how the members were offered pay for being on the board but turned it down, preferring to see the money reinvested in this hospital.

The *Journal*

George McLean's *Tupelo Journal* is now the *Northeast Mississippi Daily Journal*, with a circulation of thirty-six thousand. Lloyd Gray has been editor for a decade. The son of a past Episcopal bishop and brother of a current one, he speaks with quiet conviction, a kind of modest certainty about his work. The newspaper is his calling, and he says it is energizing "to work for a newspaper that knows what it's about." It is a for-profit paper owned by a nonprofit organization. "It doesn't stay in business to make money," Gray says. "It makes money to stay in business."

The *Journal* is about building community, as it was in McLean's day. "Newspapers help give a community its self-definition," Gray says. "No community ever rises above its newspaper." He believes that an emphasis on scandal and failure breeds cynicism and that a focus on crime and violence ("If it bleeds, it leads," the operative principle of many TV news programs and some papers) arouses inordinate fear and creates a distorted sense of how bad things are. A newspaper mirrors a community, and if that image is distorted and fractured, members of the community will find it hard to rouse enthusiasm for shared endeavors. It is no accident that George McLean's successful efforts at community building were rooted in (and served by) the editorial policy that he established and that has persisted for more than six decades. The *Journal* is one of only a handful of community-owned newspapers in the entire country.

The aim and part of the difficult balancing act of the *Journal* are to highlight real human achievement, especially in education, health care, and transportation ("not cotton-candy stuff," Gray says), while not being simply a community cheerleader or a purveyor of smiley-face news. The paper writes about serious problems; its editorials are strong, he says, but they are solution- rather than problem-oriented. "We hold politicians to account," Gray says. "Our relationship with them needs to be honest, but it doesn't have to be adversarial. . . . There's nothing to be gained by ignoring problems. In recent years we no longer have a handful of enlightened people, mostly men, to raise the problems. Doesn't work that way anymore. The way it did in George McLean's day. . . . We have to be out there now spotlighting challenges here as issues we need to deal with."

Another element of the balancing act is that the *Journal* and its employees play active roles in the community. The staffers talk about "putting legs on our editorials," that is, doing something about the problems they write about. So, for instance, after publishing several editorials about the eyesore of a block of deteriorating houses downtown, the paper bought and renovated them. It also built warehouses that helped attract the earliest furniture factories to the area. Most recently the paper has purchased below-market-rate business-incubation space. "In all of these activities the paper did little better than break even. Our goal was community development," Gray says.[12] While reporters for most newspapers are expected to be detached and (theoretically) objective observers, *Journal* staff are encouraged to participate in community affairs as members of boards and committees. "You need to be careful not to emphasize work you're involved in too much," Gray cautions. "Some people will still accuse you, but that's the price you pay for being involved." Clearly, this is not your typical newspaper. To say it bears the stamp of George McLean's convictions is an understatement. Gray marvels at "how someone who has been dead for nearly twenty years can still be such a presence in the institution [the newspaper] and the community."

Keeping the Spirit Alive

Compared to many other places, Tupelo is a model of community spirit. The long-range planning to ensure the future of the community is impressive; the cooperation that exists among educational institutions and between those institutions, on the one hand, and businesses and the medical center, on the other, is rare enough that outsiders have trouble believing it. Today, as in the past, some business leaders devote as much as 50 percent of their time to community development, believing still that those efforts will do more for their businesses than will a narrow focus on the business itself. "Once here, companies are expected to help Tupelo maintain its allure as both a place of business and a place to live," reports *The Wall Street Journal*. " 'There's an expectation that if you're enjoying the benefits of being in Tupelo, you're expected to reinvest in the community,' says John Hicks, president of North Mississippi Medical Center." [13]

But Lee County may be experiencing some clouding of its vision of the interdependent community. The dispute holding up completion of Route 6 is one sign. There are others. Some years back, Tupelo passed the largest school bond issue in Mississippi history, with 88 percent of voters in favor. The next bond issue passed, too, but with 78 percent in favor. In the year following that vote, the town failed to reach its United Way goal for the first time. Vaughn Grisham believes that civic pride in Tupelo began slipping in the 1990s. During that time, too, public perception of the Community Development Foundation changed. People began to see it as functioning more like the chamber of commerce it replaced, losing some of its broad community focus and concentrating too much on the narrower interests of business leaders. The newspaper ran a series on how the CDF had strayed from its course. Grisham himself wrote the front-page editorial suggesting that it was time for the longtime CDF director to retire because he had lost sight of the organization's historic mission. (The director did retire, and a new leader is in place.)

Over the last fifty years, Tupelo has had an imperfect but in many ways admirable record on race relations. "McLean somehow finessed the race issue," observes Hodding Carter III, son of the crusading journalist. "In most places—ninety-nine percent of them in Mississippi—race trumped all other issues all of the time." Although most of the Rural

Community Development Councils in the 1950s were in all-white or all-black communities, a few in integrated communities had members from both races who worked together—an unusual phenomenon in the South at that time. *The Wall Street Journal* observes that "in a corner of America where labor's main selling point is its low costs and where racial conflict has left deep scars, Tupelo spends heavily to build a skilled work force and acts quickly to address minority grievances. . . . In the early 1960s, Lee County was the first county in Mississippi to integrate its schools. By doing so, it avoided the public relations debacles that for years shadowed Little Rock, Ark., Oxford, Miss., and other Southern cities that resisted the civil rights movement."[14]

During the 1960s and early 1970s, Tupelo's efforts to establish biracial committees to deal with important issues helped it avoid much of the divisiveness and distrust of that era. Grisham and Gurwitt write, "In the face of deep and often violent emotions, community leaders reminded one another and the community that the county's progress had been possible only through cooperative efforts, and that the county had to continue to build consensus for the good of all."[15] In the early 1960s, Tupelo's recreation department established a policy of not letting the teams it sponsored compete against communities with segregated teams (which described virtually all of the other communities in the area). In nearly every corner of Mississippi, private segregated academies served as "havens" for whites seeking to escape integrated public schools. Tupelo pursued a different path, convincing the community that it should not allow the divisiveness that academies would create in the locality. Thus it created a public school system that garnered the support of the entire community. Today Tupelo has one of the most effective school systems in the state.[16] Nevertheless, Grisham and Gurwitt note that the family income of African Americans was considerably below that of whites during all those years, and the history of relations between the police and the African-American community has been troubled at times. Today, race relations in the area seem a mixture of unusual cooperation and the usual tensions and prejudices. As the student body in Tupelo public schools approaches 50 percent African-American, editor Lloyd Gray sees some signs of "white flight." He believes some families are choosing to live in Saltillo, the nearly all-white city directly to the north, to avoid sending their children to racially mixed schools, even though Tupelo's school system is superior according to every standard performance measure.

When eight thousand people lived in Tupelo and family income averaged $750, the argument for interdependence was powerfully persuasive. Now, with thirty-five thousand people in the town, hundreds of employers, family income at about the national average, and an influx of professionals from other parts of the country, the sense of people all being in the same boat has eroded somewhat—and in fact residents' economic well-being is not as closely linked as it was in 1940. Yes, the livelihood of the doctor recently hired by the medical center ultimately depends on the economic well-being of the factory workers who are his patients, and the effect of job losses in the area would extend beyond the people who lost their jobs, but the equation is more complicated than the one McLean taught the town's leaders in the 1940s. The closing of one factory or a slight dip in wages would not affect that doctor much. If community means mutual influence and mutual dependence, community is stretched thinner now than when there were eight thousand people in town and a drop in the price of cotton meant less money spent on hardware and fewer loans taken out at the bank. The ties are real but looser. Some of the newer professionals in town are impatient with the emphasis on the basics in the schools and on vocational skills in local colleges (part of the strategy for continued prosperity); they want more higher-level academic courses for their children.

What can be done to keep the Tupelo spirit of community development alive? Lew Whitfield worries, "I don't see people in their thirties taking on the same leadership role. We're not doing as good a job at getting younger people involved. So now we have developed a new leadership program in which after a year of training we put each young person into an organization for a year to get them involved."

"Keep telling the story," says Lloyd Gray. "Tell people the story and keep telling it." That is part of the *Journal*'s job: to tell the story and try to keep people faithful to its meaning, evaluating their actions against the principles of community development, nudging them in the right direction when they fall short. Grisham, too, is dedicated to telling the story—in Tupelo as well as elsewhere—and serving as a critic when necessary, as in the case of that difficult editorial about the leadership of the Community Development Foundation. And there are others who keep alive the spirit of Tupelo's success. Success has made the Tupelo story powerful, but it has also changed the place and made it more difficult to continue to live the story.

CHAPTER 6

{ *Lake Forest, California* }

Saddleback Church
From Crowd to Congregation

Every weekend, fifteen thousand or more people attend services at Saddleback Church in Lake Forest, California, an affluent Los Angeles–area bedroom community in Orange County. Twice on Saturday and four times on Sunday, thousands of casually dressed worshipers, mostly families and couples, park their cars in one of the vast parking lots on the Saddleback campus and pour into the Worship Center to listen to contemporary Christian music and hear senior pastor Rick Warren connect their personal strivings and sorrows to biblical texts.

Saddleback is one of the largest of what are often called megachurches (commonly defined as churches with weekend attendance of two thousand or more), though the leaders of these large churches prefer other names: "seeker church" is one you hear at Saddleback. For the most part these big, mainly Protestant churches are a recent phenomenon. Willow Creek Community Church, one of the earliest and best known, was formed in the 1970s and first held services in the main auditorium of its ninety-acre South Barrington, Illinois, campus in the early 1980s. Saddleback Church is less than twenty-five years old. In 1980, having recently moved to Orange County to establish a church, Rick Warren held his first Bible study meeting in the living room of his Saddleback Valley condominium. Seven people attended, including the real estate agent who had located the condo for Warren and his wife. A mass mailing to fifteen thousand homes in the area brought just over two hundred people to an Easter service in a high school auditorium that same year. Now, twenty-two years later, about forty-five thousand people consider Saddleback their home church and attend at least four services a year.

Religious communities are today, as in America's past, very important repositories of social capital. However, during the last third of the twentieth century involvement in many religious communities across the country slumped, just as more secular forms of community involvement did. Estimates vary in detail, but between 1960 and 2000 church membership, church attendance, and involvement in church-related groups such as Sunday schools, "church socials," and the like declined by perhaps one third nationwide. Among the so-called mainline churches (Methodists, Presbyterians, Roman Catholics, and the like) the falloff has been even greater.[1]

During these decades of general stagnation and decline, however, megachurches have grown from nothing to memberships in the thousands or tens of thousands. They now attract a significant proportion of Protestant churchgoers in the United States. Church commentator Lyle Schaller notes that 1 percent of the Protestant congregations in the United States attracted 12 percent of all worshipers on a typical weekend in 1998. Many of these people—at Saddleback, the vast majority of them—come from the ranks of the "unchurched," having given up on other churches or never having belonged to a religious group. In an era when levels of participation in collective activities of all kinds have declined, why have millions of people, many of them apparently not "joiners," flocked to these churches? Most who attend Saddleback live in typical suburban isolation, many in gated communities in towns that have no real centers and little civic life. Many have moved here from somewhere else. Their homes and workplaces are separated by long commutes on freeways, usually one person to a car. But thousands at a time come to services at Saddleback, and many eventually commit a significant share of their lives and their incomes to the church.

These very large churches are not all the same. Some have specific denominational affiliations; many do not. Some have entirely replaced sermons with Christian dramas and music; at others—Saddleback is one of these—the pastor's message remains the heart of the service, though it may not look or sound much like a traditional sermon. Most of these churches have many elements in common, though. Saddleback offers a look at how one church has drawn tens of thousands of the unchurched to its services and illustrates some of the features of the wider phenomenon as well.

Saddleback Church occupies seventy-four acres of land on the outskirts of Lake Forest, a small city of condos and private homes, parks and open-air shopping malls (misleadingly called town centers). It overlooks a couple of main roads and some hills covered with cactus, pine, and dry brush. There are no homes nearby. Everyone who comes to the church drives here; some come from more than thirty miles away. A sign by the road that curves up from the entrance reads: "First-Time Visitors Use Right Lane for Preferred Parking." The newcomers pass acres of parking lots and a youth ministry center under construction, and turn into a visitors' parking area behind the Worship Center.

A large rectangular building of stone and plaster in desert tones of sand and reddish brown, with expanses of window on either side, the Worship Center looks more like a convention hall or an unusually attractive field house than a traditional church. The only clear indications that this is a place of Christian worship are a slim tower near the entrance with a simple aluminum cross rising from it and the main entrance itself, a glass vestibule etched with biblical texts and with Saddleback's statement of purpose spanning the whole structure in letters a foot high: "Our Purposes: Magnification, Membership, Maturity, Ministry, Mission."

The interior does not much resemble a traditional church, either. The ceiling is a flat expanse of pipes and ductwork, painted white. Rows of chairs—thirty-five hundred of them—face what looks like a concert stage. Huge video screens cover the walls on either side. Two TV cameras on a platform toward the back of the hall stand ready to capture the action. Above the stage are large speakers and three more video screens, angled to give every seat in the house a direct view. A wooden lectern in the center of the stage, a visual echo of a church pulpit, seems the one element out of keeping with the general effect.

A Service at Saddleback

An hour before the first service on a hot, clear mid-May 2002 Saturday afternoon, the resemblance to a concert venue seems especially strong as musicians warm up and do sound checks. The band includes keyboards and piano, a full drum kit, two saxophones, trombone, trumpet, and electric flute. They back up a soloist and choir running through a spirited pop-rock hymn of praise. There are no choir robes, no matching outfits of any kind: they look like a bunch of young musicians rehearsing.

Greeters meet churchgoers at every turn—on the steps, the walkway, at the door to the sanctuary—smiling and shaking hands. The church even has a "parking ministry" of volunteers in red shirts with tire tracks silk-screened on the back. The hall fills rapidly with people of all ages, most of them white, some Asian, a few African-American. Many wear jeans and running shoes; some are in shorts. Some chat with people they know, exchange hugs. The video screens show flowers waving in the breeze behind the words "Please turn off all cell phones and beepers." The message changes to "Happy Mother's Day." At 4:45 P.M., music pastor Rick Muchow comes to the front of the stage and says, "Welcome to Saddleback. Sit back, relax, and enjoy being here." He and the other musicians launch into a series of songs in contemporary pop/folk-rock style, inviting the congregation to join in. Lyrics appear line by line on the video screens, some superimposed on images related to the song's theme. A song praising God for the bounty of his creation unfolds over scenes of mountains and rivers, autumn landscapes, parents and children, a cityscape at twilight.

After the music, Rick Warren steps forward. Like his congregants, he is casually dressed, wearing light khakis and a loose shirt patterned with leaves. His message, "What to Do When You're Overwhelmed" (the first in a series of "What to Do When . . ." messages on "God's principles for life's common situations"), is a blend of heart-to-heart talk, biblical exegesis, and multimedia performance. He is colloquial, direct, humorous. He has the gift of seeming to speak individually to each of the more than three thousand people listening to his words, both the people so busy they fear they will never catch up and those suffering deeper losses and crises. He uses the annunciation to Mary—Gabriel telling a teenage girl that she will give birth to God's son—as his example of overwhelming circumstances. He evokes the difficulties of Mary's situation in contemporary terms: having to tell her fiancé ("Hey, Joseph, I'm pregnant, but it's not what you think"); explaining to her parents and a community that stones women for sexual misconduct that she is still a virgin, but she is going to have a baby and that baby is God. He calls the audience's attention to the Bible's understated description of her initial reaction to the startling news: "The Bible says she was 'confused and disturbed.' Well, duh!" he adds, drawing a laugh from the audience.

In the course of his talk, he uses Mary's adjustment to her overwhelming situation as a guide to what his listeners should do when they are overwhelmed: Let go of the need to control the situation; let others help; let God give you strength. The biblical verses he quotes appear on the video screens and in the sermon notes handed out with the programs, which also have blanks to be filled in with key concepts as he explains them. His message, including the two thematically related songs and three testimonials by women that punctuate it, lasts more than forty-five minutes. One of the women tells how her faith helped her go on after her husband's death in a hunting accident; another talks about living with increasingly debilitating multiple sclerosis and raising her children alone from a wheelchair after her husband left her. Everything happens exactly on cue, in a perfectly timed and seamless performance.

There are a collection (a note in the program tells newcomers they need not contribute; the offering is for "regular attendees who consider Saddleback their church home") and a final rousing song, and then people stream out into the California sunshine. Friends greet one another;

some people head over to the shaded tables (Information, Recovery, Fresh Start, Care, and Prayer) across the plaza from the Worship Center, some head right back to their cars.

The service at Saddleback has some of the characteristics that people who disapprove of megachurches, especially other Christians, object to. Much of the criticism comes down to the complaint that these churches draw thousands to their services by offering entertainment rather than worship, that they cater to people as consumers rather than challenge them to take up the difficult task of being good Christians. Also seen as self-centered consumerism is the frequent emphasis on personal needs and problems, on Jesus as a personal savior.

The contemporary music, the video screens, the substitution (in some cases) of minidramas for sermons are, the argument goes, forms of pandering to secular tastes that distort or displace genuine Christian worship. Some critics believe church should rise above popular culture, not embrace it.

A recent *New York Times* article gives examples of what seems an even more consumer-oriented approach to church life. The Southeast Christian Church in Louisville, Kentucky, and Brentwood Baptist in Houston, Texas, have built facilities that are in effect church-centered malls or small towns, with health clubs and athletic facilities, McDonald's franchises, banks, and other amenities designed to attract people and encourage them to eat, play, and work as well as worship there.[2] There are at least two ways to look at this phenomenon, though: as an extreme version of the consumer society co-opting religion, or as religion infused into daily life—as encouraging either a more secular or a less secular life than that lived by members of traditional churches.

It is true that market research helps shape the design of services at Willow Creek, Saddleback, and other new, large churches. Since surveys show that many people decline to attend church because they find traditional music and sermons boring and traditional pews uncomfortable, such churches replace those disincentives with the kinds of music, message delivery, and physical environment that many people prefer. When

Rick Warren arrived in southern California, he surveyed people in the area to discover what they wanted in a church. (His book, *The Purpose-Driven Church*, includes a chapter entitled "Who Is Your Target?") He eventually produced a composite of a typical target individual, Saddleback Sam, a man who prefers casual meetings to formal ones, who likes contemporary music, is well educated, and would rather be in a large group than a small one. (Warren notes, "When I took our music preference survey, I couldn't find a single person who said, 'I listen to organ music on the radio.' ")[3] The Saddleback experience, from parking facilities and child-care arrangements to the music, messages, and ease of coming and going anonymously, reflects the preferences of that composite. Weekend services are as carefully shaped to "customer" preferences as any commercial product.

But Warren disagrees with the critics' assertion that the contemporary style of Saddleback services ignores or abandons the essential heart of Christianity. He contends that, on the contrary, these crowd-pleasing services are more faithful to living Christianity than "traditional" worship, which is an agglomeration of the contemporary styles of other eras. He writes, "We invite the unchurched to come and sit on seventeenth-century chairs (which we call pews), sing eighteenth-century songs (which we call hymns), and listen to a nineteenth-century instrument (a pipe organ)."[4] He says that Jesus drew large crowds by speaking directly to people's concerns in language they understood, not by insisting on traditional forms of Jewish worship, and that the church of Luther's time made no clear distinction between secular and religious music: the hymn tunes that we now think of as religious were in the style of popular tunes of the time. "There is no such thing as religious music," he says, "only religious lyrics."

Warren cites the New Testament verse "David served God's purposes in his own generation" (Acts 13:36) as his watchword, emphasizing "in his own generation" to explain that his purpose, like David's, is to reach the people of his generation in their own terms (by definition, in a contemporary style), not to preserve a particular, familiar idea of a "timeless" church. For Warren, in other words, the medium is not the message, the message is the message, and it should be communicated in whatever forms touch people most effectively.

Butch Yellott is now a "division leader" at Saddleback who oversees small-group formation in one of the areas from which the church draws its members. Pastor Rick Warren's message, and his congenial, contemporary translation of "how the scripture applies to real life," drew Yellott to Saddleback. At the Lutheran church of his youth, Yellott says, "It was the King James version, and I couldn't make the translation, the thees and thous and thou-shalt-nots. I never got that connection between church and God being part of everyday life." But now he sees that connection everywhere. At Saddleback, he says, "the teaching was so practical and easy to understand." And, he adds with a laugh, "Pastor Rick walked out in a Hawaiian shirt and no socks. It got my attention."

The crowds pouring in for weekend services at Saddleback attest to the success of the strategy, at least in terms of attracting large numbers of people. The larger challenge Saddleback and other megachurches face—and the key social-capital issue—is how to turn the "crowd" into a "congregation," to use Saddleback terms for distinguishing between the visitors, the consumers of comfort and entertainment, and the committed members of the church community. The answer is small groups.

Small Groups

On a Friday night in Lake Forest, Monique and Tim Holcomb's doorbell rings. Their two daughters rush to the door, with a yelping dog at their heels. The door opens to Sharon Carton and her two children, and the place becomes a cacophony of babies and toddlers and dogs and big girls home from ballet class. This is how the Holcombs' regular Friday-night small-group meeting starts. Once the children, the dog, and the babysitter are settled in the other room with *Cinderella*, the adults chat and pray and delve into their current topic of study: building better relationships. Questioning, talking, and listening, they strive to help one another grow as Christians. These people are comfortable enough with one another to hand kids around, to finish one another's sentences, and to stop by on Saturday mornings to visit even if it's too early to be out of pajamas.

Candid discussion of relationships has led to intimacy among members of this group. They have had to be "honest and open and ready to be vulnerable," says Sylvia Farrone. "We couldn't be superficial about it." Now, says Monique Holcomb, "I can tell them things I wouldn't talk about with other people. These are the people I would go to if I needed help."

The idea of being part of a "community" of forty-five thousand calls into question what "community" means. If it signifies real relationships among people who know one another well enough to share some trust and understanding, then tens of thousands of people cannot form a community. In any large organization, people's sense of loyalty, connection, and identification comes from being part of a smaller team or group who spend enough time together to know and be known to one another. Joining a small group is the first, essential step in being part of a megachurch rather than just attending it. In his book on the phenomenon of very large churches, Lyle Schaller notes, "Most very large congregations affirm the fact that they are a congregation of congregations, of choirs, circles, cells, classes, fellowships, groups, and organizations or a congregation of communities."[5] And in an article in the *Atlantic Monthly*, Charles Trueheart cites Jim Mellado of Willow Creek on the importance of lay-led "cells" of up to ten people, the small-group cell being "the basic unit of church life."[6] The same is true at Saddleback. Warren writes, "People are not looking for a friendly *church* as much as they are looking for *friends*."[7] He adds, "The average church member knows 67 people in the congregation, whether the church has 200 or 2,000 attending. A member does not have to know everyone in the church in order to feel like it's their church, but he or she does have to know *some* people."[8]

Part of Warren's Mother's Day weekend message on "what to do when you're overwhelmed" is to let others help, that is, to connect with other people. He tells his audience, "If you come to me with a problem, my first question is going to be 'Are you in a small group?'" He adds, "With fifty thousand names on the Saddleback list, there are people who have experienced what you're going through." He urges people not yet in a group to "pick a night and a neighborhood." A response form included with the program lists the communities that most Saddleback attenders come from and the available dates and times for groups.

People find one another in other ways, too. Saddleback periodically passes out lawn signs to its congregants. One recently on display was a remembrance of the victims of September 11, with an American flag and the words "Saddleback Church" in small print. Those signs give church members a reason to say hello to their neighbors: "Oh, you go to Saddleback, too?"

Sharon and Roger Carton were convening a new small group for the church's "40 Days of Purpose" campaign, a churchwide exploration of life's meaning and purpose. They went to every house in their neighborhood that had a 9/11 Saddleback sign on the lawn and invited the owners into a new small group. "People we've never met before in our neighborhood" have joined the group, says Sharon Carton. "Some people are at that stage where they just need somebody to ask them."

Warren cites a biblical foundation for small-group membership. He mentions that the New Testament uses the phrase "one another" more than fifty times, an indication of the importance of human relationships to Christianity. In *The Purpose-Driven Church*, he writes:

> Even a casual reading of the New Testament will show that the Gospel spread primarily through relationships. As soon as Andrew heard about Christ he went and told his brother Simon Peter. Philip immediately contacted a friend, Nathaniel. Matthew, a tax collector, held an evangelistic dinner party for other tax collectors.[9]

He points out that the metaphorical extension of the word "member"—a limb of a body—to the idea of membership in a group has a Christian origin, rooted in the belief that those in the church are figuratively "members" of the body of Christ. During his Mother's Day message he says, "If you're a Christian, fellowship is not optional."

The path to membership at Saddleback passes through an obligatory small-group membership class ("Class 101"), and the church has small groups and small-group ministries for every conceivable need and talent: couples groups, singles groups, a group for single parents of teenage children and one for mothers of preschoolers, Woman to Woman ministering, men's morning Bible study, deaf Bible study, a group combining volleyball and Bible study, groups for women with breast cancer and for men caring for women with breast cancer, a group for "teens-in-temptation," one for families with incarcerated loved ones, groups for separated men and separated women, a group for sufferers of chronic pain or chronic illness, and a "Geeks for God Ministry" for Cisco-certified networking professionals, among many others. Roughly eight thousand people are in Saddleback small groups at any one time, says Executive Pastor of Strategic Resource Development Forrest Reinhardt.

Brad Guiso spent a weekend in the San Bernardino Mountains with nine other church members and their mountain bikes. The group, which rides regularly and always prays first, completed a twenty-four-hour, two-hundred-mile relay race over the weekend, up and down mountainsides, all on one-track trails. "Where else can you find a church large enough to have a hundred fifty people on your mountain biking e-mail list?" he asks. But for Guiso, the community he has found in ten years at Saddleback goes deeper than recreational sports. He and his wife, Tammy, have been members of the same couples small group for seven years. Group members have helped one another move, seen one another through births and deaths, celebrated birthdays and children's achievements. When Brad found himself unemployed during an economic downturn, he answered the doorbell one day and found sacks of groceries and an envelope containing several hundred dollars. It was from the Guisos' small group from Saddleback.

At Saddleback, says Tim Holcomb, "You are expected to be in community; you can't live on your own. The purpose of your life is to be in community, to love and to give. When you see community work, it makes you want to be a part of it."

The church devotes extensive effort and attention to creating and supporting these groups. In addition to the flyers and the messages from the pulpit, Saddleback periodically holds small-group connection sessions, promising, "If you are tired of being a nameless face in the crowd, join us . . . for one hour and we will help you find a small-group family." At the session, people sit in sections of the hall that correspond to where they live and briefly tell one another about themselves (with a one-minute time limit; it is almost like speed dating). Five hundred or more people may connect in small groups at one of these sessions. Pastors Steve Gladen and Brett Eastman, responsible for membership and small groups, have created a small-group connection kit, which includes a step-by-step video that new groups view and follow during their first meeting. The video leads people through the process of telling their stories of how they came to the church, describing where they are on their spiritual journeys, and choosing a group leader. These new groups commit to seven or eight weeks of study together, but, says Gladen, more than 70 percent continue beyond that some for years. He believes that the biggest factor in keeping a group together is affinity: people whose concerns, ages, and backgrounds are similar tend to connect and stay together. Eastman says the groups offer "short-term fellowship that can lead to lifetime relationships."

In a church with as many congregants as Saddleback now has, one-on-one relationships between clergy and congregants may be impossible. Tim Holcomb says that he knows he could reach a Saddleback pastor whenever he needs to but adds, "It's not perfect. A small church that had the same genuineness would be in some ways preferable."

Sharon Carton agrees that close connection to clergy is something "you do miss." But, she says, "you rely on your small group for that." When she went to the hospital to give birth to her son, James, Monique Holcomb and another church member took turns caring for her daughter, Emma. "Those were the people who brought me meals," Carton says.

"I don't have family here. It has helped immensely to have people we can have that sense of community with." Carton is not alone here in being far removed from the network of family. Of the five adults in the Holcombs' group, just one has a parent who lives within driving distance.

Certainty and Commitment

The theology Rick Warren preaches is clear, certain, and consistent. He expresses the belief that the Bible is inerrant, the word of God delivered through men, and the ultimate and complete guide to how to live a religious life. He teaches that God's design gives purpose and meaning to everything that happens and that God is directly involved in the life of every human being on earth. "God has a plan for you," he says again and again, and asserts that the inevitable trials of life exist to develop character and bring people closer to God. "God will always sacrifice short-term comfort for long-term gain," he says in his Mother's Day message. "Faith," he adds, "is surrendering to God's will." He believes that those and only those who accept Jesus as their personal savior, who are born again, will be saved.

Lyle Schaller writes that "the number-one point of commonality [among very large churches] is absolute clarity about the belief system. The proclamation of the Christian gospel is organized around certainty, not ambiguity."[10] That is undeniably true of Saddleback, where the message is a confident assertion of truth, not an exploration of hopeful possibilities. And the message is delivered with unflagging consistency. Minister of Development Forrest Reinhardt says that Saddleback no longer has guest pastors at its services because their messages might be incompatible with the church's theology. For instance, the last invited outsider preached that God rewards good Christians with material success—not a Saddleback belief. He was asked to leave immediately after the first Saturday service, and staff filled in for the rest of that weekend's worship.

The message's power to comfort and inspire is undeniable. It rejects the possibility of a random, impersonal universe. It says that life in general and your life in particular have a noble purpose, that God created you specifically to fulfill that purpose. ("You are not an accident," as Warren puts it.) It says that God will guide you and give you strength if you let him. It says that sins can be forgiven and redeemed, that the world was made for us, not we for the world. It answers all the troubling questions about why we exist, why bad things happen, and what will happen to us when we die.

Warren's message is comforting but not easy. He invites his listeners to work toward the goals of a Christian life, to become as much like Christ as possible, leading a life of service rather than personal pleasure. The ultimate aim—the aim of the "purpose-driven life"—is to obey the great commandments ("Love the Lord your God with all your heart" and "Love your neighbor as yourself" [Matthew 22:36–40]) and fulfill the great commission ("Go and make disciples of all nations, baptizing them in the name of the Father and of the Son and of the Holy Spirit" [Matthew 28:19]). The structures of small-group education and spiritual development at Saddleback are designed to help people move from "the crowd" of weekend attenders to "the congregation" of those who are actual members of the church to "the committed," who are committed to spiritual maturity, to "the core" of those active in lay ministry. It is a progression, as church staff also say, from "attendees to army."

A complaint about megachurches, related to the consumerist one, is that they engage in a bait-and-switch tactic, that is, they attract people with amenities and entertaining services, asking little of them, and only later introduce them to the demands and costs of real membership, including tithing, many hours of volunteer work, and, sometimes, attending more traditional services designed for "believers" (as opposed to "seekers"). Warren would probably agree with the "bait" part, which evokes the idea of Jesus' followers as "fishers of men." He believes that attracting the unchurched with the bait of appealing, contemporary services is part of his mission. The "switch" accusation does not fit, however, because he insists from the start that the task of becoming a committed

Christian will be demanding. The services are entertaining and "easy," but he tells the crowd that they are only at the doorway to a longer, harder, more satisfying life journey. He is not afraid to make demands.

The lively, contemporary, consumer-friendly services certainly help get all of those thousands of people to services on the weekend, but entertainment value in and of itself plays only a small role in Saddleback's success. After all, there are movies and concerts and casinos available if entertainment is what you're looking for. The visitor more familiar with traditional services notices the video screens, the pop music, and the casual atmosphere first, but the real draw of Saddleback is its confident promise of a purposeful life and also its confidence in making demands on people, in telling them it can help them discover their talents and put them to meaningful use. People come to Saddleback not despite their isolation and materialism but because of them; they are looking for the community and sense of purpose that their materially successful lives lack. Butch Yellott decided to scrap the MBA program he had started in favor of working part-time as a small-group division leader for Saddleback Church. Echoing Warren, he says he is now living a life of "significance instead of success."

The Purpose-Driven Church Conference

On the Tuesday after Mother's Day, almost four thousand church leaders arrive at the Saddleback campus for a four-day Purpose-Driven Church Conference. They come from all fifty states and from thirty-five countries; they are white, black, brown, and Asian men and (some) women. They are here to learn some of the principles and techniques that have made Saddleback successful and to take lessons back to their own congregations or apply them to their own plans for establishing a new church.

One of Saddleback's aims is to stimulate the development of other churches. Forrest Reinhardt describes Saddleback as the "twenty-first-century Bell Labs for the church." He says, "We'll try a hundred different things to find the one that works and do a conference on it. We have a double focus of *application* to Saddleback and *implications* for other churches. The staff is required to spend a minimum of ten percent of their time on other churches." Comparing Saddleback's influence with Willow Creek's, he describes Willow Creek as the "mother church" that produces everything, helping to plant copies of Willow Creek in other places. Saddleback, he says, provides more of a changeable template: basic principles that will take different forms in different places.

The conference looks a lot like other conferences: groups of people with name tags carrying thick binders of conference materials; hats, T-shirts, and sweatshirts for sale; a tent of church tools and materials for sale: CDs and cassettes of religious music and sermons, instructional videos, books on church development and inspirational books, kits for youth ministry, for recovery, for developing small groups.

From one to five in the afternoon, with only one break, Rick Warren speaks from the stage of the Worship Center. He delivers something between a lecture, a sermon, and a worship service, with singers and instrumentalists providing music. Every seat in the Worship Center is taken, and hundreds of other attenders watch him in a large tent via closed-circuit television. His subject is the purpose-driven life. His underlying message is similar to the one he tells his congregation, though presented a little differently to this group of mainly church professionals.

"Meaning comes from connection, not independence," he says. "If you don't like fellowship on earth, you're not going to like heaven." He talks about mercy, learning to make allowances for others' faults: "Every church has people who are EGRs—extra grace required—and if you don't instantly think of who that person is in your church, it's you." He speaks about the great commandments and the great commission and says that their mission is evangelism: "God holds you responsible for the unbelievers in your life."

Near the end of the long afternoon, Warren's talk turns to his personal life for the first time. He describes the final illness of his father, a pastor for fifty years who helped build more than a hundred churches, physically, as a carpenter. For a week, Warren says, his father was in a kind of delirium, dreaming aloud about his life's work, reliving the building of those churches. During his last hours, he became agitated, saying over and over again, "Got to save one more for Jesus," at one point putting his hand on his son's head as he repeated the words. "That has been the theme of my life," Warren says. Behind all the market research and pop music, the videos and contemporary language, the care and feeding of small groups, evangelism is, finally, the engine that drives the very large church.

All Saints Church: Ambiguity and Ritual

All Saints Church in Pasadena is about seventy miles north and east of Saddleback—a little over an hour's drive if you're lucky enough to avoid freeway traffic. It, too, is a growing church, having almost doubled its membership since the late 1980s, when the church board decided to make an effort to grow. With thirty-five hundred members and an average total of thirteen hundred worshipers at its two Sunday services, All Saints is not quite a tenth the size of Saddleback, but it is a large church compared to most. Only one in four American Protestant churches reports an average worship attendance of more than 140.[11] Like Saddleback, All Saints draws its members from a wide area—in this case, the whole San Gabriel Valley—and people drive past eight or ten other Episcopal churches to get to this one. So All Saints, too, has bucked the trend of shrinkage or stagnation in church membership.

Some of what the church has done to attract more members parallels the strategies of very large churches, but on a smaller scale. The first change it made after reaching its growth decision was to introduce a second Sunday service. In addition to giving people more choice, the second service was a response to what seems to be a basic principle of church attendance, says Anne Peterson, senior associate for liturgy and leadership: once the sanctuary is about 80 percent full, new people stop coming, perceiving somehow that the church has no room for them.

Only additional services or a larger facility allow the numbership to increase. (The sanctuary at All Saints holds about 850 people, so it is again nearing its practical limit, with 1,300 people at two services.)

All Saints' staff also adopted the small-group idea as part of their growth plan, recognizing that pastoral care and personal connection would depend more on small communities within the greater community as the church got bigger. Their "Covenant One" groups, which introduce newcomers to the church's beliefs and to one another, are in some ways analogous to the Class 101 membership groups at Saddleback. In these meetings, group members share their spiritual autobiographies—personal, often emotionally charged stories about their spiritual journeys. As the life details spill out, people come to know one another. "I would argue that one of the pillars of community building is being heard and telling our stories," says church member Diane Norton. Sharing spiritual autobiographies is, she says, "a way of helping people to be safe and let the barriers down, and that takes time and nurturing."

Joe Duggan moved to the Los Angeles area from New York for a job. He didn't like L.A., did not know how to drive, and did not know a single person here. He did not intend to stay until he found All Saints. He became involved in small groups and church work and met the woman who is now his partner. He says, "I came for a job, and I stay as the result of relationships," most of which he traces directly to church.

There are also book groups and groups for music and social action, though of course many fewer than at the much larger church. But the differences in the small-group programs go beyond differences in scale. Whereas Saddleback and most other very large churches bring together similar people in groups, All Saints intentionally gathers people as unlike as possible, to reflect its belief in inclusiveness and the essential oneness of all people. Longtime member and junior warden Catherine Keig says, "I don't describe community as sameness; I describe it as difference." Anne Peterson says that a single group might include a former nun, an atheist, a couple of gay men, a Methodist, and people of different ethnic backgrounds, though church membership is predominantly white. Rusty

Harding, associate for small-group ministries and covenant class, describes "the magic when people tell their stories, and what used to be huge differences are transcended. People emerge from eight weeks together with strong bonds across deep divides."

Kip Petit had women friends her age and friends from work who were basically like her. In a small group at All Saints, she joined two gay male couples, a man in his mid-sixties, a single mom with young children, and a former magazine executive from Africa. Some in the group had been brought up Catholic, some Anglican, some Baptist, some Presbyterian. The group included a teacher, a gardener, a doctor, a student, and an insurance broker. "It didn't seem like anybody had that much in common," says Petit. But when the group finished its curriculum, it did not disband. Members continue to meet every week, choosing new topics of study. They have supper together and e-mail one another routinely. Petit toured Ireland with another group member. "Just having someone who's interested in you, giving you attention, is very important," she says. "I had women friends and friends from work, but they weren't the real intimate friends I have now."

Sharing stories connects members of small groups at Saddleback (and, as we have seen, it is the foundation of connections between members of Valley Interfaith and other groups we have described), but it also works here. Although some groups at All Saints do continue to meet long after the classes officially end, it is far fewer than the 70 percent of Saddleback groups that do. Affinity is a more powerful glue than diversity. While small groups seem the heart of Saddleback, the only road to commitment and connection, at All Saints they are important but not central in quite the same way.

A second service makes room for more people, but what draws them to All Saints is its unusual blending of Episcopalian ritual and tradition with political and theological liberalism. The church identifies itself as "prayerfully pro-choice." All Saints has been performing ceremonies of union for same-sex couples since 1991, and just over 20 percent of its members are gay or lesbian. Associate rector Scott Richardson says that people come to All Saints "because of our rooted history in social justice preaching," a history that includes liberal positions on Vietnam during the 1960s, on racial issues, on feminism, and on gay and lesbian issues. In the fall of 2001, rector J. Edwin Bacon, Jr., took a stand against bombing Afghanistan after the September 11 attacks that was controversial inside as well as outside the church. All Saints is deeply involved in local, national, and global social action, with ministries that work on local health, education, and safety issues (including Night Basketball and Books, a cooperative program with other Pasadena institutions to give local youths a safe place to study and play) and wider issues of nuclear-weapons abolition, environmental defense, and opposition to the death penalty. Several nonprofit organizations in Pasadena—the AIDS Service Center, the Grace Center for battered women, the Union Station home-less shelter, and the Young and Healthy health-care program for unin-sured kids—began as All Saints ministries.

A social worker in a school district that serves many children from impoverished homes in the inner cities, Barbara Ackermann spends her days with kids who have grown up without the benefits of community. To create those necessary connections, they join gangs. "A lot of kids get into gang affiliations to build community," Ackermann says. At All Saints she sees an opportunity to be part of a community that supports children. Many children in the parish have been adopted, she says, "shifted to better circumstances than they came from." All Saints, she says, embraces those kids, and the congregation becomes part of their community.

Catherine Keig says the church and Rector Bacon's sermons "connect what's going on in the newspaper with the Bible." So one thing most members have in common is liberal activism, though with all the grada-tions and differences that you would expect to find in a group of several thousand people.

Joe Duggan once studied to be a Catholic priest. His take on religion is quiet, reflective, and focused inward, but when All Saints was the tar-get of a Sunday-morning protest against its acceptance of gays and lesbians, he found himself out front, quietly directing church members around the ruckus. He stood alongside other church members in defense of a common belief. "It was the first time I had done something like that," he says—linked what he considers a political act to his faith. At All Saints, he has come to see a "necessary relationship between your faith and your politics."

More than anything else, Sunday-morning worship knits together the diverse members of All Saints. Scott Richardson says, "We locate our unity in common prayer." The service and its setting contrast at almost every point with Saddleback's. The eighty-year-old church building in downtown Pasadena could have been transported from medieval England. Gray stone, with a square stone tower, the church proper is connected to offices and meeting rooms by the stone arches of a cloistered walk. The sanctuary has a cruciform floor plan of nave and transept, stone pillars, and a high, arched ceiling of dark wood beams from which wrought-iron chandeliers hang on long chains. Kneelers fold down from the backs of the dark wooden pews.

Sunday morning, Mother's Day 2002, the sanctuary is nearly full. The congregation is a little older, on average, than the Saddleback congregation, but there are couples and individuals of all age. Some women wear slacks and some men are in shirtsleeves, but many congregants wear dresses or jackets and ties, dressing up for church. The service begins with organ music and a processional hymn as the choir, clergy, and other participants come down the central aisle, wearing white robes, some carrying candles, which they use to light other candles near the altar. There are hymns, responsive prayers, a gospel reading, an offering, and Holy Communion: the consecration of the host and the wine, followed, for ten minutes or more, by congregants moving to the Communion rail to partake.

Rusty Harding and Scott Richardson call Communion the main unifying practice of the church community, and it is worth noting that "communion" and "community" are essentially the same word, having to do with sharing, with joint participation. But it is a unity of diversity.

Every week, these same words invite people to take Communion: "Whoever you are, wherever you find yourself on this journey of faith, you are welcome." "If you come in for one day, you're welcome at our table," says Petit. "You could be Jewish, Muslim, Roman Catholic, or stopping by with your sister."

Rusty Harding, associate for small-group ministries and covenant class, says that the Episcopalian core of the service and the church is defined more by practice than doctrine; members of the community take Communion together but have, says Harding, "wildly divergent opinions of what it means." For some, it is the body and blood of Christ; for others, it is a symbolic shared meal that represents fellowship and nourishment. Anne Peterson says, "We have an inclusive vision of Christ and more ambiguity than a lot of people can tolerate." Joe Duggan agrees that this is a church community "where your questions can be honored," where it is acceptable, he says, "to live in the ambiguity." Saddleback also believes in inclusiveness, in the sense that its evangelical mission is to win over everyone, not just people who already share the church's beliefs or lead a good Christian life. So, for instance, Rick Warren refused permission to an antiabortion group that wanted to set up a display outside the Worship Center, though he himself opposes abortion, because he did not want a newcomer to the church who might have had an abortion or might be struggling with the issue to be discouraged by the judgment implied by such a display. But the goal for members of Saddleback is a clear, consistent, and explicit set of beliefs: not living with ambiguity but overcoming it.

Although the meeting of conservative ritual and theological ambiguity at All Saints may seem paradoxical, it makes sense. Lyle Schaller explains:

> Most of us need a point of dependable stability and continuity in our lives. The ideological conservative finds that point of stability and predictability in ideology and thus is free to advocate change in practices and institutional life. The ideological liberal is more open to new ideas and innova-

tion in ideology and thus looks for continuity, predictability, and stability in practices and institutional life.[12]

Schaller's comment defines a core difference between Saddleback and All Saints. He also warns that "theological pluralism and large numbers of worshipers appear to be mutually exclusive goals" and, more vividly, describes the middle-sized congregation "that boasts, 'Our strength is our diversity,' and watches passively as the vast majority of first-time Sunday morning visitors do not return, but eventually join a church that emphasizes certainty, internal consistency, and clarity in its proclamation of the gospel."[13]

All Saints' unusual mix of social activism and satisfying ritual, along with the quality of preaching and music at the church, succeeds in attracting people who seek that combination and cannot find it elsewhere, and so the church avoids the pitfall of pluralism that Schaller describes. There, as at Saddleback, a combination of shared values, shared worship, and small-group connections creates and maintains a church community. Nevertheless, certainty has a wider appeal than ambiguity, and All Saints will never draw (and does not aspire to draw) anything like the numbers of people who attend Saddleback and other megachurches.

CHAPTER 7

{ *Waupun, Wisconsin* }

Do Something
Letting Young People Lead

On November 2, 1999, about thirty sixth-graders at the Waupun Middle School in Waupun, Wisconsin, met after class in a "Town Hall" meeting to choose projects they could take on to help their school and community. Guidance counselor Stephanie Spoehr, school psychologist Richard Dary, and Kiwanian Cully Dommisse were with them but stayed mainly in the background. It was the kids' meeting, not theirs.

Following procedures almost identical to those used in Valley Interfaith house meetings to define an action agenda and build commitment to carrying it out, they divided into small groups to discuss possible service activities. Then the groups presented their ideas to the meeting and the students voted on the list of possibilities. They agreed to take on the top three: raising money for a field trip fund for students whose families could not afford to pay the fees; getting new playground equipment for the school; and convincing authorities to install warning lights at a railroad crossing on Edgewood Street, a few blocks away, where only a small sign marked the crossing and vegetation and mounds of soil obscured the view down the tracks.

The sixth-graders were the first local members of the Do Something League, a national organization established to encourage community activism and develop leadership skills among young people. Spoehr, Dary, and Dommisse, the "Community Coaches" of the group, left the meeting in the kids' hands because the first principle of Do Something is youth leadership: letting the young members choose projects, create strategies for carrying them out, do the work, and celebrate and reflect on their accomplishments. The Do Something organization provided a framework for these stages: the "Town Hall" (later renamed "Speak Out" when it became clear that the town hall concept did not resonate with children), a "Path to Change" planning tool, "Projects," and "Celebration."

Cameron ("Cam") Dary, the sixth-grader who led the railroad crossing project and Richard Dary's son, attests to the fact that adults left them free to succeed or fail on their own and probably, in this case, anticipated failure. "Some of the adults thought it might never happen," he says. "You could tell by the way they looked they were just waiting for it to fail." [1]

Dary and his fellow students presented their idea to a meeting of the Waupun City Council. "They told us that we should collect evidence to support our idea that the crossing wasn't safe," Cam says. "We decided to use a survey to ask people who lived on the street whether they thought it unsafe." The survey of fourteen people who lived nearby demonstrated strong interest in a safer crossing and willingness to support the project. Having done research to determine who could authorize a crossing signal, the Do Something kids wrote to Rodney Kreunen, Wisconsin commissioner of railroads, in January 2001:

> We are a group of 6th graders at the Waupun Middle School involved in the Do Something League. We have chosen this project because we are concerned about the safety of our community. . . . Our survey of fourteen local residents indicated that ten believe that Edgewood Drive is unsafe, twelve have witnessed people not stopping, and thirteen want a better warning device. We will be meeting with the Public Works Department February 1, 2000, to discuss our concerns.

Kreunen's reply a month later revealed that the order establishing the crossing in 1995 had specified automatic flashing light signals, which had never been installed. But the commissioner added that the amount of traffic at the crossing might not justify the cost of automatic signals. He promised to have a traffic study carried out. "Because we brought attention to the crossing, a police patrol sat next to the tracks and watched what cars did, whether they were speeding, if they stopped, and how much traffic there was," Kyle Vandezande, another student involved in the project, noted. Further correspondence went back and forth. Eventually the railroad offered a compromise: instead of flashing lights it would install a series of warning signs on the approach to the crossing and would remove the brush and mounds of soil that blocked drivers' view of the tracks.

More than a year after the students voted for the project, the railroad made the promised improvements. Cam Dary says, "I knew it would take a while, but not as long as it took. I was a little optimistic since I hadn't worked with government before."

In addition to discovering that government moves slowly, he and his fellow sixth-graders learned that adults do not always know what is possible, that you can accomplish a lot even if you do not get exactly what you wanted, and—most important—that sixth-graders can make things happen in the adult world when they are organized and persistent.

Origins and Changes

Concern about civic participation by America's young people has been growing for some years, as evidence of civic disengagement has mounted. To be sure, young Americans in the 1990s did volunteer more than the immediately preceding generations, partly because of increasing service requirements in schools, but this idealism has not spilled over into broader social and political involvement. In the presidential election of 1972, 42 percent of young people aged 18 to 24 voted, but by 2000 this figure had dropped to 28 percent, the steepest decline of any age cohort. Among college freshman in 1966, 58 percent had said that "keeping up-to-date with politics" was an important personal objective, but by 2000 only 26 percent held that view. Participation in student elections fell even faster—from roughly 75 percent in the late 1960s to 20 percent in 2000.

The long-term significance of this youthful disengagement was heightened by the fact that civic activism early in life is one of the strongest predictors of later adult involvement. For example, political scientist M. Kent Jennings and his colleagues, who have tracked the political involvement of the same people for more than thirty years, have found that those most active in middle age were those who had become engaged as adolescents. An international conference of youth development specialists meeting at Stanford University in 1999 concluded that to prepare for effective participation in democracy,

> Young people need face-to-face interpersonal experience in contexts and organizations that are meaningful to them. They should have opportunities to take part in groups and to engage in activities that advance the public good; that incorporate them in reciprocal social networks; and that embody respectful conduct toward familiar and unfamiliar individuals. Young people should acquire the knowledge and capacities that prepare them to understand and actively participate in the political system.[2]

As we shall see, both in Waupun and elsewhere, Do Something fits this prescription quite well.

The idea for Do Something originated with actor Andrew Shue and his longtime friend lawyer Michael Sanchez. Having been involved in public service as teenagers themselves and believing that their current work, though successful, lacked essential meaning and satisfaction, they met with Wendy Kopp, founder of Teach for America, and Alan Khazei, of City Year, and talked with them and other social entrepreneurs about how to create an organization that would encourage young people to become leaders and active participants in serving the needs of their communities.[3] Shue's work in the entertainment industry gave him visibility and access to individuals and organizations that could provide funding and publicity for the new endeavor. Shue and Sanchez hoped the support of organizations including MTV, Fox Family Channel, and Blockbuster and Shue's role as an actor on *Melrose Place* would help make the idea of public service seem "cool."

Starting with Newark, New Jersey, in 1993, they began establishing local chapters, choosing a chapter model because they sought to create a national movement that was also a local one, whereby people living in local communities would decide what needed to be done and how to do it. Over the next four years, they opened chapters in cities including Anchorage, Atlanta, Boston, Chicago, San Diego, and Washington, D.C. Each chapter had an executive director and typically two other paid staff members. After school and on weekends, chapter offices offered leadership training to youths and helped them develop community projects.

Before long, though, the chapter model began to reveal its weaknesses. Because the professional staff at each chapter was so small, success hinged on having executive directors who were good at everything from fund-raising to inspiring young people to office administration. Finding and keeping enough all-around experts was a problem; when a good director left, programs at that chapter stalled while the national organization scrambled to find and train a replacement. Also, says current president and CEO Anthony Welch, "We were paying a lot of money for rent and utilities that wasn't providing sufficient direct service to the communities. We had to ask ourselves what our real goal was."[4] One goal was—and remains—to come as close as possible to reaching every young person in America. That implied a vast and expensive network of chapters.

In 1997, while they wrestled with the drawbacks of their system, Do Something executives got involved in helping to plan the President's Summit for America's Future, an event chaired by Colin Powell, and met leaders of organizations doing successful work with schools. At about the same time, the Newark chapter office was discovering that working through schools was more effective than reaching out directly to individual youngsters. Also, the evolution of Internet technology into a powerful tool for connecting people and sharing information seemed to offer a new way to deliver Do Something ideas and resources to participants, one that need not depend on local chapters. (Or on expensive publications. Do Something had been investing a lot of money in a magazine,

Build, that was distributed free through Blockbuster video stores.) The Web's "scalability," its ability to multiply the number of people reached with little increase in cost, harmonized with the leadership's ambition to build a large-scale organization without devoting a lot of resources to infrastructure and communication.

Together, these factors convinced leaders to change direction and scrap the local-chapter model in favor of a school-based one. With Do Something located in and partnering with schools, the money that was being spent on infrastructure could go directly to project work. In addition, it could tap into existing social groups and existing relationships of trust and cooperation in schools, rather than having to recruit youngsters one by one. Just as the Industrial Areas Foundation in Texas attracted members and gained strength and credibility by working through church communities, Do Something would benefit by entering communities through the established institutions of local schools.

As sensible as it was, this structural change came at a cost. Orlando Watkins was in the middle of a five-month program to prepare for being executive director of the Atlanta chapter office when training abruptly stopped and the promised chapter jobs disappeared. The trainees felt betrayed by the sudden withdrawal of jobs they had so recently started. And the change meant renegotiating or ending relationships with people in the communities where the chapters existed or were being established and breaking promises about services the chapter would provide. Watkins, who stayed with Do Something and became its national training director, remembers how hard it was to rebuild trust and reestablish relationships in Atlanta. People in the community questioned the organization's reliability and whether it knew what it was doing. (In fact, it didn't; it was trying to learn.)

The new school model shifted the program's focus to younger participants. When Do Something was launched, it worked mainly with people in their twenties. The move to a school-based model meant that members would be eighteen and younger, some much younger. Welch thinks that change makes sense. "We found that the pool of interested twentysomethings was small," he says. "If people are not involved by fourteen, you've lost them. Twenty-five is too late."

At the Local Level

Do Something came to Waupun through Teri Dary, Cameron's mother. An energetic, outgoing woman with a ready laugh, Dary learned of the program when she was a third- and fourth-grade teacher in nearby Beaver Dam, where she was voted elementary school teacher of the year for 1988–1989. Earlier, she had taught emotionally disturbed and learning-disabled students. A long-standing interest in involving students in the community led her to attend a Do Something training session for community coaches, teachers, and other adults who support student activism. She then drafted a proposal to bring Do Something to Wisconsin schools "to empower students to create strong and healthy communities." That plan, along with recommendations from her colleagues, earned her a 2000 Christa McAuliffe Fellowship, which allowed her to take a sabbatical from teaching and devote herself full-time to Do Something work. She has since become professional development director for the national organization. Though a teacher in Beaver Dam, she had connections with the Waupun schools, where her husband, Rich, was a school psychologist and their older son, Cameron, was entering middle school. Cameron convinced the adults that they should have Do Something at the middle school. So Rich Dary brought a team of six Waupun educators to a training session. They still recall how it inspired them. Waupun guidance counselor Jill Walker says, "You come back from some training all fired up to try something new, but time passes and you're still doing the same old things. This time, we said, 'We have to do this now, we have to start Monday,' and we did." They talked up the program to the sixth-grade class and set up that first Town Hall meeting.

Teri Dary remains an important advocate for the program in Waupun. Cam has been involved in other projects, most notably work to get a new bike path built, and he has also become the youngest member of the National Commission on Service-Learning, chaired by Senator John Glenn. (The only other student on the commission is an undergraduate at MIT.) But Do Something in Waupun has grown beyond the Darys. It now involves forty or more youngsters in all the middle school grades and students at several elementary schools. Beginning in 2003, Do Something will come to the high school, too. The phenomenon of youth activism is become an everyday part of life in this small city.

In many ways, Waupun, Wisconsin, is what we expect—or hope— rural America to be. Along its wide, straight, quiet streets, ranch houses and some two-story Victorians sit on broad green lawns. In early spring, boats and campers wait in many driveways, ready for warm weather and vacation trips. Downtown comprises a few blocks of shops and offices along Main Street, a town hall, a library, churches. With a population of around ten thousand, Waupun is too big for everyone to know everyone else, but people nod to acquaintances as they drive by and they are likely to stop and chat with friends from church or school when they take the family to Culver's for burgers. The mayor, Bob Reinap, teaches sixth grade at Waupun Middle School. Many teachers live in the same neighborhoods as their students; some wave to their own children as they pass through the halls. It is, people here say, "a good place to raise kids."

After September 11, 2001, the people of Waupun held a quiet vigil for the victims of the terrorist attacks, lining both sides of Main Street, holding candles. A concert later in the fall raised $4,000 to contribute to the families of firefighters who had died. A recent campaign collected tens of thousands of dollars to help a local family pay medical bills. The community is not wealthy, but it is generous.

But Waupun is a particular place, not a representation of American rural life. The green lawns are surprisingly, almost obsessively trim, block after block without a weed in sight or more than a couple of inches of variation in height. One longtime resident acknowledges the quiet, steady social pressure to keep them that way. And doing yard work or any work on Sunday, the Lord's day, is frowned on in Waupun, so all the mowing and weeding happens at other times. Then there is the fact that about a quarter of the city's population is prisoners in the Waupun Correctional Institution, a maximum-security prison almost as old as the city itself, and the Dodge Correctional Institution, an assessment and evaluation center for state prisoners. A visitor asking about the effect of the prisons on the town gets a mixed sense of their importance and visibility. Waupun Correctional occupies twenty acres a couple of blocks from Main Street, its thick walls and guard towers directly across from rows of pleasant homes. The prisons are the city's largest employer, but several people readily volunteer the information that many employees commute from other places, as if suggesting that the prisons are in Waupun but not of it. Some teachers mention having the children of guards and other blue-collar prison employees in their classes, though, and describe their efforts to convince some of those parents who have not had a lot of educational success themselves that it is important for their children to get good grades.

Waupun suffers from the same kinds of problems and sorrows that afflict all communities, openly or in secret. There are vandalism and domestic violence. Brian O'Donovan, the police liaison officer at the middle school and high school, says that a couple of dozen kids cause most of the problems at the schools. There is the occasional teen pregnancy. A couple of years ago, the middle school was shocked by a student's suicide. Last spring, a sixteen-year-old girl died when she lost control of her car and hit a tree. School psychologist Richard Dary, together with the district's Pupil Personnel Services team, worked to help the high school deal with the blow, which hit doubly hard because the girl's mother teaches at the school.

Residents talk about changes they have seen over the past couple of decades. People say they never used to lock their doors but now they do. O'Donovan (known as "Odie") talks about kids being openly rude to teachers in ways they never were in the past. Dr. Alain Holt, district administrator, says "families are more spread out now" to explain children's need for the kinds of connection with older people that they used to get within extended families. Maybe most surprising in light of clichéd expectations about rural, midwestern America is that person after person talks about being too busy, about the damage too much work, too many meetings, too many cell phone calls and e-mail messages do to personal and family life in Waupun. Odie talks about the problem of two-parent families with two jobs and too much going on in their lives who toss their children a twenty-dollar bill to get them out of their hair. The slower, saner pace that harried inhabitants of larger cities and suburbs sometimes dream about is not found in Waupun.

This is where Waupun Do Something kids are learning to play an active role: a community racially more homogeneous than most larger cities, churchgoing, with a solid sense of community values, but also more fragmented and harried than in the past and experiencing, on a smaller scale, many of the problems and pressures that trouble the country as a whole—a good place to live, but no paradise.

The fall Speak Out meeting at Waupun Middle School, where students decide on projects to undertake during the year, draws thirty or more, most of them sixth-graders, and a mixture of kids who belong to different groups in the school, or no group at all other than Do Something. Coach Stephanie Spoehr says that openness to everyone has been an explicit aim of the program. Do Something offers a new community for kids seeking a place for themselves in the school who do not necessarily fit the traditional niches of "jocks," musicians, and the "popular" group. Some of the most active kids in Do Something have moved to the town in the past couple of years; Do Something has been a way for them to fit into a school where many of the other students have known one another since kindergarten. Spoehr mentions, too, that a couple of kids who had been known as troublemakers and generally poor students discovered a potential for leadership in Do Something, with the experience changing their sense of themselves and their reputation in the school system. Whether because the program is relatively new or because it calls for particular kinds of talents or is about caring for other people and thinking in communitarian terms, it attracts an unusual mixture of students, who seem to get along well with one another. "I knew a lot of the other kids that joined [Do Something] when we were in sixth grade, but I got to know some people that I never would have gotten to know so well otherwise . . . people from different groups in the school," says Cody DeHaan.

Bob Reinap, the middle school teacher who is also the mayor of Waupun, emphasizes how much the program is "genuinely youth driven, not run by adults planning behind the scenes." Beyond giving students opportunities to learn how things really work in the world, youth ownership has led to addressing needs that might otherwise have been ignored, says Reinap. Kids are "geographically aware," he explains. "They notice things riding around on their bikes that you probably wouldn't see driving by in your car." One of their current projects is a proposed bike path along the river that will connect Pine Street Park, a city park, with the Fond du Lac County Park, which is now accessible only by way of a high-speed county road. Once the sixth-graders became involved in the project and presented the idea to the city council, they discovered that a plan to build a bike path had been proposed several years earlier. It had foundered, partly because the city had not been able to obtain an easement from a property owner along the proposed route. When the students from Do Something came to the city council with a proposal for the bike path, the council helped them think the proposal through, suggesting contacts with the Department of Natural Resources to design and plan the path, and with the property owner whose land would be crossed. Scott Hermsen, director of public works for the City of Waupun, remembered being impressed by the way the youths worked to persuade the property owner: "There was one other meeting where I went over to the middle school and we met with the property owner for this trail. We wanted to impress upon him that this was important to the kids, important to the community, and it just so happened that his property was a great place for the path. That was a neat thing, to see the kids express their ideas to this property owner."

Once the city had obtained a verbal OK from the property owner, Scott Hermsen and the rest of the city staff were able to apply for DNR monies to build the path. In September 2002, Waupun received a DNR Stewardship grant to cover 50 percent of the cost of the bike path. The City of Waupun in cooperation with Fond du Lac County will fund the remaining 50 percent. The portion of the property owner's land that the path will cross will be deeded to the city. Path construction is slated to be completed in the summer of 2003. Scott Hermsen praised the students and Do Something, giving them credit for breathing life into a project many adults in Waupun thought would never come to be: "The contacts made by the students of Do Something with the city council, the DNR, and the property owner were really crucial to securing the land, designing the trail, the grant process—the successful building of the path." Ross Dary, Cameron's younger brother and also involved in the project, made comments that reflected the pride of having done something many adults said couldn't be done: "The path is being built because we put a lot of time into it, we have done the work that needed to be done, and we have done it really well."

At Jefferson Elementary School, too, project ideas come out of the children's own experiences. Because one of the Do Something fifth-graders had been in the hospital, she suggested giving stuffed animals to "frightened children," and her proposal was adopted by the group. They put "Pennies for Pals" buckets in the halls and collected enough money to deliver stuffed animals to the local hospital and the police and fire departments, and still have some left over. They gave some of the extras to People against Violent Environment, a shelter for victims of domestic abuse in Beaver Dam. A coach comments that one of the students who helped make the connection with that organization has a deeply troubled family life. The project gave this student an opportunity to help others, and that was a powerful feeling for someone who had experienced helplessness. The coach added that the information about this resource gained during the project could be helpful to the student—and to the student's family.

Maybe the most impressive aspect of the youths' participation is their persistence. Almost anyone can get excited about a need or an injustice. The hard part, for adults as well as kids, is carrying out the often long and frustrating process of following through. Both the railroad crossing project and the bike path work have been long and complex. "When I first got involved in the bike path project, I thought it would happen fast. I mean, how long could it take to build a path?" says Katie Nagle, one of the student captains involved in the project. "All of the meetings, talking to all of these different people, finding money, it all took so much work and time, I couldn't believe it." The students' continuing commitment and unflagging energy are striking and are due, to a significant degree, to the fact that this project belongs to them. Of course, sixth-graders have energy to burn, but teachers and parents know the lethargy that overcomes them when they are being pushed to follow someone else's idea of what they should be doing. Their dedication to these projects shows how much the projects belong to them, how the usual separation between "appropriate" activities for adults and kids is gone. *Everything* about these projects belongs to them: decisions about what to do and how to do it, gathering information, speaking with officials, raising money. Do Something legitimizes talents and understanding that they seldom get to exercise; it gives them power.

If it is done right. Like everyone else—probably more than most—children know when they are being offered a charade of empowerment. Cam Dary, now a ninth-grader, articulates this directly: "Some adults try to control even though they don't know it." Other students make the same observation by pointing to adults whom they perceive as having contributed to the Do Something process appropriately, that is, from the sidelines rather than from the field. Kyle Vandezande, a student who worked on the project, comments that when they presented the bike path project to the city council, "They didn't try to take the project over, they just listened and gave suggestions and we made the next steps." Another student notes the acceptable role of the adult when talking about the involvement of Do Something coach Richard Dary. Cody DeHaan states, "When we were working on the bike path project, we made a presentation to the city council about why we wanted to do the project. Mr. Dary helped us put together a PowerPoint presentation. He put down what we wanted to say and let us talk, though."

Everyone has experienced the supposedly open discussions manipulated toward a predetermined outcome, the supervisor who welcomes all ideas as long as they coincide with his own, the language of empowerment used to disguise control. The temptation to guide kids toward the better choice or the "right" answer is strong. Winnie Smith, an assistant coach at Jefferson Elementary School in Waupun, says, "When you start coaching in Do Something, you have to back off. That's the hardest part if you're a teacher and used to being in charge." That is why Do Something literature and training emphasize a continual focus on letting youth lead, on coaching and supporting, not directing.

Coaches and professional leaders believe the Do Something model works better than requiring a specified number of hours of community service for high school graduation, the "service-learning" approach in many communities. The idea of working on something as long as it takes to accomplish your purpose is a valuable lesson in itself. It also creates flexibility: students can choose to commit to modest projects or ambitious ones. Probably most important of all, requiring a set number of hours tends to make community service seem a chore to be gotten through rather than a goal or even a way of life to be embraced. The middle school children working on the bike path project are not counting hours; they are getting a bike path built.

In its third year in Waupun and as it expands to more schools—as it achieves results—Do Something is becoming more and more visible to the community as a whole. The local papers feature stories and photographs of Do Something accomplishments. The middle school group recently got a fan letter from a woman who identified herself as "a granny person," thanking them for their work on the railroad crossing. Dr. Holt believes that the program has created a bridge between young people and the adult community. Through Do Something the students have established a relationship with the city government. Holt also says that the program contributes to connecting the schools to the community, making them places of social awareness and social gathering, rather than isolated education factories that children disappear into each day.

The students have also taken note of the connections they are making with adults in the community and the ways in which these relationships lead to positive outcomes. "I learned that it takes a community to do this, not just one person," comments Kyle Vandezande. When asked to explain his statement, Kyle responds, "The city council listened to our plan and gave us ideas about who we could talk to about the path, like the DNR and the property owner whose property it would cross. We met and talked with everyone, and when we walked through the woods to see where it [the path] could go, it was me, the other [Do Something student] captains, the property owner, the DNR person . . . and someone from city council. We all went together. That is why it got done." Katie Nagle, a soft-spoken, thoughtful middle school student, comments, "The first time we went to the city council meetings everyone was afraid. But we began to see that they were just people, too, and they thought we had good ideas and we started to feel like we were working together with them and others to do it."

Cam Dary adds, "I learned that even though some people think adults don't respect kids, they actually do. Most of them do listen to the kids' ideas." He paused and reflected for a moment before adding, "And I learned that kids actually have the power to do stuff, without adults doing it for them every step of the way."

Gradually, adults not directly connected with the schools are getting involved with the program. The first was Cully. Almost everyone connected with Do Something in Waupun talks about him. Cully Dommisse was head Community Coach at Jefferson Elementary School until he died early in 2002, only a couple of years past his sixtieth birthday. He had retired to Waupun after a career in the Air Force and opened a small business downtown, but he spent much of his time volunteering, involved in Kiwanis and other community groups. He was the first Do Something coach not employed by the school system. Stories of his enthusiasm and kindness came from everywhere. The children at Jefferson who worked with him collected money for a memorial bench under a shade tree on the playground, a tribute to the care and comfort he brought into their lives. When they talk about Cully and remember going to the memorial service in his honor, they become subdued for a moment. They are a little sad, a little awkward, but you can also sense a hint of pride among these fifth-graders, because they have been granted entry into an adult world where people die and kids can find their own way of honoring someone they care about.

In addition to connections between kids and adults, between students and community members, Do Something Community Coaches see the program as preparing students for responsible participation in society in adulthood. Guidance counselor Stephanie Spoehr has encouraged Do Something students to make presentations to the Kiwanis Club and the Rotary Club on a regular basis. These are rarely requests by the kids for assistance, but rather presentations to keep the club members informed about Do Something activities. Spoehr notes that building these connections not only develops relationships between the students and the community, between kids and adults, but educates students about community-based organizations and government. She hopes the experience will lead to involvement in these organizations later in life. She also encourages the students to invite community representatives to the Speak Out each year; members of the police department, Kiwanis, Rotary Club, and other organizations often attend. "Building understanding on both sides is key," Spoehr notes. "We want them to get involved in community-based organizations later in life, to take an interest and do something. That is being a responsible citizen. Actual involvement teaches the kids this far more than isolated character education possibly could." We cannot know yet if the experience of Do Something will foster higher levels of involvement in society in the future, but one student, Kyle Vandezande, says, "I learned that it is not just the mayor that makes decisions, it is the whole council. I could see being on the council someday."

When asked about the Do Something Web site—there is one for the students and a separate one for coaches—the youth of Waupun talk about it mainly as another place to tell their story. They are more excited by the idea that people in New York or Los Angeles may read about what they are doing in Waupun than they are by the opportunity to read about activities in those cities. CEO Anthony Welch says that the youth site has so far not been as active an electronic meeting place for young people as he expected. Some of that may have to do with the site's design— the chat features need improvement—but it may be more a result of the power of local Do Something communities, the satisfactions of localness. The fact that student participants here generally think of Do Something as *their* program, with a minor contribution of posters, materials, and occasionally some money from a national organization also called Do Something, may not reflect the credit that the wider organization deserves for training and support, but it demonstrates how successfully the leadership and coaches have lived up to the principle of local youth ownership.

The one Do Something activity where local youths feel connected to the rest of the country is the annual "Kindness and Justice Challenge" in honor of the Martin Luther King, Jr., national holiday in January. The national organization publicizes the event widely, seeking to engage even schools with no other Do Something participation. For two weeks, students around the country fill out forms describing every act of kindness they carry out—washing dishes or cleaning up without being asked, for instance, or helping another student with homework—and every act of justice, such as standing up for someone being bullied in the courtyard. (One Jefferson fifth-grader remarks that kindness is a lot easier than justice, a valuable truth.) They compete with their own goal and their achievement of the year before—three thousand acts of kindness and justice—but part of the satisfaction they feel comes from knowing that students in thousands of other schools around the country are doing the same thing and that their three thousand acts contribute to a national total of more than three million. During those weeks, kindness and justice are shared national student activities.

The youth Web site describes activities carried out in particular schools as a way of sharing ideas, but Do Something activities vary from place to place, with youth leadership the only consistent theme. In Newark, the only big city where the organization maintains a chapter office, Do Something youths from several schools have banded together to increase their political influence. In the spring of 2002, they created a platform that they urged mayoral candidates to support. In suburban Los Angeles, a Do Something school in a well-to-do suburb has partnered with a less affluent school to work on a community project together. How many of the projects are similar from place to place? How many are unique to one location? That information is hard to come by. Because of its commitment to local creativity and autonomy—and local coaches' commitment to the same principles—the national organization does not know the full scope and variety of Do Something projects. That is partly good news—the local organizations have independent lives—but leaders are working to learn more about what is going on locally in order to have more information to share and to use in evaluating the program nationwide.

The first goal of an evaluation study under way at Brandeis University has been to set up a system for coaches to report on local activities and provide information on staffing and time spent on the projects being carried out. Alan Melchior of Brandeis says that the long-term goals include developing a full assessment portfolio that will measure the effects of the program on the youths involved, on their schools, and on the wider community. The evaluation process will include surveys of youngsters before and after their Do Something participation to judge its effect on them, and community and school surveys with similar purposes. The evaluators hope to assess the differences that the activities of Do Something schools make to their communities, both to learn what works best and to provide data that will, they hope, gain new support for the program and greater participation in it. Melchior sees this as a multiyear process not only because formulating and carrying out the evaluation is complex but because it takes time to influence children and affect their communities. He says, "Although people want to know what the result from this year is, the effect on kids is likely to build up over several years."

Wisconsin Dells: Training and Connecting Coaches

"Let young people lead" is the mantra repeated again and again at the two-day Community Coach training session in Wisconsin Dells. Educators and community members from Milwaukee, Greendale, Waupun, Antigo, and Shawano—some already experienced coaches, some new to Do Something—have come to be trained as coaches and to learn techniques for a new pilot initiative: infusing the Do Something model of youth leadership and activism into the classroom curriculum. From the introductory session through the days of training, session leaders from national headquarters in New York urge participants to say it with them: "Let young people lead." The slogan is like the Texas Industrial Areas Foundation's Iron Rule: "Never do anything for anybody that they can do for themselves." Getting things done in schools and communities is important, but it is secondary to the aim of developing the skills and the habits of leadership and participation among young people. A coach intervening to direct students toward a "better" project or to correct flawed planning would be putting the service goal ahead of the developmental one. In many cases, the intervention would not necessarily be an improvement, if the quality of student choices in Waupun is any guide. Take the railroad crossing project. As Cam Dary's remarks suggest, a "helpful" adult probably could have told them that they were unlikely to get the automated gate and flashing lights they wanted. The equipment was expensive; the road was not a main route and carried what would be considered light traffic in most towns and cities. The letter they received from the railroad commissioner made exactly those points. But their efforts paid off. The railroad cleared away the brush and mounds of soil that blocked the tracks from view, and it put up a series of signs on the approaches to the crossing to replace the single "RR

Crossing" sign that had been there, cemented in a bucket that was often tipped over. So a project that more experienced adults might have dismissed as hopeless achieved useful results. Sometimes not knowing that something can't be done is an advantage. The kids learned, too, that community action can be successful even when the outcome is not the one you sought.

A roomful of mainly teachers—forty or so at this training session— has a particularly lively quality, a feeling of being let out of school that is also literally true. Most people are casually dressed; there is a lot of laughter and friendly teasing, some gossip, plenty of stories swapped about life in the classroom. But when the session leaders ask them to develop brief presentations in small groups, they get right to work, and you realize that most of them were once eager students. They are here, giving up a good part of their weekend, to find new ways to help students they care deeply about. A lot of their conversation is shoptalk, comparing notes about teaching. They complain about a statewide cap on teacher compensation increases that, because of rising insurance costs, means that their take-home pay has been going down. But that has not made them stop caring about their work. With the Waupun group is Dawn Breckenridge, Cully Dommisse's daughter. She is not a teacher, but now, a couple of months after her father's death, she is learning how to be a Community Coach so she can continue his work.

One of the aims of the session in bringing together teachers from all over the state is to begin to build a support network of Do Something coaches and the principals of Do Something schools. As professional development director, Teri Dary has been instrumental in bringing them to the training. She and the national leaders hope that these days together will help form a community. They come from very different places: the large contingent from Milwaukee represents a single, urban school district many times the size of the tiny town of Antigo. Their interest in Do Something and their commitment to teaching give them some common ground. Dary has established an electronic meeting space for them to share ideas and experiences, especially as they begin the new process of bringing Do Something into the classroom. But the teachers mainly sit in their local groups and do not connect as much as the organizers hoped they would. Later, Dary remarks that organizers should have made specific efforts to move people around during the training to increase cross-community interaction.

The first day of training focuses on Community Coach philosophy. Matthew Heyd, Do Something's chief operating officer, talks about citizenship as a learned skill. He emphasizes early and continuous engagement, youth-adult partnership, and, above all, youth ownership of the projects. Tari Costello of Waupun, Wisconsin high school teacher of the year, reinforces the point: "You have to learn to sit back and watch, to let things develop." Later, presenters go through the basic elements of Do Something participation: the Speak Out (vision), the Path to Change (planning), the Projects (implementation), and the Celebration (reflection and recognition).

On the second day, the session turns to the new Do Something initiative: "infusing" the program's principles and techniques into the school curriculum, finding classroom opportunities to connect learning with community action, and—an even more revolutionary idea—inviting the students themselves to devise and plan those activities. Leaders and participants are aware of some of the difficulties, including the long-standing habit of teacher control of the classroom and the danger that students will not "own" Do Something in the classroom as they do the voluntary, after-school version of the program. The infusion plan is driven by an ambition to change the nature of teaching and bridge the traditional separation between classroom and community. It is also meant to involve more students in service more of the time in order to make active community participation a central part of the school experience, not a part-time elective. Alan Melchior of Brandeis comments, "When we want kids to learn something, like math, we make it part of their curricular activities K to 12. Just being exposed to a service experience doesn't work well."

The infusion pilot is the latest example of the change and innovation that have characterized Do Something from the beginning, most dramatically in the shift from chapters to school-based programs. Program Director Lara Galinsky, who has been with Do Something for six years, says the organization has always responded to the lessons offered by the experience of members. In the first year of using the school-based model, she says, they gave the thirty Community Coaches in the pilot project a week-by-week curriculum to follow, but that left coaches believing they were failing when they fell behind. The next year, in reaction, they were too loose. Only in the third year did they arrive at a system that works: the key mandated events (Speak Out, Path to Change, Project, Celebration) and guidance by Community Coaches that Galinsky describes as the "grab-able core" of Do Something. She thinks the strength of the organization comes from a combination of clarity about its essential principles and behaviors with a willingness to change in light of experience and the creative work of kids and their coaches. Alan Melchior agrees: "They're committed to the idea of being a learning organization. They want to know what's working and what isn't." So there is a useful and maybe crucial consistency between how flexibly Do Something works internally and its aim of encouraging youth to take charge and learn from their experience.

Do Something's national leaders and the organization itself come across as a mixture of modesty and ambition. The commitment to local youth leadership scatters the organization's power around the country. At the Wisconsin meeting, Dary, Heyd, Galinsky, and Director of Curricula Eve Bois seem more like cheerleaders and coaches than directors of a national organization. They react with pleasure and almost surprise to stories of what Do Something youths have done, as if amazed at the power and independent life of what they created. At the same time, though, they want nothing less than to reach every young person in America and convince them all of the deep satisfaction of a life of public service. Pleasant, polite, and modest as they are, the leaders are unmistakably on a mission. Heyd proudly reports that they now engage fifteen thousand educators and four million students in at least some aspects of

Do Something. By infusing Do Something into the curriculum, they seek to engage many more and, beyond that, to transform how education happens in this country. "Infuse" is a telling word choice, different from, say, "apply." It suggests working Do Something principles deep into the bones of classroom experience, redefining education as more active and participatory. This new initiative reflects the same basic beliefs: that the only way to learn participation is to participate; the only way to become a leader is to lead.

The Do Something students at Waupun Middle School have kept scrapbooks that chronicle three years of Do Something at the school: photographs of the Speak Out meetings at the beginning of the year, where they decide which projects to work on; copies of letters to and from the city council about the bike path; results of the survey of homeowners near the railroad crossing and copies of correspondence with the railroad about making the crossing safer; clippings from local newspapers about their accomplishments; photos of the Do Something cleanup of Rock River, which runs through the school grounds.

The young people radiate a serious delight in discovering their ability to make things happen in the adult world on their own terms. They talk excitedly about the plan they had to donate a couple of benches to the city to put on Main Street so people would have a place to sit and "old people could rest," as their letter to the city council explained. But at their meeting with the Do Something kids working on the project, the councillors raised objections. Thank you very much, the officials said, hand over the money. Student Ross Dary explains what happened:

> There was one project where we wanted to put benches on Main Street but the City, we went to them and did a couple of presentations to them about that. But they didn't want it, and they told us we could get garbage cans to put on Main Street and they told us what kind and what color they would be. But then we said no, we don't want to because they were making

all the decisions about what we were going to have. So it wasn't us doing the work, they were doing the work and we were just going to pay for it. So we said no.

Some adults in the town, even Do Something supporters, are still shocked by that particular display of independence. But the kids love that story.

CHAPTER 8

{ *Cambridge, Massachusetts* }

The Harvard Union of Clerical and Technical Workers

"The Whole Social Thing"

If there was one critical moment when what would soon become known as the Harvard Union of Clerical and Technical Workers chose the path that led to a new kind of union, it came in the middle of August 1985. That was when the group separated from the United Auto Workers, the parent organization that had been supporting the drive to convince Harvard's mainly female research assistants, lab technicians, secretaries, and other clerical workers that they should vote to unionize.[1]

In mid-August 1985, the small group of Harvard organizers, led by Kris Rondeau, a former research assistant at the Harvard School of Public Health who had become a full-time union activist, found itself with no money, no office, no equipment, and no backing from any established union. That lack of resources and affiliation, which one might have expected to bring organizing efforts to a halt, was likely the best thing that ever happened to the Harvard organizers. It helped turn the unusual way they did their work into the union's philosophy and identity, and led to a successful vote to unionize Harvard University's clerical and technical workers in 1988, fourteen years after organizing started.

The parties to the 1985 split agree on this: that the Harvard group's methods differed from usual union tactics and that the UAW wanted the campaign to conform more closely to those standard practices. The Auto Workers and other traditional unions typically attracted members by telling workers what they could get for them and emphasizing the grievances against employers that they had the power to address. Rather like a political campaign, their campaigns used handouts, telephone surveys, and large meetings to get the message across. Instead, the organizers at Harvard were slowly building relationships with the employees, 85 percent of them women, whom they hoped to enlist in the union. They had multiple one-on-one conversations with them over coffee and lunch during which the employees could talk about their work and their wishes and tell their personal stories. The organizers held small meetings that similarly focused on the stories and concerns of individuals, rather than on a union agenda or on extracting a commitment to support the union.

Their methods resembled the relational organizing of Valley Interfaith and other Texas Industrial Areas Foundation organizations, which make personal stories and trusting relationships the foundation of collective action and let their agendas arise from thousands of conversations. In fact, organizer Marie Manna remarks that she, like Ernie Cortés, learned some organizing principles from Saul Alinsky's IAF, especially the importance of "knocking on every door." (She notes, though, that she and the Harvard Union of Clerical and Technical Workers [HUCTW] rejected Alinsky's idea of organizing against an "enemy"— a subject we will return to later.) The organizers never presented the union as a powerful (and parental) third party that could do things for the employees, nor did they exploit the idea of uniting to battle terrible working conditions and insufferable bosses. Most of Harvard's technical and clerical workers wanted more recognition and reward for their work, but many liked their jobs and liked being at Harvard.

This style of organizing was slow, because listening to everyone takes time and building trust and relationships takes time. And the campaign was not aggressive or confrontational. Arnold Zack, former president of the National Academy of Arbitrators and a member of the Harvard University Board of Overseers Visiting Committee on Human Relations, says of organizer Rondeau,

Kris's way of organizing is a great shock to the labor movement. I know it has caused her problems with some union people because of her time-consuming approach. The old-timers of the labor movement are oriented toward handing out leaflets at factory gates and expecting men (primarily) to act fast and support the union, for all kinds of macho reasons. But when organizing women, and particularly cerebral women, Kris has gone against the grain of the conventional wisdom for union organizing and focused on winning over the loyalties of women who have traditionally been loath to join unions ("I will not be working that long," "I don't want to offend my boss," "I don't really need a union since I am a professional," etc.).

And it has worked. Indeed, it has worked so well that she has been able to organize the workers without their losing their loyalty to the employer or their commitment to their professionalism. The test of that is in the current situation at Harvard, where Kris has offered to come up with money-saving improvements for the university, something unions *never* do outside. So my read is that what Kris has done is not only important for those she has organized, but it is crucial and perhaps the key to union survival and growth in a largely antiunion environment. Sure, it takes more money, and sure, it takes more time, and, above all, sure, it takes a different approach to organizing, but it has worked where traditional organizing techniques have failed.[2]

As the twentieth century drew to a close, it was becoming clear that conventional union organizing was failing almost everywhere throughout the industrialized world. Union membership in America had peaked in 1954, when nearly one third of all nonfarm workers (32.5 percent) had belonged to a union; by 1998 that figure had nose-dived to 14.1 percent. By the 1990s this dramatic decline was mirrored in virtually all industrialized countries. Many explanations were offered—the changing structure of the postindustrial economy, aggressive employer resistance, and adverse changes in labor law, among others—but as an authoritative group of U.S. labor experts argued in 1998, "The American labor movement is at a watershed. For the first time since the early years of industrial unionism sixty years ago, there is near-universal agreement among union leaders that the future of the movement depends on massive new organizing." Nevertheless, they reported, "most unions have continued to run fairly low-intensity traditional campaigns that relied on gate leafleting, mass mailings, and a few large meetings." In the first half of the twentieth century unions had represented a vital source of social capital—and thus, too, of political power—for the American working class. In the course of its long decline in the second half of the century, however, the main-line American labor movement settled into the conservative, top-down role of "business unionism," mostly managing contracts for existing members rather than pursuing an aggressive bottom-up strategy of recruiting new members through time-intensive, grassroots, face-to-face organizing.[3]

Ted Barrett, Rondeau's boss when the union was still affiliated with the UAW, describes the differences between her work and "normal" UAW organizing this way:

> Her whole concept of organizing was different. In the UAW, we'd convene a meeting in a hall and tell people why they ought to join the union. At Harvard they'd go to someone's house and have coffee and talk about it. It was the whole social thing.[4]

That "social thing" is the social-capital heart of this story. It is what makes HUCTW unusual and interesting. Also, in the opinion of participants on both sides of the unionizing contest, the social thing is why the union won at Harvard.

First, some background.

Union Organizing at Harvard: An Uphill Battle

Two earlier attempts to unionize a group of clerical and technical workers had failed at Harvard.[5] In 1977, employees of the Medical Area Group voted 436 to 346 against forming a union. Those workers at Harvard Medical School, the School of Public Health, and similar facilities were one segment of the larger clerical and technical group that Rondeau's organizers were working with in 1985. In fact, in 1975 Harvard had formally objected to the National Labor Relations Board that the medical-area workers did not constitute a genuinely distinct group and therefore had no right to organize separately from clerical and technical workers at other Harvard facilities. The NLRB eventually decided in favor of the union organizers, but the dispute put off the election for two years. John Hoerr, author of *We Can't Eat Prestige*, a study of the union's development, believes the delay was instrumental in its defeat.[6]

A second vote, in 1981, failed by a similar margin, 390 to 328. Hoerr and others point out a contradiction, or at least a powerful tension, between Harvard's opposition to these efforts and the espoused pro-labor positions of many Harvard faculty members and especially then-president Derek Bok, a legal scholar whose writings include much on the value and validity of organized labor.[7] Bok and those who worked with him seemed to believe, however, that this particular union was not good for Harvard. They argued, too, in print and in meetings of medical-area employees, that it would not be good for the workers either, reducing their freedom by putting them in the hands of a third party that would force them to strike or require them to give up their Harvard health insurance for the much weaker plan offered by the union.

In any case, Harvard unquestionably brought its legal and persuasive power to bear against the medical-area unionizing efforts, and its power succeeded. In the mid-1980s, when the organizers' connection with the UAW ended, Kris Rondeau was leading an effort to organize for another vote, this time among approximately thirty-six hundred clerical and technical workers throughout the university, not just the hundreds of medical-area workers. (The National Labor Relations Board had reversed its 1977 ruling that the medical-area workers formed a distinctive enough group to be represented by its own union, in part in response to some organizational changes at Harvard.) Harvard's opposition to unionizing had not diminished.

In 1976, Rondeau had taken a job as a research assistant at the Harvard School of Public Health. She did not dislike the work, but the limitations of the job became apparent fairly quickly. The pay was low; no real opportunity for advancement existed; much of the work was repetitious and isolated; and research assistants, like other technical and clerical workers, found themselves on the receiving end of condescension because the intellectual elite they worked for saw their work as menial, and because most of them were women. Rondeau did not immediately embrace the union effort, but the campaign, led by Leslie Sullivan, who had also started at Harvard as a research assistant in the School of Public Health, attracted her attention. Rondeau thought it was reasonable and fair for medical-area workers to have a say in the conditions of their work. In 1977, she began working as a volunteer for the union effort. In 1979, she quit her Harvard job to work full-time for the union, becoming an employee of District 65, the common name of the Distributive Workers of America, a small New York–based union of office and retail workers, the national union supporting the Harvard medical-area drive. Within a few months, that union merged with the United Auto Workers, from which the Harvard group would break away six years later. By the end of 1981, Rondeau was leading the Harvard campaign.

Rondeau, Marie Manna, and others who participated in the union work then have a hard time explaining the precise origins of their organizing philosophy or pinpointing the moment when they realized they were doing something very different from typical unionizing practices because, says Rondeau, "It was an organic process that Harvard workers created together."[8] Reflecting back on the late 1970s and the 1980s, they describe using methods that seemed natural to them. ("We did a lot of things because we didn't know they were wrong," Rondeau says.) Their methods turned out to be the most effective way of winning the support of those particular people in that place: getting to know individuals, putting as much emphasis on finding out about them as on telling them about the union. The fact that Rondeau and Sullivan before her had held medical-area jobs themselves was a factor; they organized from the inside out, not the outside in.

"They know my shoe size," says Joyce Guarnieri, who has worked in Harvard's University Alumni Office for thirty years.[9] "They do the one-on-one stuff. They go to your desk, they make sure they know who you are . . . [and] it's not just that they stop at your desk. They remember everyone's name and everything you do and where you sit and 'she has child-care issues' or 'she has elder-care issues.' I'm talking hundreds of people. When someone comes to your desk and cares about you, yeah—that makes a difference."

Most of the organizers and the organized are women. Neither Rondeau nor Manna thinks of this as mainly a feminist story, certainly not one that makes unbridgeable distinctions between men and women, and even less one based on gender hostility. But both of them believe that relationship building is a characteristically female approach to life and that a male-dominated union would have been more likely to emphasize issues and conflict than relationships and collaboration. The titles of some of the writings about HUCTW call attention to the gender issue. An issue of *Labor Research Review*, published by the Center for Labor and Community Research, is called "Women's Ways of Organizing," and John Hoerr's book about HUCTW, *We Can't Eat Prestige*, has as its subtitle *The Women Who Organized Harvard*. It is not impossible that male leaders would have used similar methods—Ernie Cortés took a related approach to Industrial Areas Foundation organizing in San Antonio in the 1970s—but it seems unlikely. So gender is not the whole story. But it matters.

Ken Tivey, a secretary in the Harvard Department of Economics, comments, "I think it [the HUCTW strategy] comes almost directly from the fact that the majority of membership in the union is female. And the way women comport themselves in the workplace is very different from the way men do. . . . A male-based union looks at things in a more confrontational way."

Finding Their Voice

Whatever the immediate circumstances of the Harvard organizers' split with the United Auto Workers, the root cause was the two groups' incompatible ideas of organizing. From the UAW's perspective, the drive was going too slowly and the women running it seemed to ignore the traditionally effective techniques of emphasizing the power of the union and the stinginess and stubbornness of the employer. From the Harvard organizers' point of view, the union's plans to speed up the process would undermine years of patient work creating trust and commitment. The UAW wanted to conduct a telephone poll of potential union members, which Rondeau considered exactly the wrong approach; she believed that anonymous callers from an outside union asking questions about grievances and issues would subvert the relationships being built through shared conversations. When she told UAW officials that she could not deliver the twelve hundred names they requested for the polling, they suggested handing out free panty hose in Harvard Square to encourage employees to sign up. Again, exactly wrong, she believed. Whereas the organizers were trying to nurture trust and a sense of community, the UAW wanted to buy involvement with a trivial, insulting gift.

Because the relational approached developed naturally, Rondeau and her team were not fully aware of what they were creating. Rondeau says, "We realized by the time we won that workers needed to get a sense of connection and community from their workplace. We hadn't started out knowing that."[10] But they did sense that a less relational approach was wrong. The break with the UAW may have been a shock at the time, but in retrospect it seems almost inevitable.

Anne Taylor, general counsel for Harvard, who led the university's campaign against the third unionization effort in the late 1980s, believes the loss of UAW backing was "the luckiest thing that ever happened to them." She explains, "They couldn't afford even to photocopy a leaflet. They were forced to go talk to people one-on-one. I think this model was emerging before then, but it got crystallized."[11] In her *Labor Research*

Review interview, Kris Rondeau says much the same thing: "We had no paper. We had nothing. So we stopped putting out a newsletter altogether." She adds: "Not depending on literature requires everybody to eventually talk to somebody about the union. . . . When you rely on one-on-one organizing, people don't have the safety valve of literature anymore. If they want to know what's going on, they have to approach somebody." [12] Interviewed with Rondeau, Gladys McKenzie, organizer for the American Federation of State, County, and Municipal Employees (AFSCME) at the University of Minnesota, reinforces the general relational point:

> We live in the midst of paper where nobody knows anybody and everybody is isolated from everyone else and memos come down in droves and that's not what we want to build. We don't want to be pen pals. We want to connect with a face. [13]

In an era when some see the wide availability of information—on paper or via the Internet—as the glue of universal community, many people and groups have arrived at the contrary insight McKenzie expresses: that transmitted information does not ease isolation or connect people in genuine relationships. The memos that "come down" from the top may serve useful purposes (sometimes), but creating community is not one of them. Valley Interfaith and other Industrial Areas Foundation organizations are nearly paperless because they, too, are about building relationships of trust that can be formed only over time and face-to-face. The same principle helps explain why groups from Arkansas and North Carolina traveled to meet Vaughn Grisham in Oxford and talk to people in Tupelo and (as we shall see) why United Parcel Service managers rely heavily on face-to-face meetings.

Organizing without printed material gave the union a tactical advantage. Harvard was skilled at fighting paper with paper. In the past, the university had responded to union organizers' published aims with barrages of counterargument. Now the union's agenda was invisible; there was nothing to make a case against. More critical, though, and more of an advantage, was the positive side of this paperless campaign, the person-to-person relationship building that was now the union's main activity. Relationship itself became and remains the union's agenda and its strongest selling point.

Anne Taylor remembers hearing, during the campaign, a Harvard employee explain why she was active in the union: "I live alone. I'm not from this part of the country. I'm not married. I go to work. Work is really important to me because that's where my circle of friends is. Now I have someplace to go after work. I have people who care about me and ask about me and who want to hear my story."[14] Taylor adds, "I realized right then we were going to lose to these people. I could sell them a good benefits package; I could sell them competitive wages. But I couldn't sell them a sense of belonging, of being part of something bigger."

Guarnieri, who has served on the union's executive board, counts fellow union members among her strongest allies—inside and outside the workplace. When her elderly mother died of cancer, a contingent of HUCTW members filed into the Charles Keefe Funeral Home in North Cambridge to attend the wake. The next day, there they all were again, this time at St. John the Evangelist Church for the funeral.

"You just get wrapped up in everyone's life," says Guarnieri. During her mother's long illness, she says, people she knew from the union would call: Did she need them to go grocery shopping? Did she need a ride anyplace? Could they come do the laundry? "You get to know them better, and then you wonder how you could ever live without these people," Guarnieri says. Involvement with HUCTW has been "a meaningful, life-changing experience." She says, "Most clubs you sign up for, or organizations you belong to, don't do that—you have your membership card, but so what? They don't change your life, necessarily . . . this does."

Part of relationship is listening; part is being heard. In conversation with Rondeau, the word that comes up again and again is "voice." She talks of the (mainly) women in the union "finding their voice" in a situation where they had had none. She has talked about how powerful the experience of "finding our voice" was.[15] Having a voice means not only learning to speak up but also having others pay attention to what you say. During the unsuccessful unionizing campaign of the late 1970s, the Harvard administration sent a letter to medical-area workers that said "WE HEAR YOU" in capital letters and promised to address the workers' concerns if they voted against forming a union. Then Harvard won—and forgot its promise. The university's turning a deaf ear to the workers it had claimed to hear helped ignite the next campaign.[16]

Again, the organizers of Valley Interfaith and HUCTW seem to understand the same lessons: the importance of people finding their own voices, rather than repeating words given to them by well-meaning organizers. Marie Manna says, "We didn't have a platform; we didn't say, 'Join the union and you'll get this and that.' It is about people participating and deciding. We can't tell them what to do."[17] Valley Interfaith and HUCTW also understand that people can find their voices only if leaders and organizers are patient enough and quiet enough to give them a chance to speak, especially if their gender, training, and status have accustomed them to silence. "Workers were not used to using their voices at this time," Rondeau remarks. She says, "This is not a place where the loudest person will be leader. Our meetings were small; our tone was moderate. We tried to create a union that was a safe haven for people. When John Hoerr was working on his book, basically living here, he came out of a union meeting and said, 'I get it. The union's for shy people.' We wanted it to be a place where people could try out their voices."[18]

"You couldn't have found a more shy person than me," says Guarnieri, agreeing. But she found herself called upon to speak to other potential union members, even standing to speak at a union rally. "After a while," she says, "you develop your own confidence."

The voices sang as well as spoke. The union's singing group, the Pipets (named after the glass tubes used in laboratories to measure small amounts of liquid), continues to gather and sing, although not as often as in the past. Perhaps the singing group is not a central part of the story, but Anne Taylor says, "An employer will never beat a union that has a singing group. Singing together builds unity and harmony and commitment."

Evan Keely, a fellowship assistant in the Office of Career Services, sings with the Pipets now. That is, in fact, how fellow union members tend to introduce him—"Evan sings in the Pipets." Keely recalls members packed into a standing-room-only rally at a Cambridge church. The Pipets performed a Hooked on Classics spoof: labor lyrics set against a classical background. It brought the house down.

Then everybody sang a rousing chorus of "Solidarity Forever." Songs don't have the power to change contracts. But, says Keely, "the spirit that engendered among the membership" was something impressive to behold. (Group singing was a regular feature of Rural Community Development Council meetings near Tupelo in the 1940s.)

The organizers continued to work for more than a year without union sponsorship and essentially without pay. (One of its slogans at the time was "Too dumb to quit.") Toward the end of 1986, they affiliated with the American Federation of State, County, and Municipal Employees, which provided financial support but agreed to let the Harvard group continue its own campaign, with its own style of relational organizing. John Hoerr tells how the new affiliation came about. When Robert McGarrah, an AFSCME director, was attending a summer course at the John F. Kennedy School of Government, he happened to walk through the basement of the school, where he saw a large poster with "We Believe in Ourselves" printed at the top. More than a thousand signatures appeared below. That accumulation of signatures for what seemed a grassroots effort impressed him enough to make him seek out the union and led, some months later, to the new affiliation, one that has continued.[19]

In 1986, HUCTW began putting the slogan "It's not anti-Harvard to be pro-union" on T-shirts, bumper stickers, and posters. Borrowed from a speech by Massachusetts Congressman Barney Frank, the sentence expresses the union's belief in cooperation and engagement rather than an us-against-them stance. It extends the idea of relationship and shared participation to the employers who are usually considered labor's opponents. Rondeau says:

> Our group is bizarre in the labor movement. We try to solve conflict in a way that deepens the relationship between labor and management. We're trying to create a community. So we model that. How long can you last by building a community that demonizes the enemy? You burn out. People aren't looking for a fight when they come to work. They want a good job and good relationships. It hurts to come to work and fight with your employer and be miserable all the time. It is damaging to their souls.[20]

When Harvard's clerical and technical workers voted to unionize in 1988 (by a close vote of 1,530 to 1,486), they had an opportunity to discover whether that belief would work in practice.

To some degree, it has. Credit for creating a relationship between what had been opposing sides in the unionization campaign goes to Rondeau and her group, but also to Harvard, especially in the person of John Dunlop, the emeritus professor appointed chief negotiator by the university. HUCTW laid the groundwork for a relationship by not demonizing Harvard during the union drive; it genuinely sought a working partnership with Harvard after the successful vote, in a situation where victory could have tempted it to pay back the university for some of the tactics it had used to fight the effort. Dunlop began meeting one-on-one with Rondeau and advising Derek Bok even before Dunlop's official appointment. He counseled the president to recognize the union voluntarily rather than pursue a possible legal challenge to the election. And he suggested that the university request a sixty-day transition period for informal discussions before official bargaining began. In other words, he, like HUCTW, sought relationship rather than confrontation. And Bok, to his credit, agreed, despite pressure from some at Harvard to challenge the validity of the union vote.

John Hoerr describes the seven meetings of Harvard's and HUCTW's transition teams during that sixty-day period as an opportunity "to learn something about one another and to measure intentions and trustfulness."[21] During the meetings, the university group explained details of employment information and finances; HUCTW brought in employees to tell stories of their work and their lives outside work, explaining, Rondeau says, "what it means to work at Harvard from a very personal level."[22] The meetings led not only to informal mutual understanding but also to a written "Understanding" that recognized for the first time that support staff, such as faculty, administration, students, alumni, and boards, should participate in the process of governing the university.

The contract negotiated in 1989 included a significant salary increase for employees. More remarkably, it avoided the usual spelling out of management rights and union rights, of detailed descriptions of the responsibilities of particular jobs, and of the grievance procedures that would come into play when workers believed the terms of their contract had been violated. Instead, the contract described a problem-solving process designed to encourage employees to participate in resolving issues, rather than turn them over to union professionals. Local problem-solving teams of union members and management representatives were expected to work together on problems. A university problem-solving team would handle issues that had not been solved locally; mediation and arbitration procedures would come into play only when neither the local nor the university problem-solving team had been able to resolve an issue. The fact that only six cases went to mediation and none required arbitration during the first seven years the system was in place demonstrates its success.[23] These unusual contract features reflect John Dunlop's longtime commitment to problem solving and the union's desire for a working relationship with Harvard.

"We talk every day about things that happen all the time," says Guarnieri. "So that when the contract is up, we don't have to sit there and fight." She says that she is constantly reminded of a basic philosophical principle of the union: "No matter how hard things get, no matter how hot things get, no matter how controversial things get, we always have to treat each other with kindness and respect." The "each other" she refers to means fellow union members and also Harvard management. Margot Chamberlain, a staff person in Harvard's Edwin O. Reischauer Institute of Japanese Studies, describes HUCTW as "totally different" from other unions. "It's based on relationships," she says. "The tactics, rather than being adversarial, are . . . built on conversation and humor. They're not alienating. . . . There's an inclusiveness about it."

Ken Tivey, the Department of Economics secretary, sees the relational approach as strategically driven and strategically useful: "Harvard is a very large, powerful institution, and if you start confronting it directly head-on, your chances of success diminish."

Rondeau sees striving to maintain a partnership with the university as a way of maintaining the spirit in which the union was created:

> We were trying to keep the joy that we felt in building the organization alive once the organization had been officially created. One of the things we figured out was that we might be able to do it by not having rules, but using relationships to work out issues. The idea was that using a problem-solving process as opposed to a grievance mechanism could bring the labor and management people involved closer, and [make them] more able to solve bigger problems because of the relationship they have.[24]

HUCTW organizers have applied the lessons of Harvard to other campaigns. Beginning in 1991, Rondeau and fellow organizer Elisabeth Szanto spent five years doing person-to-person organizing for AFSCME at the University of Massachusetts Medical Center in Worcester—putting down "deep roots," Szanto says.[25] Their 1997 success in winning a pro-union vote contrasts with an earlier, failed effort by another union— the typical phone and media blitz by organizers who never really got inside the organization. One of the stories from that election is of the union rep who challenged the vote of an employee in the medical center library because he did not know and refused to believe that there was a library.[26] After winning the vote, the AFSCME union worked to build a cooperative relationship with management, as at Harvard, and (also as at Harvard) with positive though mixed results. Rondeau says, "Managers start out hostile, but it's a hospital: you have to get the work done.

Once they figure out that you can help them get the work done, that changes things quite a lot."[27] In addition to representing several thousand workers at the medical center, and in two small Cambridge-based organizations, the union is also involved in a major drive to organize the clerical and technical workers at nearby Tufts University.

The years since the first Harvard contract was signed have not been one long period of mutual respect and deepening relationship, however. After Neil Rudenstine became president of Harvard in 1991, relations soured, mainly, Anne Taylor says, because the Harvard administrators who began dealing with the union at that point believed in "a very traditional, hands-off, adversarial approach." It takes two to make a relationship, and the change in Harvard's attitude toward the union led to a situation much more like traditional labor-management confrontation. Taylor characterizes the 1992 contract negotiations as "very bitter." She believes, though, that HUCTW's commitment to a cooperative relationship with the university is real and that the union has resorted to more militant tactics as a last resort: "They picketed this building [Massachusetts Hall] for about six weeks back in '97 over health benefits for part-time workers. But they were only out there picketing because nobody was talking to them; they didn't have any lines of communication. That was a relationship problem. They were kept at bay, so they marched around in the winter for weeks and weeks until the issue was resolved."[28]

In many labor unions, and other groups as well, having a common enemy is a powerful source of solidarity. Groups define themselves not only by who is inside but by a common view of the outsiders who oppose them. People pull together in a crisis; they are unified and energized by a fight, as the long, angry history of wars and political and religious disputes has shown. So one of the challenges facing HUCTW is how to maintain its spirit and solidarity after the union has been established and, more important perhaps, when it strives to work with rather than against management. Rondeau talks of keeping the joy alive by working with the university to solve problems, but problem solving may be less stirring than the call to win the right to unionize in the first place or the periodic battles that other unions engage in. Maintaining the spirit over time, when many of the people now in the union have no direct experience of the early days, is a challenge. Anne Taylor remarks, "This is all built on relationships and process. That means you have to keep an enormous number of people energized and active. If you succeed, then you really build a community, but it's very hard to keep going."

The difficulty of keeping such a community going—the expense of time and energy required to build relationships one by one—may help explain why more unions have not followed this model.

Continuous Organizing

The poster that Robert McGarrah saw in the basement of the Kennedy School now hangs in HUCTW's office on the second floor of a Harvard-owned building across Massachusetts Avenue from Harvard Yard. About four feet square, it communicates a complex message of both individuality and solidarity. "We Believe in Ourselves" and some printed text occupy approximately the upper quarter of the whole. Long columns of handwritten names beneath those lines fill the rest of the poster: more than a thousand signatures, each different from all the others, each personal, but together forming an impressive mass, like rows and rows of seats in a meeting hall packed with people who are both individuals and a group. Think of the lines from Walt Whitman, poet of the individual and the collective:

> One's-Self I sing, a simple separate person,
> Yet utter the word Democratic, the word En-Masse.

The office is cluttered and informal, full of what look like hand-me-down desks, chairs, and a few sofas. It looks homey and maybe a little improvisational, like the apartments of graduate students who do not have much money or who care more about thoughts than things. There is no display of power and status such as you might expect to find in a union headquarters. A small meeting room with a sofa and a couple of chairs is made even smaller by a curtain running its length, with stacks of paper and other supplies piled up behind it. Most of the walls and cubicle dividers look like some people's refrigerator doors: crowded with photographs, some capturing moments in HUCTW's history, but also family photos, along with drawings by children, postcards, notes, cartoons.

The organizers who work here are consciously engaged in the effort to build and maintain community, to ensure that membership in HUCTW provides the intangible social benefits of community and not just decent salaries and fringe benefits. They want to be sure that new members know that is what the union is about. All of them continue to do organizing in the workplace; none is a full-time administrator or manager. Several hundred union members, all volunteers, are actively involved in organizing. The union participates in a thousand "problem solvings" each year, working with Harvard to resolve individual problems raised by union members.

Recruiting methods have not really changed over the years, although new clerical and technical workers at Harvard do get a small packet of printed material—a copy of the contracts and some pages of other basic information. The established union is not entirely paper-free, as it was in its early years of struggle. But the process of drawing new members to the union still includes a series of one-on-one conversations over coffee or lunch and then invitations to small meetings that give everyone a chance to talk, to find and use a distinctive voice.

Two weeks after Margot Chamberlain started work, some union people came by to introduce themselves. "I thought it was the weirdest thing I'd ever seen," she says now. "What were they doing here that they just came by to say hello? I didn't get it." She gets it now. When new employees come on the job, Chamberlain is one of the union people who stop by to say hello.

There are other ways to bring new members into the fold of community. Shauna Cagan, who joined the union when she came to work at Harvard just two years ago, plays second base and short field on the HUCTW softball team.

"One of the things I think that happens," Cagan says, "is that we kind of hang out with people who are like us. This team has a really wide range of people. It has older people who have been on the team for a long time, old-school union members, and then a group of young guys that I wouldn't necessarily know." After games, you can find them at Kendall's or Charlie's in Harvard Square. Much of Cagan's networking at Harvard happens directly through the names on that lineup card. "The Harvard system is pretty big," Cagan says. "It's definitely nice to feel like you have connections there."

In January 2003, the union launched a major effort to create more affordable housing in Cambridge, Alston, Somerville, and adjacent communities. The union expects that it will take decades to realize results. This initial period is one of learning and discovery, as the union funds partners who can help them learn about housing. "We are not taking a position that Harvard should provide housing for our members and not for others," says Rondeau. "I know it may sound corny, but this is about the process and not the outcome. There have been great concrete rewards—child care, health benefits, salary, and even a week off over Christmas when we got an agreement to close Harvard down for one week—but this is not what we organized around. If we do the process right, we will get to the outcome we all want."

More than 90 percent of Harvard's clerical and technical workers belong to HUCTW. Its contracts guarantee parental leave and other quality-of-life benefits as well as decent salaries. But employee turnover is high. There are new people coming in all the time, and Rondeau recognizes that integrating them into the union and keeping its original spirit alive is a major challenge. As Taylor notes, keeping an energetic and active community going is an enormous task.

Rondeau believes that the last couple of years have brought a renewal of energy after a gradual loss. One area she says union members hope to influence is work design. By doing so, they would fulfill more of the early promise of participation in the governance of the university than the union has so far realized. HUCTW has developed a project called New

Work Systems at Harvard to think through work processes and put more emphasis on working in teams, because that can be a better way of working in many situations and an antidote to isolation. Twenty-five joint union-management councils have been put into place to address issues of work design, with the goal of raising this to a hundred such joint councils in a few years. Results so far have been limited. Rondeau says that Harvard, unlike the University of Massachusetts Medical Center, "is not yet interested in productivity." This may be true partly because Harvard has a lot of money and partly because, in some quarters, people believe that the Harvard way of doing things is by definition the right way.

Nevertheless, work design may be one area that the union will give more of its energy to and derive energy from. "We've addressed good benefits and good pay, but there is still something broken about the work experience for most of our members. Work for many of them is a pretty dispiriting experience. The hierarchies don't work. The way they are compartmentalized doesn't work. This is the deepest interest we have. If we can solve it, it will give both our members and the employer far more flexibility," Rondeau says. Like any living organization, HUCTW is permanently in process and its future shape is unpredictable. The presence of men in the union has increased from about 15 percent at the end of the 1980s to about 30 percent. Whether that change—or trend, if it is a trend—will have any significant effect remains to be seen. Unchanged, though, is Rondeau's commitment to the ideas that shaped HUCTW more than twenty years ago. Her energy and Manna's are still evident after two decades, as is their sense that they helped create something unusual and important. Labor organizers in national offices may well be right that using "the social thing" is a very expensive way to organize, but, unlike more conventional strategies, it seems to be working.

CHAPTER 9

Experience Corps
Bringing "Old Heads" to the Schools

For years the headlines about Philadelphia's public school system have told the same story: low test scores, troubled classrooms, high drop-out rates, kids not learning to read or calculate well enough to succeed in today's world. The apparently dire state of Philadelphia's public school system has led to a contract with Edison Schools to see if private enterprise can succeed where public efforts have apparently failed.

Stories in newspapers and magazines in recent years have also discussed another problem: the increasing number of retirees who would soon be leaving the workforce in historically unprecedented good health to live comfortably on Social Security and savings in Arizona or Florida, supported by the payroll taxes of younger generations struggling to support the swelling, unproductive ranks.

Taken together, these stories make what has been going on in (pre-Edison) Philadelphia elementary schools surprising. Take the Cook-Wissahickon Elementary School in North Philadelphia. With approximately 60 percent African-American and 40 percent Caucasian students, it is one of the relatively few genuinely integrated schools in the Philadelphia system, says school principal Rosemary Cataldi. Eighty percent of the students are eligible for free lunches, the standard measure of poverty levels in schools.

A two-story tan brick building in a tidy neighborhood, the school does not look or feel like a school in crisis. The corridors of Cook-Wissahickon are clean and quiet, the walls covered with bright murals, drawings and writings by students, pink and red hearts for Valentine's Day, and a large ethnic-heritage "quilt"—a patchwork of student collages illustrating their African-American, Italian, Mexican, English, German, and Latin American backgrounds. In the library, a seven-foot-tall "Recyclosaurus" made from soft-drink cans flashes jagged teeth. At a table in one corner of the library, Dr. Simeon Cole, a retired dentist, listens while an eight-year-old reads to him. Dr. Cole gently helps the boy puzzle out some unfamiliar words. And in a classroom on the second floor, a grandmotherly woman sits at a small table with a shy second-grade boy.

"What do you want to read today?" she asks him.

He chooses a book from a small pile on the table: a retelling of the Aesop fable about a contest between the sun and the wind. She points to the words as he reads aloud. When he hesitates and starts guessing, she writes the unfamiliar word on the nearby blackboard, sound by sound, to help him decipher it. By the time he finishes the story, there are three words on the board. She asks him to use each in a sentence—"Stronger: I am stronger than you"—and write the sentences. While she makes notes about the reading lesson, he breezes through a page of subtraction problems: he finds reading difficult but loves math. The session ends with praise, a sticker for good work, a gentle pat on the arm, and "See you next week."

Across the room, Dolores Johnson-Beckles, another woman of retirement age, listens as a young girl whom we'll call Letitia reads from a book about children at school planning a party. This woman's style is different, more challenging, almost confrontational. When Letitia pauses in the middle of a sentence, Johnson-Beckles says, "Why are you stopping? Do you see a period there? I don't." But when the lesson ends, they chat comfortably together. Letitia talks about a girl in the school and says, "She's pretty."

"As pretty as you?" her tutor asks.

Letitia gives the question a moment's thought and says matter-of-factly, "Yes."

Here, too, Johnson-Beckles offers a good-work sticker and some words of praise. Letitia gives her a quick hug and goes back to her classroom. A visitor comments that she seems like a sweet child.

"She's sweet," the woman says, "but she's not a child. She's *old*, with all she's been through." Letitia has been taken out of a troubled family and placed with caring foster parents, and that seems to be making a real difference in her life.

Dr. Cole and these two women are among ten Experience Corps volunteers at the school, mostly women, all retired, ranging in age from fifty-something to their seventies and eighties. Each of them commits a substantial fifteen hours a week to the school, tutoring four to six children three times a week. Some additional volunteers give a few hours a week and work with one or two students. Dorothea Davis, who tutored in the program for several years herself, now acts as field coordinator at Cook-Wissahickon, helping to solve problems, meeting regularly with principal Cataldi and reading coordinator Barbara Pratt-Richardson. Davis works for Temple University's Center for Intergenerational Learning, which manages the Experience Corps program in a dozen Philadelphia elementary schools and for the last two decades has been devoted to bringing generations together to meet community needs.

Older volunteers tutoring children have long been a part of our communities, through programs such as Foster Grandparents and Big Brothers Big Sisters. Harris Wofford, founding CEO of the government's Corporation for National and Community Service, one of the founders of the Peace Corps, and a former senator from Pennsylvania, knows volunteer programs well, and he singles out Experience Corps as distinctive.

Experience Corps from the beginning wanted to crack the atom of "senior power" to really solve some of our big problems. To do this, you need to attract a much larger and more diverse group of seniors [than previous programs did], and you need a far deeper commitment from the participants. You must appeal to people's talents and skills and build esprit de corps. It is far more compelling to many seniors . . . if they see a chance to do work not as a single volunteer in a school, but as part of a team with a mission.[1]

In other words, the design of Experience Corps incorporates elements of social-capital building to magnify the impact of the individual volunteers. Philadelphia is one of fifteen American cities that have such programs. The nationwide Experience Corps network is overseen by Civic Ventures, a nonprofit organization "dedicated to transforming the aging of America into a source of individual and social renewal."[2]

Vibrant and enthusiastic, Cataldi talks about what Experience Corps does for Cook-Wissahickon, how much value the school gets for a $28,000 annual contribution to the program—four fifths of the school's entire Reading Excellence grant. Class sizes averaging around thirty make it impossible for teachers to give concentrated help to students having difficulty with reading and math. The three half-hour sessions a week with an Experience Corps volunteer can make the difference between a child who keeps up and one who falls behind, and between a child who thinks of himself or herself as a failure and one who enjoys success and comes to expect it. The consistent positive attention matters as much as improved reading skill—possibly more. Cataldi remarks on the commitment and consistency of older people—qualities missing in the home lives of some of these children—and talks about their devotion to the kids and how well they fit in with the life of the school. "They're part of us," she says. "They go on field trips with us; they come to awards ceremonies when one of their kids gets an award. Three times a year they have breakfasts for parents that bring parents, students, volunteers, and staff together." She adds, "And the kids see elders doing something worthwhile; they're learning more than reading."

Sitting in the Experience Corps classroom with coffee and doughnuts before they begin the day's tutoring, the volunteers explain why they joined the program. One retiree says, "I was bored after a year of retirement." Heads nod. Another adds, "I was sitting at home doing nothing. I wanted to stay active and get out of the house." The fifteen-hours-a-week volunteers receive a monthly stipend of just under $250. For some, that money makes participation possible, paying for transportation, lunches, and other expenses related to the program. But no one is in it for the money. They all talk, in one way or another, about wanting to do something for the children: "They need to be shown love and care," "There's a need for grandmothers," "I've had a good life; now it's time to give something back." Most say they are getting as much out of the experience as they give to it. One comments, "If you pay attention, they learn and you learn." One volunteer got a computer lesson from one of her students; she was thrilled to receive her first e-mail, and he got the pleasure of being the giver rather than the receiver of new knowledge.

The volunteers clearly enjoy being with one another. "If this room wasn't here," says one of the Cook-Wissahickon volunteers, "we'd be in bad shape. We're a family here." The volunteers encourage one another and exchange knowledge about what does and doesn't work with the kids. They are a "community of practice," a term that refers to informal groups of people who share knowledge and support one another in their common work. "These are relationships with a purpose," note Marc Freedman, one of the founders of Experience Corps. "They're a lot like the relationships the retirees used to have at work."[3] Although the purpose of the program is to offer a way for retirees to help schoolchildren, the program also offers the satisfactions and comforts of new relationships among the participants.

Amid conversation about the rewards of spending time with "our children," there are a few complaints about the amount of paperwork the retirees have to do, the requirement to keep careful records of each session with each child and, it seems, to fill out a variety of other forms. "I'm here to volunteer with children," one says, "not to do paperwork." Program managers recognize that the volunteers should spend as much time as possible working with the children, but they say that most of the paperwork is necessary and useful. In addition to allowing the program to assess its impact on children and provide information that gives Experience Corps credibility with the community, the school, and funding sources, it helps the volunteers themselves gauge the effects of their efforts. Whether or not that argument convinces the volunteers, there is no question that their dedication to the children is absolute. No one is talking about leaving the program, only about making sure they can continue to work with their kids. Some have been part of Experience Corps for four years or more, practically from the beginning.

The Experience Corps Idea

Launched as a pilot program in five cities in 1996, Experience Corps was inspired by earlier programs and by ideas that date back to the 1960s. Experience Corps cofounder Marc Freedman traces the creation of the program and the history of ideas about appropriate roles for seniors in society in his book *Prime Time: How Baby Boomers Will Revolutionize Retirement and Transform America.* One key inspiration was Foster Grandparents. That program got its start in the 1960s, when Sargent Shriver, then director of the Office of Economic Opportunity, had an "Aha!" insight during an official visit to Cincinnati. Immediately after touring a public hospital where he watched three harried nurses try to care for as many as a hundred babies crying for attention, he visited a nearby "old people's home" whose residents, also starved for human contact, complained that they had nothing to do. Shriver said, "For God's sake, why don't we just take those old people out of this one building—which was in easy walking distance of the place where the children were—and put them to work doing just what those nurses said that the babies needed."[4]

Turning that thought into a functioning program took some doing, among other reasons because of the lingering myth that old people were unreliable and incapable of doing "real" work—the image of elders "put out to pasture" or settled into rocking chairs. At first, many institutions that could have benefited from their help were reluctant to participate and turned down the government money that was offered. Some expressed the fear that seniors might carry diseases they would pass on to the children. Freedman describes the hard work undertaken by program organizers to persuade the first few institutions to take part. Today, the Foster Grandparents program involves more than twenty-five thousand older Americans relating one-on-one to a hundred thousand children a year. It is, according to Freedman, "a hidden triumph of social policy."

Freedman's own early understanding of the value of caring and mentoring relationships between adults and children came from a study of mentoring programs he and colleagues conducted while working for Public/Private Ventures, a nonprofit organization that evaluates social policies and programs. Analysis of one of those programs, Big Brothers Big Sisters, revealed what he calls "a staggering improvement" in kids in the program, compared to kids on the waiting list for it. But the waiting list was thirty thousand names long. Where would that many volunteers come from? With the midlife generation overwhelmed by work and family demands, the answer seemed to be retirees, who had been given, and could in turn bestow, the gift of time. In the late 1980s, Freedman also visited the Work Connection, a small Boston-area program that connected retired blue-collar workers with youths who had gotten in trouble with the law. He saw how life experience had given the retirees patience and made them credible in the eyes of those rebellious and skeptical youths. The strength of the relationships they had developed impressed him, and he found evidence of the benefits to young people whose lives had seemed headed in the wrong direction.

In the early 1990s, Freedman heard John Gardner, former secretary of Health, Education, and Welfare and founder of Common Cause, deliver a talk entitled "Reinventing Community." After the talk he approached Gardner and told him that he thought one source of community rebuilding might be older Americans relating to and assisting the younger generation. Freedman describes how Gardner reached into his briefcase and pulled out a paper he had written in 1988, "The Experience Corps," that expressed the same idea in a few succinct pages. Gardner's brief essay argued for an institution that would draw on the "talent, experience, and commitment" of older Americans, providing a mechanism for them to give back to society while enjoying an opportunity for learning and satisfaction for themselves.[5]

When the Commonwealth Fund of New York asked Freedman to write a study of how older Americans might contribute to community service, he elaborated on Gardner's argument, drawing on his own observation of the strengths and limitations of existing senior volunteer programs. The basic principles he articulated in that study have given Experience Corps its particular character and—although this was not his intention—have contributed to making this a social-capital story of relationship and engagement, not simply a story about a volunteer program.

Commitment is one of the principles—the stipulation that Experience Corps volunteers would commit to work for a specific, significant amount of time (fifteen hours a week became the standard) to be eligible for the monthly stipend the program offers. Some who volunteer for the program work fewer hours, but that regular commitment has been the foundation of trusting relationships between tutors and students and tutors and teachers that could not have been formed through brief or intermittent contact. Rosemary Cataldi says that hard-pressed school staffers are, naturally enough, unwilling to invest in relationships with volunteers who show up infrequently or only when they feel like it. There are many other demands on staff more important than spending time with people who have good intentions but will not be there week after week, helping to educate the children.

Freedman called for a *critical mass* of participants in each school because he saw the difference a group of eight Foster Grandparents volunteering twenty hours a week made at the Reiche Elementary School in Portland, Maine. Freedman argued that the Experience Corps program should place enough volunteers in an institution to have a real presence there, to change things—the kind of visibility and effect that a volunteer or two could never have. Robert Tietze, senior program director at Temple University's Center for Intergenerational Learning, who has overall responsibility for Experience Corps in Philadelphia, says, "It is extremely difficult for one or two volunteers to affect a school community. Usually they are invisible except to the teachers they work with. The program needs to have a presence, and when we have a team of volunteers we create a critical mass of time, energy, and commitment. It is the only way to change a school's culture and environment."[6] In addition, having groups of that size has created a supportive community of peers for the volunteers themselves—an experience very different from the isolation volunteers in schools sometimes experience.

The plan also specified that Experience Corps volunteers would have opportunities to take *leadership* roles in the organization and to introduce innovations that allowed them to use their particular talents to benefit the young people. As some of our other stories suggest, lasting commitment and a sense of genuine participation and connection often depend on having opportunities to develop new skills and take leadership roles. Simply being a "foot soldier" or doing the same thing over and over does not build social capital as readily.

When Tom Endres, director of the National Senior Service Corps, convinced Congress to appropriate $1 million for pilot projects that could demonstrate the potential contribution of volunteer seniors, Freedman had a chance to turn these ideas into reality. A final, critical part of the plan came from Dr. Linda Fried of Johns Hopkins School of Medicine. An advocate for public education (and a parent of school-age children of her own) as well as a geriatrician, she was convinced that elementary schools needed help and suggested to Freedman that Experience Corps choose children in elementary schools as the population to be served. Like Shriver, she saw a natural fit between a group that needed attention and a group that could provide it. So, in 1996, Experience Corps pilot projects were launched in the South Bronx; North Philadelphia; Minneapolis; Portland, Oregon; and Port Arthur, Texas.

Theory into Practice

Finding volunteers proved difficult at first. Because the program was new, no word of mouth existed; there were no Experience Corps veterans who could tell friends and neighbors about the program and its satisfactions. And no obvious mechanism existed for matching willing volunteers with volunteer opportunities in the schools. Building such a mechanism, filling that vacuum, was one of the program's aims. Help came from the American Association of Retired Persons. Membership in AARP, a national organization that anyone over fifty willing to pay dues can belong to, does not typically bring people together; contributing to a national lobbying or interest group is not like joining a club or committee. But AARP had two things that made it useful in this case: a database of the names and addresses of people over fifty and a good reputation. When AARP mailed thousands of announcements about the Experience Corps opportunity to members who lived in the vicinities of several of the pilot locations, enough responses came from suitable candidates to staff all of the pilot schools with the sought-after critical mass of volunteers.

Six years later, several of the volunteers at Cook-Wissahickon and Bayard Taylor Elementary School, also in Philadelphia and one of the schools chosen for the pilot program, remember first hearing about Experience Corps through an AARP mailing. A few have been with the program since the beginning. Others learned about it from the original volunteers. Now word-of-mouth does exist, and recruitment is easier. One volunteer at Taylor, Howard Shub, was brought into the program by his wife, Norma, who began as a volunteer and is now field coordinator for Taylor and another site—his boss, he says.

Who are these volunteers? In North Philadelphia, they are predominantly African-American. Most are women, some in their fifties or sixties, others in their seventies or eighties. They are all alert and generally healthy and youthful, though several use canes and one needs a walker to get around the school. Many have had long careers in education, but there are also former federal and municipal employees (including a mailman and a sewer worker), the retired dentist, someone retired from the insurance business, and veterans of other professions.

These are the people who would have been out on the front porch in the past, watching over the life of the street, keeping an eye on the neighborhood kids. They have worked and raised families and gained a lifetime of experience. They are the "old heads" that Elijah Anderson describes in *Streetwise*—responsible, experienced older adults who befriended and encouraged youths, surrogate parents who passed on their values and understanding but who lost their authority as neighborhoods declined.[7] Now, Freedman says, "The porch has moved inside the school." He sees Experience Corps as a way of reviving and formalizing some of the teaching and mentoring roles that elders have traditionally played in communities. "Experience Corps is a new way of doing old things," he adds. Like the "urban village" concept inspiring efforts to revitalize the Dudley Street neighborhood in Boston, the program hopes to reweave some of the traditional fabric of community life, connecting generations and giving retirees the opportunity to take an active, useful role as village elders who instruct and guide the young.

The volunteers teach reading and math—the primary educational aim of the program is improving the literacy skills of children at risk of falling behind their classmates and maybe never catching up. But education is not the sole aim of the program or necessarily its most valuable contribution. Robert Tietze says, "It isn't just tutoring, it's community; it's about working with children to establish relationships that have a social, emotional, and educational impact." Consistent, reliable, positive attention is perhaps the most important contribution the volunteers make to the lives of the children, some of whom live in family situations where such attention may be scarce—for instance, with a single parent who works long hours, in some cases at multiple jobs. Part of what the children learn from these relationships is that they themselves are worth paying attention to: someone willingly spends half an hour three times a week with just them, helping them learn, listening to their thoughts and feelings, caring about their progress and their future.

The relationships also give the children a positive example of what seniors can be like in a culture that sometimes portrays old people as foolish, helpless, or selfish. Tietze says the mission of the Center for Intergenerational Learning is "to break through walls of separation between generations." Karen Kolsky, principal of Taylor, describes what she considers an important benefit of Experience Corps this way: "We connect the five-year-olds and the ninety-year-olds. The children see older adults who are active, engaged, knowledgeable, and caring—they get a positive sense of what an eighty-year-old can be." She nods toward Norma Shub, the Taylor field coordinator and a vibrant woman in her mid-seventies. "Norma is what we all want to be at that age."

The children's "extracurricular" learning includes a living connection with what might otherwise seem abstract and ancient history. One of the Cook volunteers who was active in the civil rights movement in the 1960s shows students her photographs of events from those times and recounts her personal experiences. This is a clear example of "bringing the front porch inside the school," reviving the traditional role of elders passing on a community's history to the youngest generation, bringing their shared heritage to life.

Building that connection to the past is one of the particular benefits of matching children with senior volunteers. There are others. One is the natural ease possible in relationships between children and grandparents or those of grandparent age. It is a common experience in families: adults whose relationships with their own children were fraught with the usual anxieties, tensions, and misunderstandings have much more relaxed and supportive relationships with their grandchildren (who are almost certainly locked in the usual battles with *their* parents). Freedman remarks, "Seniors have a special relationship with time," one element of which is patience: a willingness not only to work at the pace that suits their individual charges but to take whatever time is needed for trust and a sense of connection to grow. He believes that some of the least successful volunteers are the ones who push an agenda of scheduled improvement goals too hard, instead of valuing the relationship for its own sake and attending to the natural pace of their students' development. But the elders are impatient, too, reluctant to spend their valuable time and energy on anything that gets between them and the children, such as paperwork.

In Philadelphia and elsewhere, the sympathetic connections between tutors and students, and tutors and teachers, are at the heart of the program's success. Volunteers connect with teachers not only to discuss the children's work but to attend staff development sessions, sometimes serving as mentors for new teachers as well as young students. When a new and inexperienced teacher took over a class in the middle of the year at one of the schools, the Experience Corps volunteer helped her settle in, explaining how the previous teacher had done things and building a bridge between the students, who knew the tutor well, and the newcomer.

That all of these ties quickly become important to the volunteers is shown by their response to being offered opportunities to transfer to schools closer to their homes. When some of them joined Experience Corps, no schools in their own neighborhoods were involved in the program, so they went to more distant sites. As the program has expanded, schools closer to home have become available. With only a few exceptions, the tutors have turned down the school closer to home, preferring to travel (often by public transportation) rather than give up the relationships they have established. They want to stay with "their" children, "their" teachers, and "their" fellow volunteers. Freedman sums up the importance of relationship in the program: "Social connectedness is the heart of Experience Corps, and the connections radiate in so many directions."

Freedman notes that many volunteers have expressed less sympathy for parents and less sense of connection with them, feeling that many do not spend enough time helping their children to learn. Volunteers, often of a different generation and different income level than many of the parents, have been frustrated by children coming to school without an adequate breakfast, poorly dressed, without a good night's sleep. They disapprove when no one at home reads to the student or helps with homework the night before. To try to bridge this gap, to get parents more involved with the school and their children's education, many Experience Corps schools have begun to hold regular parent breakfasts to bring together volunteers, teachers, kids, and parents. These breakfasts were introduced by the volunteers. The get-togethers have made some difference. In some instances, parents choose to "shadow" volunteers, observing tutoring sessions to learn techniques they can use at home to help their children improve their reading. But of course a few breakfast meetings cannot neutralize all the problems of overworked and overwhelmed parents, of unstable home lives and troubled neighborhoods. With its locked doors and barbed wire to discourage break-ins, the Taylor school in Philadelphia feels more like an enclave or a refuge than an integral part of the distressed community that surrounds it. The Industrial Areas Foundation actions to improve schools in Texas recognized that schools could not be meaningfully improved in isolation; they needed to be seen and treated as part of the larger community.

To signal and reinforce the legitimacy of the volunteer group as a real, functioning part of the school, the Experience Corps insists that volunteers have mailboxes in the school office alongside the teachers' boxes. Tietze explains, "We have learned that some elements are critical to the successful integration of the program into the school. Some, like the mailboxes, may seem insignificant, but we have found that such apparently simple things can make or break the program. If a school is unwilling or unable to work with us to establish these elements, it may be a sign that the relationship is not going to work, and we will choose not to establish a program at that particular site." He adds that the enthusiastic support and participation of the principal and teachers are basic requirements. If support is lacking or halfhearted, the relationship will probably fail. If the principal is enthusiastic but the teachers are not, the program cannot work. "Sometimes you have to be willing to walk away," he says. "Otherwise you may be placing your volunteers in a tenuous and stressful environment."

The emphasis on volunteer leadership has borne fruit of various kinds. Dorothea Davis at Cook-Wissahickon and Norma Shub at Taylor are volunteers who have followed a "career path" within the program, becoming field coordinators after a couple of years' experience as tutors. This kind of opportunity provides a triple benefit: keeping people in the program who might otherwise leave after stints as tutors; developing field coordinators with experiential knowledge of the work they are co-ordinating and credibility and connections with the schools and their fellow volunteers; and creating a further example of what older adults are capable of doing. Though the opportunity for volunteers to assume leadership was always part of the plan, in the early years very few volunteers were interested. Many had left careers where they had organizational responsibility, and they wanted the chance to do direct service as volunteers. It was only after several years that volunteers expressed interest in assuming leadership responsibilities.

Individual volunteers have also invented program features unforeseen in the initial plans. Martin Brown, a former postal worker, created an internal postal system at the Taylor School, installing a real U.S. Postal Service mailbox in the main hallway for students to deposit letters in. He and a student assistant regularly deliver mail throughout the school. His innovation has spurred student letter writing (and writing skills) while supporting a sense of community at the school. Another volunteer, who had worked at a food stall at the Thirtieth Street train station, operated a mobile kiosk in the school, in effect continuing his career with a younger and generally more appreciative clientele. Valley Interfaith's Alliance Schools program has had the same experience with retired volunteers bringing into the schools services that mirrored their occupations.

Tietze says that maintaining high standards and communicating frequently are necessary parts of ensuring the credibility of the program and the continuing support of the schools. Volunteers in Philadelphia undergo fifty hours of training at Temple University (an exercise in team building as well as skill development) before they can begin work in a school. Rosemary Cataldi comments, "Volunteers are so well trained when they come here." Some who want to be part of the program are not accepted. Tietze explains, "The basic criteria are caring, patience, enthusiasm, dependability, ability to communicate, and willingness to learn. If a candidate does not have those attributes or is unwilling to work as part of a team, they will not be accepted in the program." (Temple's Center for Intergenerational Learning makes an effort to find other volunteer opportunities for seniors who may not be a good fit with the Experience Corps.)

Tietze believes that the rare serious problems that do arise must be dealt with quickly and decisively. When one volunteer began making inappropriate comments to the teacher he worked with, school administrators called Tietze to request that he be transferred to another teacher. But Tietze decided that was a half measure that would not be in the best interest of the school or the program, and the volunteer was asked to leave. "The schools have to know that we'll take care of problems and maintain the integrity of the program," Tietze says. Constant communication does that. Communication is the main job of the field coordinators, who conduct volunteer meetings and regular monthly meetings with the principals. "Some principals don't want regular meetings," Tietze says. "They say, 'I'll call you if there's a problem.' But we want to avoid problems. That's why we meet."

Results, Measurable and Intangible

Some of the effects of Experience Corps are measurable. The reading scores of 75 percent of Experience Corps students in Philadelphia have increased one grade level. Attendance among the students tutored has improved. Surveys of volunteers taken at the beginning of their participation in the pilot program and at the end of the two-year pilot show a significant increase in their sense of purpose and energy and a significant decrease in loneliness.[8]

Other results, less tangible, are probably more important: the greater pride and hopefulness of students; the lessons they learn about caring and civility; greater connection and respect among generations; a richer school environment; a new sense of the possibilities of what Freedman, in a phrase coined by Monsignor Charles J. Fahey of Fordham University, calls "the third age."

The engagement of seniors with schools and children may have wider effects on society, especially if they begin to participate in large numbers. Freedman cites an example from Miami, Florida, in the late 1980s to suggest the power of participation. At that time, the city made a major effort to involve seniors in the schools as volunteers. Several years later, Freedman says, this group of several thousand seniors who had worked in the schools led a campaign to pass a billion-dollar school bond issue. Contrary to the image of retirees with no children of their own in school opposing such measures, more than 80 percent of the older population voted for it, ensuring its passage.[9] Engaging with particular people in particular schools (rather than thinking about an abstraction called "the schools"—often preceded by adjectives "failing," "violent," or "inefficient") probably made the difference. As with so many of our stories, being there and connecting person to person created understanding and support.

The Miami story and the success of the Experience Corps volunteers suggest a better future than the one imagined by those who foresee a huge population of unproductive, self-indulgent baby boomer retirees draining the nation's resources while younger generations struggle to provide for their own needs and their elders' demands.

The Future of Experience Corps:
Problems and Possibilities

The aim of the Experience Corps's two-year pilots and the intent of the "demonstration project" funding that supported them was to test principles of successful senior volunteering that could be applied to other programs, existing and new. Civic Ventures, a nonprofit founded by Marc Freedman that oversees Experience Corps nationally, shared pilot results with established programs, such as Foster Grandparents, but change is hard and the Experience Corps experiment has not led to all the broad changes that Freedman and others hoped for. At some future date, more of the program's most successful features may be adopted elsewhere, but the original idea of Experience Corps as a demonstration project has given way to an ongoing and expanding program. In Philadelphia, the Center for Intergenerational Learning will expand to forty new schools over the next four years, for a total of fifty-two, with approximately 520 fifteen-hours-a-week volunteers and another 300 who work fewer hours without stipends. That growth will be funded as part of a $6.8 million grant from the Robert Wood Johnson Foundation to expand the program nationally so that it reaches many major metropolitan areas over the next decade. Along with recent grants from the Atlantic Philanthropic Service Company and AmeriCorps, Experience Corps will be adding 2,000 volunteer positions nationwide over the next four years. Tietze says that continuing structured expansion should not be the only goal: "A program like this is the starting point, not an end in itself. Ultimately we hope schools will emulate the program and we'll see a spontaneous generation of this type of program across the country."

Expansion is a sign of success, but it also creates new challenges. Tietze recognizes that "managing a hundred volunteers takes more than triple the effort of managing thirty; everything changes: administration, training, everything." Maintaining the spirit of the program and the close connection and constant communication that characterize it now will become harder as the program expands. The volunteers' concerns about paperwork should alert program directors to guard against the likely (but maybe not inevitable) increase in bureaucracy as Experience Corps grows.

The current nationwide emphasis on standardized testing will probably have mixed effects on Experience Corps. Improving reading scores is a worthy goal. It provides a focus for the tutors' work, and testing may offer useful objective information about the program's effectiveness. A demonstrable positive effect on basic reading skills would undoubtedly make it easier to get continued funding. At the same time, Experience Corps is not just about measurable academic progress. Too much pressure to improve test results might distract from the social and emotional goals of the program or lead critics and supporters alike to pay less attention to the essential intangible benefits.

In Philadelphia, uncertainties about school funding and management might make the continued presence and future expansion of the program difficult, too. At Cook-Wissahickon, the two-year Reading Excellence grant that has supported the program ended at the close of the 2002 school year. Cataldi is determined to keep the program going but uncertain, at the moment, where the money to do that will come from. As we write, the Philadelphia school system as a whole faces an uncertain future. The broad conclusion that Philadelphia public schools are failing and something must be done—a reflection of real problems that nevertheless ignores the particular accomplishment of the principals, teachers, and Experience Corps volunteers at schools like Cook-Wissahickon and Taylor—threatens to sweep away some of the good with the bad.

A broad generational issue raises another question about the future of Experience Corps and programs like it. The seniors who volunteer now are mostly part of a World War II generation that has consistently demonstrated a commitment to service, to "giving something back," in the words so many of the volunteers use when asked why they give three days a week to the program. Will the next generation of seniors show the same spirit? In *Bowling Alone,* Putnam marshals evidence that the postwar baby boom generation does not share that ethic of service to anything like the same degree. The subtitle of Marc Freedman's *Prime Time—How Baby Boomers Will Revolutionize Retirement and Transform America*—is, so far, a hope rather than an observable fact. So the question of whether that generation will also want to give something back remains to be answered. One of the points of Freedman's book is that we lack effective mechanisms for connecting retirees who want to do valuable work with the work that needs to be done. He believes that Experience Corps and programs like it can provide an infrastructure for service that will encourage participation and make available meaningful opportunities to contribute. And the sheer size of the baby boom generation means that participation by even a significant minority would translate into an unprecedented flood of volunteers.

How these issues and pressures will play out over time cannot be predicted; the future scope and shape of Experience Corps are unknown, and the question of whether it will inspire similar programs or even the spontaneous initiatives in schools and communities that Tietze describes cannot be answered now. In the meantime, though, more than a hundred Experience Corps volunteers spend three days a week in a dozen Philadelphia schools, helping more than six hundred students to read and do math, as well as teaching them about kindness, commitment, connection, and the world that made their world. In more than a dozen other Experience Corps cities, seniors sit with the children they tutor, listening, talking, encouraging—reliable, patient, engaged, enjoying themselves. Rosemary Cataldi of Cook-Wissahickon still marvels at their dedication. "It may be terrible weather, it may be snowing," she says, "but you look out in the morning and see them coming up the steps of the school, some with canes, one with a walker, to be with the children."

CHAPTER 10

{ *Everywhere, U.S.A.* }

UPS
Diversity and Cohesion

In the mid-1960s, the United Parcel Service was overwhelmingly an organization of white males, many of them Irish Catholic, many with a background in the military. Aspects of the company parallel military behaviors and values: not only the brown uniforms worn by all UPS drivers, but careful training in standard operating procedures and a culture of teamwork and loyalty. (Loyalty has been such a fundamental UPS value that, for many years, no one who left the company for any reason would ever be hired back. Even a student sorting packages part-time at night to finance a college education was disqualified from future employment if he gave up that job.) As in the military, people who succeeded at UPS rose through the ranks, proving themselves as package handlers or drivers before they moved into management positions. Leaders of the company were UPS lifers, with twenty or thirty or more years of experience in the organization behind them, usually acquired in various jobs at numerous facilities around the country. Though geographically dispersed, the managers of the firm were remarkably homogeneous and close-knit, with extensive networks of acquaintances among people who had worked together in the course of careers that spanned more than a quarter of a century.

In the summer of 1965, the Watts neighborhood of Los Angeles erupted in riots and Title VII of the Civil Rights Act, prohibiting employment discrimination based on race, color, national origin, religion, or

sex, went into effect. Walter Hooke believes UPS hired him as East Region personnel manager at about that time specifically to help the company address the requirements of Title VII and the challenges of social
turmoil in the 1960s. The assassination of Martin Luther King, Jr., on
April 4, 1968, would spark riots in cities across the country. The black
power and antiwar movements, hippies, the sexual revolution, and the
drug subculture attested to a divided populace contending over values,
justice, politics, and different ideas of what being an American meant, or
should mean.

It is easy to imagine UPS responding to that stew of unrest and apparent instability—so unlike its own culture—by trying to turn inward, pro-
tecting itself by taking even greater care to hire only "people like us,"
resisting legal and social pressures to change. Instead, along with other
diversity efforts it made, the company accepted Hooke's plan to launch a
community internship program that would put managers in social service programs in America's turbulent cities for six months at a time.
Hooke convinced company leaders that the only way to understand people who, they believed, would be future employees and future customers
was to engage them and their problems.[1] He pointed out that UPS package cars (as the chocolate-brown delivery trucks are called internally)
had not run in Cleveland, Los Angeles, Baltimore, and Washington during riots there: what had happened in the cities directly affected the
company's ability to do its work. Ignoring people and problems was bad
for business, he argued.

UPS has been and remains a no-nonsense, results-oriented company,
with a fervent emphasis on efficiency and focused hard work. At the
same time, it maintains a practice of service to the community that
goes back to cofounder James E. Casey, who set up the Annie E. Casey
Foundation, one of several public services established by his family and
the company. For many years now, a highlight of the annual senior managers' meeting has been the presentation of the Jim Casey Community
Service Award to the UPS worker—as often as not a part-time package
handler—who has made the greatest volunteer contribution to the

community. So a combination of practical and ethical considerations supported the internship idea. The first internships were set up in Philadelphia and at the Henry Street Settlement in New York City.

More than thirty years later, the program is still in operation. Program sites have included Pittsburgh; Oakland, California; and Montgomery, Alabama. Today, selected UPS managers take part in community internship programs in Chicago; New York; Chattanooga, Tennessee; and McAllen, Texas. They live and do community work in those places for four weeks, not six months, but the aim is the same: to learn about the lives of potential UPS employees and customers by being there, listening to people speak for themselves, and working with the programs and agencies that support them, and, in the process, to become aware of life issues that probably affect some of the people they currently supervise. Although the "alumni" of this program constitute only a fraction of all UPS managers, many of them (such as Lea N. Soupata, senior vice president for human resources and a member of the UPS board of directors) now hold key corporate positions. The fact that busy, up-and-coming managers are often assigned to the program indicates the importance of equal opportunity and cross-cultural understanding within the firm. Through their internship work these managers contribute to the communities, but the main target of the program is the managers themselves; its central purpose is to give them experience and understanding that will make them better managers in a diverse company.

If America's social-capital deficit is to be addressed, it is hard to imagine how that can be done without carefully considering the links between the workplace and community. At the beginning of the twenty-first century more Americans are working outside the home than ever before. Some evidence suggests that they are spending longer there, as well, although experts disagree about the trends in work hours.[2] The issue of social capital and work has two facets:

· Work can affect social capital *outside* the workplace (as, for example, in corporate-sponsored volunteering or workplace flexibility that enables employees to reconcile their professional obligations with their family and community obligations).

· Work can affect social capital *inside* the workplace (as, for example, in the ways office architecture or supervisory practices affect relations among coworkers).

The UPS community internships illustrate the former, but UPS is hardly the only company in America to provide opportunities for community service. UPS is, in fact, an even more interesting story because of the role of social capital within the workplace itself.

We picked UPS, not Ben & Jerry's, because it is a very large, profitable firm in a highly competitive global industry. UPS does not represent "boutique capitalism," and it is not a cushy place to work. Although we have not done a scientific survey, we believe that UPS has pursued a more social capital–intensive strategy than many comparable firms. UPS management has followed this strategy not out of altruism, but because of a hard-nosed business calculation that it is a good way to make a profit, just as HUCTW builds community as a good way to organize a union and Saddleback builds community as a good way to save souls.

Diversity and Cohesion

UPS in 2002 looks very different from the all-male, all-white company it was in the 1960s. African Americans, Hispanics, Asian-Pacific Americans, and other minorities now account for more than one third of the firm's employees. Minorities hold 27 percent of managerial positions. Women are 21 percent of the UPS workforce in the United States. Women constitute 27 percent of management and 25 percent of supervisory personnel. In 2002, UPS ranked twenty-fifth among *Fortune* magazine's "50 Best Companies for Minorities," the fourth consecutive year it appeared on the list. DiversityInc.com ranked UPS third in its list of top ten companies for diversity in 2001.

UPS's culture of hard work, cooperation, connection, and loyalty remains surprisingly similar to what it was thirty years ago, despite changes in the wider culture, expansion to new business and therefore employees with new skills—IT (information technology) professionals and air freight pilots, for instance—and increasing diversity. But our discussion of the company's cohesive culture and, we believe, relatively high level of organizational social capital needs to be placed in a cautionary context.

First, no dispersed organization of nearly four hundred thousand people can be all one thing. The experience of individuals and groups will necessarily vary. At UPS as elsewhere, there are good managers and bad, people who like their jobs and people who do not. It would be easier to write about social capital at any one of a number of small, "friendly" companies, but UPS is interesting precisely because it is a large firm in a highly competitive industry that has survived and maintained its strong culture for almost a hundred years.

The social-capital landscape at UPS is further complicated by the fact that the company includes three fairly distinct groups of workers. UPS depends on a large number of unionized part-time workers to sort and load packages in its many hubs and centers. UPS drivers also are unionized—and we will say more about the Teamsters and UPS later. Although many current managers have been drivers or package handlers, they have moved into work that is different from what their unionized fellow employees do. The turnover rate among managers is less than 2 percent; among part-time package handlers it is as high as 50 percent or more, depending on location. Pay for part-time work at UPS is no longer dramatically higher than for almost any other part-time employment, as it once was, although part-timers do get fully paid health care and pensions—rare benefits in part-time work.

It is possible to ask, though, whether UPS is one company or two—or even three. To an unexpected degree, it seems to be one company and one (complex) culture. To begin with, the work brings package handlers, drivers, and managers together. UPS's core work of sorting and delivering packages is grueling, more demanding physically than an outsider can imagine. Completing those tasks is a daily challenge that can be met only when people cooperate. Always fighting the clock, sometimes fighting the weather, UPSers share the daily drama of getting a tough job done. Even drivers, who spend most of their time on the road alone, depend on the package handlers who load their vehicles: a poorly loaded package car makes their work impossible.

Tales of cooperation are part of the company's folklore. The Christmas holidays provide prime examples of workers banding together to sort and load impossible volumes of packages, including instances of senior managers helping out at the conveyor belts when there was no other way to get the job done. Drivers describe making their deliveries when bad weather kept FedEx and Airborne Express off the roads. Experienced drivers vividly recall their first days on the job, when the workload seemed not just difficult but nearly impossible. Ken Black, who has been driving a package car in the Greensboro, North Carolina, area for more than two decades, says that the best advice he got from veterans when he started was "Don't quit at the end of the day, wait until the next morning." They knew he would be tempted to give up, as they had been. Even with that advice, Black says, his first day of making solo deliveries, a Friday, was almost his last: "I got lost; at nine-thirty at night I was still trying to deliver packages. I got back to the center so late, there was nobody there to tell I was quitting." Over the weekend, Black recovered and drove the route on his own. Monday went a little better, and twenty-two years later he is still at it.

The very difficulty of the work draws people together. Being able to "hack it," showing the strength and persistence the work demands day after day, defines what it means to be "a real UPSer." Displaying those qualities generally trumps ethnicity or background when it comes to gaining acceptance or respect.

The focus on difficult work and the clarity about what it requires have helped this widely dispersed global company of 370,000 maintain its culture and sense of cohesion over decades of growth and change. There are other sources of unity, some of them visible and symbolic. Like any uniform, the brown uniform worn by every driver represents membership in a collective enterprise, commonality over individuality. The shared, explicit standards and practices that define many jobs at UPS also contribute to unity. All drivers go through the same extensive training to learn the "340 methods"—detailed standard techniques designed to ensure safe, prompt deliveries.

A number of less tangible factors contribute to the connectedness and coherence of the UPS culture—to its social capital. Many of them are the same as the important sources of social connection in other organizations we have looked at that, in most ways, seem very different from this one: Valley Interfaith and HUCTW are two examples. Like them, UPS is rich in conversation and storytelling. Like them, it devotes much effort to finding and developing leadership ability in its members. To a remarkable extent in a company characterized by standard practices, it allows and encourages decision making at all levels. As Valley Interfaith and HUCTW exemplify relational organization, UPS exemplifies relational work. As Ernie Cortés says, "The answer is relationships."

For a large, global company that values efficiency almost to the point of obsession, UPS is surprisingly hospitable to face-to-face conversation. Every morning, in every UPS hub and center, drivers gather for a brief prework communication meeting, or PCM, before they go out on the road. Every day, all around the country, drivers meet at lunchtime in parks and parking lots to talk, mixing social conversation with work: veterans help newcomers find obscure addresses or solve other problems; the drivers exchange missorted packages or balance their remaining loads to make sure everything gets delivered on time.[3] Hub and center managers are out on the floor, talking with the people they supervise. (Managers who hide in their offices are noted and criticized.) District and regional managers spend much of their time traveling to work sites in their areas of responsibility. Being there, shaking people's hands, asking them about their work, and talking directly to them about company policies and expectations is the norm. Paul Funari says that he brings together the staffs he manages in Maryland and Atlanta every month so that they can have ongoing direct contact. One senior manager remarks, "We are not a memo kind of company," and former CEO Jim Kelly says, "I don't even know the phone numbers of the people on our management committee because I never pick up the phone if they're in the office. We just walk into each other's offices when we need to talk."[4]

Like other large companies, UPS uses e-mail to distribute data and information, and it tracks package movements electronically, but, unlike many firms, it does not see electronic (or even phone) communication as a substitute for face-to-face contact. It does not go in for virtual teams, which many organizations have embraced in the name of speed and economy. (Funari's monthly meetings would be considered an unnecessary expense in many large companies today. Those companies would opt for conference calls instead.) But building and maintaining the trusting relationships on which the company depends require more direct connection.

A lot of the conversation takes the form of storytelling. Some of the stories are formalized. At Jim Casey Night at the annual senior managers' meeting, current leaders recall and discuss aspects of the founder's work and the values inherent in them. Veteran drivers recount tales of their early difficulties to encourage newcomers and to communicate some of the tricks of the trade. They also recall the veterans who shared stories with them when they were new: the tales, for instance, of winter deliveries in rural Wisconsin that include tips for preventing ice from forming on the steering wheel and how you are likely to find your farmer-customers at different places, depending on the weather. Longtime managers tell stories of their own experiences as package handlers or drivers twenty or more years earlier. It is a way of creating a connection with people currently doing the work by building credibility: managers demonstrate that they know what the job is like.

Valley Interfaith and HUCTW build strong relationships in part by putting decision making in the hands of members and by developing leaders from among their memberships. In addition to believing that members know the most about their own needs and problems, the professional organizers recognize the role genuine participation and shared power play in relationships of trust; just giving marching orders to people is unlikely to create commitment and connection.

UPS seems an unlikely environment for encouraging employee decision making. The company's unambiguous aims and its standard practices seem to leave little room for autonomy or even choice. The "340 methods," for instance, spell out drivers' actions in extraordinary detail, even instructing them to insert the key in the ignition with the right hand while fastening the seat belt with the left to save a second or two of time. But on larger issues and within the framework of these standard techniques, the drivers decide how best to get their work done. So when a major customer in the Boston area requests an earlier pickup and delivery time, the center manager asks the driver how he thinks he might provide the requested service and still serve his other customers. Similarly, part-time package sorters decide when they should leave their posts to help a coworker who is falling behind; they do not need management permission. In a way, having clear norms and goals frees up people at all levels to make decisions consistent with accomplishing their tasks. A driver comments, "I'm not going to call my supervisor to ask if I should go back to pick up a package later in the day. I already know what he'll say."

UPS is no democracy, but trusting the people who do the work to make the decisions necessary to get it done has been part of the company's culture for a long time. In 1956, long before business thinkers began talking about empowerment and distributed decision making, then-CEO George D. Smith said:

> It should be noted that it is considered desirable to have authority for decisions and actions as far down the line as possible. This is decentralization of authority in contrast to autocratic, centralized big-boss control. In this way, decisions should be more in keeping with the needs of the job, which have a better chance of being known where and when the needs occur.[5]

Leadership development—providing opportunities for people to advance within the company—is a key goal. Like Valley Interfaith organizers, who continually seek new leadership talent, UPS managers are on the lookout for the hourly workers who get the respect and attention of their peers and may make good future managers. Promotion from within remains the norm. The overwhelming majority of the senior managers who attend the annual management meeting have been with UPS more than twenty years. The annual Employee Relations Index survey, taken voluntarily by more than 85 percent of employees, focuses on questions of opportunity and recognition: Is good work recognized? Are managers open to new ideas? Are opportunities for advancement available? Managers are required to address problems indicated by survey responses immediately.

In recent years, business journals have announced that loyalty is dead, that each employee should think of himself as a "company of one," developing critical skills that will allow him to jump from organization to organization whenever a better offer comes along or when he loses his job. The widespread firing of employees that many organizations consider the first step to lower costs and increase profits—the dreaded downsizing—lends some credence to the death-of-loyalty idea. Although UPS has temporarily laid off workers when its volume of work dipped, it has always hired them back, often within days, usually within weeks. It fires employees only if it judges that they are not performing adequately, never for the purpose of shrinking the workforce or (as is the case with some organizations that practice "rank and yank") firing the lowest-rated 10 percent of workers every year, using fear to keep employees up to snuff. UPS recognizes the mutuality of loyalty—you have to give it to get it—and eschews the downsizing and devil-take-the-hindmost firing policies that damage connection, disrupting networks of relationships. The expectation that employees (with the exception of most part-time package handlers) will make UPS their lifetime career and that their commitment to the company will be rewarded by the company's commitment to them is the foundation of the organization's social capital.

UPS, the Teamsters Union, and the "Occupational Community"

Three features of employment practices at UPS have had a profound effect on patterns of social capital within the firm. First, Jim Casey invited unionization by the International Brotherhood of Teamsters very early in the firm's history. We'll explore the implications of that fact shortly.

Second, as we noted earlier, UPS has what labor economists term a strong "internal labor market." That is, jobs (including the top jobs) are filled mostly from within. This type of personnel policy typically leads to low turnover and high worker loyalty, and that appears to be true of full-time employees at UPS. It is the opposite of the disposable-employee philosophy that became popular in some American businesses in the 1980s and 1990s. Unlike its major competitors', UPS's wages are relatively high (not unrelated to the fact that the firm is unionized). All these conditions have produced what is sometimes termed an "occupational community," that is, relatively dense and cooperative connections among the employees. Although this sort of workplace was once common in American industry, it is now much rarer, at least among blue-collar workers.

Linda Kaboolian, a labor relations expert who has followed UPS and the Teamsters for many years, reports of UPS that "employee groups and union locals are very active in civic life—there is a real occupational community among UPS workers. Historically, there has been more union democracy and less corruption in UPS locals than in other parts of the Teamsters. I attribute these virtues to the existence of the occupational community."[6]

Third, nearly half of the UPS workforce is part-timers, and they are not nearly as integrated into the occupational community as full-timers. The part-timers bear the brunt of the seasonal nature of this work for the full-time employees, who aren't laid off during slack times. Turnover among part-timers is much higher, and their loyalty to the firm is probably lower. Even though internal surveys of workers suggest that UPS has engendered more worker loyalty than most other major employers of similarly skilled workers in America today, the distribution of opinion tends to be bimodal, with a significant number of discontented employees. We don't know for sure that those discontented people are disproportionately part-timers, but that seems likely. There are, to be sure, important exceptions to this general picture, since some part-timers are quite happy with their positions and some full-timers are disenchanted. In general, however, UPS seems to represent a dual-labor-market firm, with social capital much higher among the full-time "lifers." While some UPS policies do foster social capital, not everything that UPS management does contributes to social capital. Some of its policies (like this dual labor market of part-timers and full-timers) have the effect of undermining the occupational community in certain respects.

Discussion of loyalty and cooperation among employees of UPS inevitably raises the question of the 1997 Teamsters strike. Drivers and package handlers struck in part to demand that UPS convert more part-time jobs to full time. The fifteen-day strike cost the company $750 million in lost business, and it deeply troubled managers.[7] It was the first nationwide Teamsters strike against UPS in eighty years of unionized labor at the company. Chief of human resources Lea Soupata has described it as an "aberration" in the relationship between the company and its unionized employees.[8]

That is true in one sense, given the long history of agreements arrived at without walkouts—a very different history from that of, say, the West Coast docks, where strikes have been a regular and bitter part of the relationship between management and labor. But the proportion of part-time jobs and the compensation for those jobs are real issues. Kaboolian suggests that a strong union can help enforce a "moral economy" through its collective bargaining for wages and benefits, and its mechanisms to resolve disputes over discipline and job assignments. In effect, the union provides a counterweight to the intense competitive pressures that would otherwise tend to keep wages low.

In the summer of 2002, UPS and the Teamsters agreed on a new contract more than two weeks before the contract that had ended the 1997 strike expired. The new, six-year contract also addressed the issue of part-time work, including an agreement to convert ten thousand part-time jobs to full time and to raise the wages of part-time employees six dollars an hour over the life of the contract, an increase that is a dollar higher than that for full-time workers.[9] Having experienced one costly strike, UPS undoubtedly wanted to avoid a similar disruption of its business, but the successful negotiations this time also reflected a desire to improve and maintain relationships with hourly workers and probably a recognition that significantly higher wages for part-time workers must be part of effectively addressing the issue of high turnover.

Employee-Run Committees

Many of these issues—the struggle to develop a stable and satisfied part-time workforce and the sources of social cohesion we have discussed (conversation, distributed decision making, leadership development)—come together in the employee-led committees on health and safety and employee retention. Tested first in a pilot program in Maine in 1997, a "Comprehensive Health and Safety Process" has put the core of the company's health and safety efforts into the hands of the employees. Safety committees before that time were management driven and not nearly as effective as the new process is proving to be. The new process establishes committees cochaired by an hourly worker, who devotes all of his or her work time to health and safety issues, and a manager. Cochaired employee retention committees are similarly structured. The committees at the UPS hub in Greensboro, North Carolina, one of the largest in the United States, have been especially successful.

The Greensboro hub is a large, low brick building surrounded by acres of asphalt where several dozen gray tractor-trailers with "United Parcel Service" printed on the side are parked. The building's wide doors and rows of loading docks suggest its function as a sorting and distribution center for some of the thirteen million packages and documents UPS delivers daily. Inside are chutes and conveyor belts, trains of wagons hitched to motorized carts for hauling heavy or irregular packages, and broad expanses of open floor where the familiar brown package cars will line up to be loaded and unloaded.

Because Greensboro is a hub, the tractor-trailers ("feeders," in company parlance) bring packages here for sorting and loading onto other feeders, which carry them to smaller UPS centers, where they will be transferred to the package cars and delivered to customers. (Packages with Greensboro-area addresses are loaded on package cars here for local delivery. By 8:30 A.M., the package cars are ready to go, about twenty of them lined up inches apart, backed against the conveyor belt that carries the packages to the vehicles.)

The hub also handles outgoing traffic: the packages drivers pick up as they make their deliveries are unloaded and sorted when they return at the end of the day and loaded on feeders for distribution to other parts of the country. Every day more than four hundred thousand items enter and leave the Greensboro hub, millions of pounds of computers, car parts, mail-order clothing, documents, sports equipment, and the myriad other items that people and companies ship one another via UPS.

Sorting, loading, and delivering all that merchandise is demanding and potentially dangerous work. Five shifts of part-time workers sort and load packages here, four hours per shift. Some members of the "preload" crew, which loads package cars in the early morning hours, wear T-shirts that say, "It's not just work, it's a workout" or "Body by UPS." Their job demands physical strength and endurance and a fair measure of experience and judgment to keep up with the flow of packages, organize the package car loads to make drivers' work easier, and deal with the hazards of the job: especially heavy packages, items with sharp edges, moving conveyor belts, occasional leaks of hazardous materials from their shipping containers.

The drivers' work is demanding and potentially dangerous, too. Drivers face the possibility of accidents on the road, as well as strains and bruises from carrying packages. Greensboro drivers have their own health and safety committee.

The cochaired health-and-safety committees and the similarly structured cochaired employee-retention committees embody two basic convictions: that the people who understand the work best are the ones who do it, and that people usually respond best to help and advice from their peers. As Kisha Boyd, hourly cochair of the noonday shift employee-retention committee, says, "Management are on the outside looking in. We're on the inside." Even though many managers have risen through the ranks and once did similar work, they have been away from it too long to be sufficiently credible as peers, as much as that past experience may create at least a small patch of common ground. At committee meetings, typically held every two weeks, the management cochair acts as a resource who can take responsibility for issues that require some sort of management approval or intervention. The hourly-worker cochair runs the meeting, and most other committee members are hourly workers.

At an employee-retention committee meeting for the twilight shift in July 2002, hourly-worker cochair Katie Harris runs through a brief list of issues. She notes that not all full-time supervisors have been talking to new hires at least once a day, as they are required to do. Kevin Hunter, the management cochair, says he will talk to the supervisors and make sure they comply. Harris reminds hourly-worker committee members of their responsibility to introduce themselves to every new worker. "Unload with them when you talk to them," she says, "so they won't be backed up." She reports on the reasons for recent turnovers: one person who left had gotten a full-time job elsewhere; another had never consistently shown up for work, and efforts to reach him have failed.

Each committee member talks about a new hire he or she has responsibility for, describing how well the person is handling the work and noting any apparent problems and how the committee members might help. During the open discussion at the end of the carefully organized meeting, the committee discusses why one group has managed to retain all of its people so far this year. A member who knows the group especially well says, "Their supervisor is a real people person. And they're a good team; they help each other. When someone falls behind, the hourly beside him will flow down to help. It's a home away from home for a lot of them."

A meeting of the noonday-shift retention committee the next day follows a similar pattern. A report that one worker has lost his usual ride to work leads to a decision to approach others who live in the same area to see if one of them can provide transportation. Hourly-worker cochair Kisha Boyd reminds committee members to introduce new hires to "the whole belt"—all of the people working together in one area. She herself works alongside each new hire for an hour. Employee cochairs of health-and-safety or employee-retention committees do not entirely give up the physical labor of sorting and loading. Sometimes they will climb on the back of a package car to demonstrate a safer way of working or will work alongside an employee while they talk. In addition to keeping the work flowing, sharing the job demonstrates more powerfully than any words that they are peers who genuinely understand what they are talking about.

Alphonso Becote, the hourly-worker cochair of the noonday health-and-safety committee, attends the retention meeting. Health-and-safety and employee-retention cochairs regularly attend each other's meetings, in part because the two issues are so closely related. Inexperienced workers are more likely to be injured than experienced ones. At the Greensboro hub, 60 percent of injuries occur among employees who have less than six months of experience.[10]

Becote has been a part-time worker at Greensboro for more than eight years. The day before, he had gone to the hospital with a man who suffered an asthma attack during the noonday shift. He reports to the group on the man's progress. Becote spends most of his time on the hub floor, looking for safety problems and talking to workers, praising them for safe work as well as pointing out errors and demonstrating the right procedure himself. He encourages workers to watch out for one another's safety so that, for instance, when one tries to pick up a hundred-pound package, a coworker will remind him to ask for help. Becote also works on analyses to determine the causes of accidents, though as of the summer of 2002 his shift had gone the whole year without a single injury serious enough to result in lost work time.

Becote sees himself as a bridge between hourly workers and management. He emphasizes the importance of putting safety in the hands of the people who do the work. Even standard advice about how to lift packages or wearing proper footwear gains credibility by coming from people who are in the trenches with you. And some issues evident to the package handlers themselves are invisible to outsiders. For instance, only experience can show how tiring it is to stand on a metal grate for four hours while sorting packages and how fatigue makes errors and accidents more likely. The hourly cochairs pushed for a change because they understood a problem that hub designers did not anticipate. They came up with a cheap, effective solution: to use worn rubber conveyor belts as floor padding, rather than throw them away. Similarly, drivers' health-and-safety committee members understood exactly where in their vehicles they were most likely to slip and where strips of nonskid material would do the most good. The way these committees work expresses the same values and beliefs that motivate the community internships: that you have to be there doing the work yourself to understand it; that you can help people effectively only when you build a relationship with them.

Statistically, these worker-run committees have proven their value in Greensboro. Accident rates there have dropped year by year from eighty-one accidents per 200,000 work hours in 1996, just before the cochaired committees formed, to six per 200,000 hours in 2002. Several shifts had no accidents at all in 2002: this despite the potential hazards of the work and the fact that reportable accidents include sprains and cuts, not just accidents that require hospitalization or other serious medical attention.

Retention rates among part-time workers have improved, too, from turnover of almost 50 percent in 2001 to less than 30 percent through June of 2002, though it is hard to judge how much that improvement is due to the employee-retention committees' work. Their efforts to stay in contact with all new employees and help them solve personal problems that prevent them from coming to work probably contributed to the drop, but the economic downturn beginning toward the end of 2001 may have been more important. With fewer decent jobs available, more good workers apply to UPS and fewer are tempted away by opportunities elsewhere. Retaining part-time package handlers remains a major challenge for the company. The recent union contract that raises their pay significantly over time, in combination with these retention and healthy-and-safety programs, may make an important difference.

Several longtime managers, including the regional health-and-safety manager Mike Smith and district manager Bob Severson, attend this particular noonday retention meeting. For the most part, they just listen. Smith finds some opportunities to praise the group's work. When an hourly worker who has been on the job for less than two months talks about how difficult he found the work at first and how, even now, he cannot imagine ever being as good as the more experienced workers around him, Severson, a UPSer for thirty-two years, responds by telling about his first job with the company unloading packages and how many times he banged his head carrying items out of a particular model of package car with low rear doors.

Living Up to UPS Values and Other Challenges

Sometimes UPS's policy of opportunity and talent development comes up against the hard realities of business conditions. Near the end of the noonday shift meeting in Greensboro, articulate and energetic Alphonso Becote complains to Severson that he was told when he started at UPS that he would have a shot at a full-time driver's job after four or five years. Now, after eight years of package handling and work as the hourly chair of health and safety, he still sees no sign of being considered for one of those coveted jobs. Severson tells him that no manager had the right to give him a specific timetable: there is no way to predict in advance how many driver positions will open up. He reminds Becote that the downturn in package volume after September 11, 2001, limited openings for new drivers. Other managers praise the part-time employee's work and say they would like to see him move to a full-time position. None of this is particularly satisfying; it doesn't solve the problem. On the other hand, Becote's willingness to speak plainly to the district manager is impressive, and the manager responds respectfully. No one disputes the right of a part-time employee to challenge a senior manager.

As the company has grown and to some degree diversified not just its workforce but its work—into air delivery, supply-chain management, and even financial services—some of the old absolute clarity about what defines a UPSer and how he or she works has been eroded. The need to hire people with specialized talents (pilots and software programmers, for example) has meant that promotion through the ranks is no longer universally the case, although it remains the norm. Two decades ago, longtime employees could take commonality of experience and outlook for granted. As employees without that formative experience as sorters or drivers move up through the management ranks, the character of UPS may begin to change subtly and the firm may begin to lose some of the cohesion that has characterized it for almost a century.

But UPS maintains an usual degree of connectedness and coherence in comparison with many other large corporations. Public relations manager Dan McMackin, who started as a part-time package handler more than twenty-five years ago and then worked as a driver, says that most of the people who come into the public relations department from more volatile outside firms take on the characteristics of UPS: "They start talking about 'we' instead of 'I' and about spending the rest of their careers here." While virtual work and e-mail exchange play larger and larger roles at many corporations, the culture of conversation continues to thrive at UPS. In contrast to a general corporate climate where long tenure among employees and leaders is increasingly the exception, not the rule, lifetime careers and the leadership development and loyalty they imply are still the norm here, and are considered critical to the company's success. The experience of UPS reminds us of the important values of an "occupational community" as well as the challenges of fostering it in an increasingly competitive global economy.

CHAPTER 11

{ *San Francisco, California* }

Craigslist.org
Is Virtual Community Real?

The stories in this book are varied and, in some cases, possibly surprising in what they tell of how people are building relationships—developing social capital—to accomplish a range of purposes. For the most part, though, they are stories of social connection formed in familiar ways: people who live or work in close proximity to one another meeting and talking, discovering common interests and mutual concerns. The technology of electronic connection plays, at best, a small supporting role in these cases. The Do Something Web sites offer resources to community coaches and a place for Do Something kids to report on their projects and learn what kids in other parts of the country have done, but the enthusiastic engagement of participants seems to have everything to do with local activities and little or nothing to do with cyberspace, at least in Waupun, Wisconsin. The Chicago Public Library Web site provides information about the Library and access to some of its materials, but that story is about why the Internet has not made the physical public library obsolete, as some predicted it would. Saddleback Church has a Web presence, but that institution lives in its services and small groups. Other groups we have looked at—Valley Interfaith and HUCTW are the clearest examples—ignore or eschew Internet technology entirely.

Ever since the World Wide Web caught the public imagination and began to grow in the 1990s, however, we have been hearing about the promise of online community. Some of the discussion has focused on the idea of electronic communities of interest—groups of people who may live thousands of miles apart coming together on the Web because of their common involvement in a particular subject or issue. (Support groups for victims of rare diseases and their families illustrate this sort of Net-based community.) Proponents of these communities have argued that ties of mutual interest mean more than the accident of physical proximity. Many such groups exist; whether they are communities in any but the very loosest sense of that word and whether they create new social capital, as we understand the term, are open questions.

Internet-based connections can be broadly divided into those that link you to people you already know and may have met face-to-face (such as e-mail) and those that link you to people whom you don't know and who may even be anonymous (such as chat rooms). (Of course, some uses of the Internet, such as listservs for common-interest groups, may involve a mixture of these two types.) Much of the hype about "virtual community" has revolved around the latter form of impersonal, even anonymous connection, but in terms of actual usage thus far, the former, more personal type of connection is far more common. For example, the authoritative UCLA annual survey of Internet usage found that the average user spends nearly twenty times more hours e-mailing than in chat rooms. As of 2002, "62.5 percent of all Americans send e-mail or instant messages."[1]

E-ties to people you don't know are, by definition, purely virtual, but e-ties to people whom you also know offline constitute a kind of alloy that combines the advantages of both computer-based and face-to-face connections. E-mail, instant messaging, and similar techniques join the ease, reach, and immediacy of electronic communication with the trust, sensitivity, and durability of relationships based on repeated face-to-face communication. Like the telephone, these forms of electronic communication can strengthen, broaden, and deepen existing personal ties. For example, e-mail (combined with the relative ease of tracking long-lost acquaintances through the Web's astonishing powers of information retrieval) can make it dramatically easier to renew personal ties with former schoolmates or distant family members. The UCLA survey in 2002 found that more than half of all users say that the Internet has increased the number of people with whom they stay in contact.[2] Similarly, in many parts of the world Internet entrepreneurs are seeking ways to use technology to foster greater communication within a single neighborhood. Such use of electronic communication as a supplement (not an alternative) to face-to-face communication may ultimately prove to be the most important effect of the Internet on social connectedness.

On the other hand, use of electronic means to communicate with people we already know offline, however much it permeates our lives, is not likely to produce entirely new forms of community. The more revolutionary potential of Internet technology is the possibility of creating connections among people who don't (or at least didn't) know each other offline. So in exploring the potential of the Internet for social-capital success stories, we looked especially hard for cases that seemed to promise the creation of new social ties among people who did not initially know one another.

We are in no position to judge authoritatively how much real community building and social-capital building happen on the Web. Although we looked hard for candidates for a case study of online social capital, our investigations usually turned up less solid evidence of new social capital than we had hoped. Some apparently promising sites were in decline; some turned out to be commercial ventures with a veneer of community vocabulary; most offered no clear evidence of members' building the relationships of trust and reciprocity that we understand to be central to social capital.

Obviously we cannot generalize about the vast and changing content of the World Wide Web, and we make no claim to a definitive survey. But we judged craigslist, which we examine here, the most interesting candidate for a social-capital case among the sites that came to our attention. It stands out in terms of longevity, growth, and the persistent commitment of its founder and users to the idea of a noncommercial electronic community meeting place owned and shaped by the people who post messages there. Craigslist began in San Francisco, and its San Francisco site, by far the most active of more than a dozen craigslist sites, is the one we examine. Studying craigslist will not answer all the important questions about social capital and cyberspace, but it can provide some useful insights and perspective.

www.craigslist.org

Visit the San Francisco craigslist and you find a site that most closely resembles an electronic version of a newspaper's classified ads, with listings of jobs and housing, services, activities, items wanted and for sale, and personals. There are also discussion forums on topics including the arts, computers, parenting, pets, politics, and recreation. Compared with most Web sites, it is shockingly plain. There are no banner ads, no eye-catching colors, no animations—no graphics of any kind, in fact. What you see is a plain gray background and columns of text: lists of subcategories under the basic headings of "jobs," "housing," "personals," "community," etc. Click on a subcategory ("admin/office/cust serv," for instance, one of two dozen items under "jobs") and you find a list of jobs organized by the date they were posted (seventeen new listings on September 5, 2002, in this one area). Most of the job postings are similar to what you would find in the newspaper, though more detailed, since longer items cost no more to post than short ones. Many listings of houses and apartments for rent are similar—fairly detailed, but not much different from rental listings elsewhere. So what is going on here? What gives craigslist a possible claim to community and social-capital creation?

From One Dozen Users to 1.6 Million

Craigslist started small. In 1995, Craig Newmark worked for Charles Schwab, "evangelizing the Net inside the company," he says, talking to management about the role the Internet could play in the investment brokerage business. "I saw a lot of people helping each other out on the Net," he adds. "I figured I could do that, too."[3] Initially he sent e-mail messages to a list of about a dozen friends, telling them about technology events and arts events that he thought might interest them. The list of recipients grew as his friends forwarded the messages to their friends, and the kinds and amount of information increased as well. Within the year, Newmark replaced the e-mail list with a Web site. Job and housing leads became the core content; new categories and discussion forums were added as participation expanded, growing out of the interests of the people who used the site.

As of the spring of 2003, craigslist ranked among the 200 top Web sites in the world in terms of activity—actually 187 and climbing—with about 2.8 million unique visitors a month at its sites in nearly two dozen cities. The majority of activity occurs on the San Francisco site. But Newmark says the participation in the New York City site "took off" in 2001, and if its current growth rate continues, he expects it to equal or surpass the San Francisco site's sometime in 2004. All postings except job offers are free; those cost the posting organization seventy-five dollars for each listing. Because of their volume, the job listings generate enough revenue to support a staff of fourteen full-time employees.

The high level of activity on the San Francisco site may be one factor arguing in favor of craigslist as community or, at the very least, as deeply embedded in community. Craigslist has a presence in San Francisco. It has become a feature of the city's social landscape, something many people (especially but not exclusively those in their twenties and early thirties) use and discuss, something people who live there know about, part of the culture they share. The experience of one new user, Katherine Rose, shows how widely it is known and how closely it is identified with San Francisco. When Rose graduated from an East Coast university in the spring of 2002, she and some school friends decided to move to San Francisco. None of them had jobs lined up, but they trusted they would find work when they got there. Having grown up in the Boston area, Rose wanted the experience of living somewhere else.

She remembers, "As soon as I told people, 'I'm moving to San Francisco. I have to find an apartment,' they said, 'Have you looked on craigslist?' My mother's college roommate, who lives in Oakland, also suggested craigslist."

Once in San Francisco (she and her roommates rented a Russian Hill apartment they located through the site), Rose found that "everyone here says, 'Look at craigslist' for jobs, for furniture, for whatever you need." Many Web sites that are familiar to Internet enthusiasts seem to be invisible or unknown to the culture at large. In San Francisco, craigslist is an exception.

Then there is the fact that even in requests for housing or postings of rooms for rent, many people reveal much more about themselves on the site than we usually expect in such transactions, sharing the kinds of information we exchange when we are building a social connection with a new acquaintance. This excerpt is fairly typical:

> I am an adventurous, outdoorsy and athletic person when I am not hunkered down at my desk during the prime hours of the work day. CD's in rotation right now: Radiohead, The White Stripes, Beatles, Stones, and Coldplay. I am not a raging party guy but enjoy nights out on the weekends and good wine buzz from time to time.

as is this one:

> I am a 21 yr old student (biology major)/bartender/assistant private investigator. I take school very seriously. I enjoy going out on the weekends, or some week nights if all my homework is in place, and I usually stay out till pretty late (2-3am). I am a pretty clean person, some would consider me anal, but I don't push it upon others to clean as vigorously as I do. I just like cleaning (weird, I know).

and this:

> We like intellectuals, hippies, poets, musicians, writers, auto mechanics, gardeners, techies, yogis, and many other types of persons as well. If you

are rich and beautiful, that helps, but it is not necessary. If you are "normal," don't even bother. We like persons who can pay rent on time. We like eating healthy and organic. We like persons who have radical ideas, but who are also willing to clean the bathroom.

Personals are often many paragraphs long. Some are mini-autobiographies or short stories about failed relationships or little essays about what makes life good or horrible or the writer's hopes for the future. Craig Newmark has commented:

> Because we're not charging by the word, people can say as much as they want. And in their postings, people reveal something of themselves—and others feel a sense of connection. One woman told me that she reads our lists just for the personal stories. It's a window into what's going on around her, and it provides a sense of connection and intimacy with others. That's the common theme: What's going on around us?[4]

Newmark believes that the physical proximity of the people who visit craigslist, the fact that they all know and experience the same metropolitan area, is crucial to the sense of community it generates. Although technology commentators have often emphasized the globe-spanning potential of the World Wide Web, Newmark insists that the localness of the craigslist sites is what keeps them alive and growing and what makes it possible for people to feel a community connection online. Studies of e-mail use conducted by Barry Wellman and his colleagues at the University of Toronto support the idea of local focus rather than global reach. Their research found that a significant majority of e-mail traffic passes between people who live within thirty miles of one another.

Periodically there are craigslist parties, announced in open invitations to anyone who visits the site to get together at a restaurant or bar for a few hours on a particular night. But only a tiny proportion of craigslist users ever attend these gatherings, and Newmark does not believe that actually meeting in a group is essential to feeling part of a craigslist community. He says:

> The idea that these are people in your neighborhood is what matters, that these are people you might know or see around town, or at least have a sense of the same local considerations. The idea that people *might* be around is more important than actual face-to-face contact.

Most of the postings are locally rooted by references to the events, locations, and vocabulary of the area. Because of that, and also because most postings are tied to specific needs (for housing, jobs, companionship, help in a crisis), these electronic messages feel much more grounded in the daily life of the city and more social than, say, the entries you find on "blog" sites. (These are sites where "bloggers"—authors of Web logs—post running commentaries about their smallest experiences in often excruciating detail, frequently without any sense of where they are or who might be interested in what they have to say.) On craigslist, some messages, posted where a million people might read them, have a startling immediacy and localness:

> Looking for a lunch partner today. I'm at Market and 4th and could use some good food and conversation at about 1:00.

and:

> Anyone up for sushi tonight?

and:

> I'll be washing clothes shortly at 25th and Clement. Would anyone like to join me for a game of backgammon while the clothes spin?

On the community bulletin boards, along with people looking for ride-sharing arrangements, musicians hoping to join bands, people seeking and offering child care, and others making similar requests that you might also find in the classifieds of many newspapers, you come across people asking for advice and support on intimate matters that we usually think of as shared only among close friends:

I feel so ignorant for asking this question, but I was wondering how early you can tell if you are pregnant? My husband and I just got married three weeks ago and I feel like I am—symptoms like that time of the month, only more severe—very moody, have to pee all the time, dizzy—and I have this weird bloaty sort of feeling in my belly. I am just wondering if I am wishful thinking or if I could really tell this quickly?

and:

All this week when I tried calling my son I have been told he is not available or asleep. Last night when I called I was told by his grandfather not to call his house anymore. This has me really distraught and I am leaning on this community for some help advice & support.

In the discussion forums, the almost-real-time conversations made up of e-mail questions, responses, and comments sometimes have the character of conversation among friends who meet in a café or who have lunch together in the cafeteria at work and talk about the latest movie or some news item that has captured public attention. So, in the "parenting" forum, half a dozen participants talk about whether or not they lost their single friends after they had children. In the same forum, another group goes back and forth about what to think of the news of a baby killed by a bear in a state park: Were the parents negligent in leaving the baby outside in a carriage? Did they deserve sympathy or censure? Another thread of discussion deals with the question of whether women can have a full-time job and raise children without becoming totally exhausted, discouraged, or crazed.

These discussion are *like* conversations with friends in the local café, but of course they are different, too, and different in ways that are important to community and social capital. Written messages lack the physical expressions and gestures that are such an important part of face-to-face conversation, clarifying and deepening the meanings of the words while adding their own unspoken meaning and providing an instantaneous response to what is being said. That combination of spoken language and body language helps us understand the tone and substance of what is being communicated and also helps us judge whether we should trust the person we are speaking to, and to what degree. In face-to-face conversation, we also get signals we use to judge *our* contributions: whether we are puzzling people or making them angry, boring them or fascinating them. The rich attributes of face-to-face conversation are one key reason why members of Valley Interfaith and other IAF groups go door-to-door in their communities to talk with people directly. (The other most important reason is that the investment of time and energy in showing up at people's homes demonstrates commitment and respect.)

Lacking all of the elements of conversation except the words, the exchanges of messages in the craigslist discussion forums are more fragile than "real" conversations. Without tone and gesture as guides to meaning, readers can easily misunderstand the intent of the writers. Without the (usually) moderating influence of facing the person you are speaking to, it becomes too easy to become extreme or abusive (hence the prevalence of "flaming" in e-mail exchanges), and some of the discussion boards in fact include messages that are much harsher than you would find in most face-to-face conversations. Finally, people can leave the online discussion in an instant, maybe joining in for only a few seconds to drop a bombshell into the conversation or disappearing as soon as they get bored or read something they do not like. If part of building the trusting relationships that define social capital is sticking with the conversation, hearing one another's stories, and working toward some mutual respect and understanding, then the disembodied and volatile world of online discussion is a flawed medium for creating social capital.

Trying to Understand Web Community

To argue that the million-plus people who visit the San Francisco craigslist site every month form a "community" would, we believe, reduce that word almost to meaninglessness. The people who use craigslist simply to find a job or an apartment or those who visit the site for fifteen minutes for the voyeuristic pleasure of reading other people's personal ads can hardly be called members of a craigslist community. As our discussion of online conversation suggests, even some more actively engaged users who participate in forums about parenting or technology or politics connect with one another only in a limited and tenuous way.

Experience in the Blacksburg, Virginia, electronic community network suggests that "when you overlay an electronic community directly on top of a physical community, that creates a very powerful social pressure to be civil. If you're going to yell at somebody on the 'net, or flame them out, you may run into them at the grocery store, and they may turn out to be your neighbor."[5] Alloys of face-to-face and e-based ties can sustain social capital.

By contrast, building trust and goodwill is not easy in the largely anonymous, easy-in, easy-out, surf-by world of pure cyberspace. Craig himself clearly understands how delicate are the norms of civility, reciprocity, and trustworthiness—the social capital—that undergird his site's success. "We're trying to figure out how to run the site as a commons, yet avoid the tragedy of the commons," Craig tells reporters. "We still have a ways to go. There's always going to be something." And "the culture of trust we've built is a really big deal. We have to re-earn that every day."[6]

But there are indications even beyond the intimacy and trust of the postings we have quoted that many craigslist users *feel* connected to a community and see their participation in the site as part of their identity. Like members of other groups, they share a specialized vocabulary that separates insiders from outsiders: not only "CL" (for craigslist), but "420," (marijuana), "MC" (missed connection), and "flags" (objections to postings) as well as standard ways of advertising for roommates who will not cause a lot of fuss ("no drama"). Newmark says that one indication that craigslist was becoming more than just a bulletin board was that, much to his surprise, he started getting fan mail. Past fifty, balding, soft-spoken, he describes himself as having been one of those nerdy kids in school who wore taped-together glasses and a plastic pocket protector—an unlikely candidate for adulation. But craigslist habitués look up to him as the founder and protector of "their" site, as a central and admired personality in their community. Newmark has been invited to a number of weddings of couples who found each other through craigslist personals.

Which brings up an important point: However much craigslist may be a community itself, it unquestionably functions as a tool to create community by bringing people together, by helping runners, soccer players, readers, theater lovers, wine enthusiasts, Asian Americans, rock climbers, sports fans, and European expatriates find one another. Many hundreds of groups, clubs, and teams have been formed or populated through craigslist.

Newmark says that the WELL, an early online community, was one of the inspirations for craigslist. Created in 1985, the WELL was exhibit A in Howard Rheingold's argument in *The Virtual Community* that electronic meeting places can be genuine communities.[7] At the time Rheingold wrote about the WELL (an acronym for "Whole Earth 'Lectronic Link"), it had a lot in common with what we see today on craigslist. Localness mattered. The WELL was also based in San Francisco, and its members lived mostly in that area. Many regularly got together at "real" gatherings as well as online: at picnics and parenting groups, and at a variety of social get-togethers of people who first found one another in cyberspace. More than Newmark does with regard to craigslist, Rheingold credited these get-togethers with making the community a real one. He commented, "The WELL felt like an authentic community to me from the start because it was grounded in my everyday physical world," and he mentioned the weddings, outings, and parties he had attended.[8] The WELL had a similar range of topics and forums growing out of the interests of users (though not the housing and job lists that are a central part of craigslist). "WELLites" had their own vocabulary ("IRL," meaning "in real life," and "Thanks to everyone for your generous WELLbeams, good wishes, prayers . . .").[9] Most of all, the WELL, like craigslist, had strikingly intimate, trusting exchanges as people posted messages about relationships and medical problems, their work and their aspirations. Rheingold's strongest evidence for the WELL as a community was the exchanges he quoted.

Once considered *the* outstanding example of an online community, the WELL has seen its presence and reputation fade. Now a commercial discussion site owned by Salon Media, it has lost its localness and much of its community sense. Even aside from the important question of financing, craigslist may thrive where the WELL failed in part because of the centrality of job and housing listings on craigslist. The job listings are certainly the least personal category on the site, and housing less personal than many of the others. But these are the categories that most attract new people to craigslist, that create a mass of potential community members. Also, our observations of other social-capital-creating groups show mainly people coming together for purposes other than creating new social ties—for political action or economic advantage, for instance. Having an important aim other than simply being together or meeting new people—finding a job or a place to live—may provide a useful foundation for robust social capital.

Newmark himself attributes the WELL's decline in part to a membership mechanism that was not as free and open as he believes it could have been and in part to inattention to real human needs in other cities. "Their membership model didn't seem to be right," he says. The founders of the WELL identified free access as a goal but admitted that they could not survive without charging a fee. Certainly the current, commercial version of the WELL, with its sign-up and monthly fee required before a newcomer can join the conversation or even eavesdrop to discover whether the conversation is worth joining, does not feel like a welcoming community. The idea of paying to meet people is unsettling.

Craigslist, on the other hand, is as free and open as possible. Anyone can read all the postings and discussion threads simply by clicking on them—no need to pay, sign in, or provide any information about yourself. Posting a listing is almost as easy (with the exception of the fee-based job listings). Posters do have to give their e-mail address so that they can be sent a "self-publishing kit," but otherwise they are entirely free to create a message of any length, indicate the category it belongs in, and see it quickly posted on the site. The whole process happens without staff intervention.

This openness and ease of use must certainly contribute to the amount of traffic the site gets, but it raises another question about community. Since communities generally define themselves by both what they are and what they are not, by the norms that represent common community behavior, how can a Web site that is open to everyone, and has more than a million people at least "passing through" every month, be a community? How can it establish and maintain community norms?

Remarkably, for the most part, craigslist seems to do exactly that. Newmark says, "Norms were originally based on the idea that people should give each other a break. People have built a culture of trust on the site, managing the amount of abuse." They manage it through the mechanism of "flagging." Every posting on the site (except in the discussion forums) includes a "flag for review" feature that allows any reader to indicate that he or she thinks a particular posting should be removed: because the item is miscategorized, is "spam" (Internet junk mail), is an example of ticket scalping or other unapproved commercial scheme, or is unacceptably abusive. Until recently, craigslist staff reviewed postings that received a certain number of flags and decided whether or not to remove them. Now the process has been automated. As soon as a posting receives a set number of flags for the same reason, the site's software automatically removes it and returns it to the poster.

The system is not foolproof. Newmark says that he knows it can be abused, but generally it is not. It in fact seems to function reasonably well as an automated, community-managed system for defining and maintaining community norms of acceptable and unacceptable behavior. Disagreements exist, including objections to the removal of items that are offensive to some and not to others, but those electronic discussions sound very much like the discussions that go on in any community as it defines and refines its values. Such user-controlled social machinery is not common on the Web, but William A. Galston, in "(How) Does the Internet Affect Community? Some Speculation in Search of Evidence," suggests that collective definition of norms is a feature of many Internet groups: "Internet groups rely to an unusual degree on norms that evolve through iteration over time and are enforced through moral suasion and group disapproval of conspicuous violators . . . the medium is capable of promoting a kind of socialization and moral learning through mutual adjustment." [10]

The amount of user influence on the content of craigslist means that users have as much or more power than staff to shape the sites in various cities. Newmark says, "The sites will evolve, sometimes in unexpected ways. Over time, I'm hoping people who live in these places will set the tone." So far, the clearest differences are between sites like those of San Francisco and New York City, which have a lot of traffic, and those of Boston, Denver, Seattle, and other cities, which have much less. The first thing you notice when you look at those smaller sites is that there are dramatically fewer categories and postings. But you can also find differences between San Francisco and New York that reflect the characteristic preoccupations of people in each city. So, for instance, San Francisco has a computer forum and a "transport" forum, where you find discussions about how to keep salt air from rusting cars and comparisons of Honda and Toyota hybrid cars. The New York craigslist forum has nothing about cars (not surprisingly) or even computers, but it has a "nightlife" forum, where people ask for recommendations for dance clubs and bars, and an "eateries & cuisine" forum, where people respond to questions like "Are there any good bakeries in the Gramercy Park area?" and "Where should I take my parents to dinner when they visit?" You could almost certainly guess which city the participants live in by dipping into their discussions. The user control over norms and content that is gradually differentiating these sites from one another argues in favor of there being at least a core of genuine community at craigslist.

Newmark is deeply committed to maintaining craigslist's character and sense of user ownership. It is no surprise that a site that is among the top few hundred sites on the Web in terms of traffic would attract commercial interests. In 1999, Newmark turned down an offer for the site that would have made him a wealthy man. The buyout offers continue. Recently, he says, "I got a call from some investors who wanted to buy it, but when they heard we were publicly committed to no banner ads, they gave up." Commercialization would unquestionably change the character of the site, destroying the sense of user ownership and control and, probably, the sense of community.

With the qualifications that we have expressed here, we think that craigslist has elements of community to a surprising degree and that its community nature has a great deal to do with elements that we see in other forms of community: localness, member participation in defining the norms of the group, aims and purposes beyond that of simply being together. This example does not imply a future in which masses of people will migrate from local, traditional communities to communities of interest in cyberspace—quite the contrary—but it does suggest a role for the Internet in the mix of ways that people come to know, trust, and connect with one another. Newmark himself is relatively unconcerned about whether what happens on craigslist meets any particular definition of community or social capital:

> People started telling me that they felt connected in some kind of community sense. I used to be doctrinaire about definitions and I didn't feel it was a community site, but I eventually said, if people feel connected, it must be a community.

CHAPTER 12

{ Portland, Oregon }

Portland

A Positive Epidemic of
Civic Engagement

In February 1974, after a hard-fought struggle of more than two years, the city council of Portland, Oregon, established a new Office of Neighborhood Associations. In the ensuing years the city government recognized roughly ninety neighborhood associations, each encompassing roughly four thousand to five thousand citizens. At first glance this development seems administrative arcana of interest to only the most ardent specialist in municipal history. Yet it turns out to be one key to solving a most remarkable puzzle about civic engagement in contemporary America.

A Civic Puzzle

In the "all power to the people" era of the late 1960s and early 1970s, such experiments in neighborhood decentralization were not uncommon in urban America. To be sure, unlike most such initiatives, the Portland experiment drew on a strong local tradition of neighborhood activism, and the original draft ordinance was repeatedly amended to accommodate grassroots pressure for greater neighborhood autonomy.[1] Nevertheless, as we have discovered in analyzing a massive archive of two decades of survey evidence from Portland and the rest of America, civic activism in Portland in 1974 was virtually identical to that of other comparable metropolitan areas.[2] Portlanders in the early

1970s were no more and no less civically engaged than any other Americans.

Over the next two decades, however, a gulf steadily widened between Portland, which experienced an extraordinary civic renaissance, and the rest of the country, which slumped slowly into isolated passivity. Elsewhere in America in the 1970s and 1980s, as Putnam reported in *Bowling Alone,* public meetings emptied, local organizations atrophied, and "good-government" groups expired. In Portland, by contrast, in these same years civic activism boomed.

The two charts in Figure 1 illustrate this remarkable and steadily widening disparity between Portland and the rest of urban America. In 1974, 21 percent of Portlanders attended at least one public meeting on town or school affairs, compared to 22 percent for residents of comparably sized American cities. By the early 1990s, the figure for the rest of the country had been cut in half (11 percent), whereas the figure for Portland had risen steadily to 30–35 percent. In 1974, 4 percent of Portlanders reported that they were members of "some group interested in better government," slightly below the national figure of 5 percent. By 1994, the Portland rate had nearly tripled, while the national rate had halved.

The massively growing discrepancy between Portland and comparable metropolitan areas also applies to other forms of civic engagement. Rates of writing letters to the editor were identical in 1974 (6 percent), but by 1994 the rates were 17 percent for Portland, compared to 4 percent elsewhere. Portlanders were slightly more likely to sign petitions in the mid-1970s (50–60 percent versus 40 percent elsewhere), but by the mid-1990s, the petition gap had become huge (75 percent versus 25 percent). In the early 1970s, an identical 15–16 percent of Portlanders and their counterparts elsewhere reported that they had served as officers or committee members of some local organization in the previous twelve months. Twenty years later the figure in Portland had risen to 28 percent, compared to 7 percent elsewhere.

In sum, by many different measures civic engagement in Portland

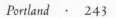

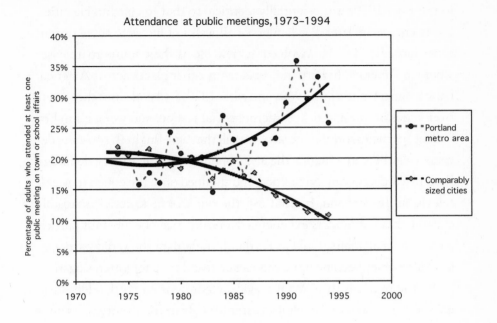

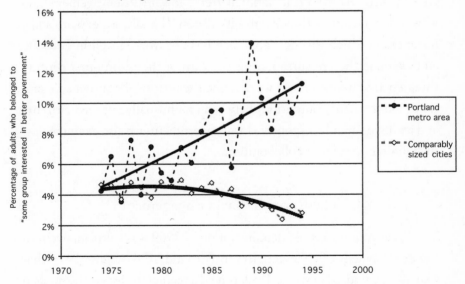

Portland's civic renaissance

in the early 1970s was essentially identical to that in comparable cities, but twenty years later, Portlanders of all walks of life were three or four times more likely to be involved in civic life as their counterparts elsewhere in America. In Portland, as in many other places across America, baby boomers in the late 1960s and early 1970s had gone into the streets over issues of war and peace, racism, social justice, and women's rights. Talk of "participatory democracy" was all the rage. But in the ensuing decades elsewhere in America the aging boomers left the streets, discarded their placards, gave up on politics, and slumped onto the couch to watch television. In Portland, by contrast, the ranks of civic activists steadily expanded as Portlanders experienced a resurgence of exuberant participation in local affairs. Only in Portland, these data show, did participatory democracy become more than a faded and then forgotten slogan.

So the puzzle is this: What magical elixir boosted Portlanders' civic engagement and social capital so astonishingly in the twenty years after 1974? In this chapter we examine the roots of Portlanders' newfound civic activism. We seek to understand how and why this metropolitan area bucked the powerful national trend toward disengagement and what it has meant to the city and its citizens. Finally, we explore some instances in which this new approach has not worked well in Portland and examine the pressures that at the turn of the twenty-first century threatened to weaken it. As we describe the history of unusual cooperation (and frequent contention) between an unusually engaged citizenry and an uncommonly responsive local government, we also examine possible limitations of that collaboration.

The Roots of Civic Engagement

The Riverfront for People demonstration of 1969 was a crucial event in the development of civic activism in Portland.[3] On August 19 of that year, three hundred or so Portlanders held a picnic/protest on the median strip of the four-lane Harbor Drive, which ran along the Willamette River at the eastern edge of downtown. They were demonstrating against a proposal to use the demolition of a large building between the Drive and Front Street as an opportunity to widen the riverside roadway. As the group's name suggests, the Riverfront for People activists wanted less highway, not more. They wanted improved and not diminished pedestrian access to the river. And they won. Two years of discussion, the completion of a bridge that provided a new traffic route, and the willingness of the head of the State Highway Commission to consider a park as an alternative to the highway led to the demolition of Harbor Drive and its replacement with Tom McCall Waterfront Park, a mile-long esplanade along the river, an early example of the river walks and waterfront parks that have been a part of urban improvement in San Antonio, Texas; Providence, Rhode Island; and other cities.

Thirty years later, the park remains one of the attractions of an appealing, "user-friendly" downtown. On a Saturday in mid-September 2002, visitors and locals enjoying an unusual persistence of warm, sunny weather sat on its benches and lawns reading (Portlanders spend an average of 37 percent more money on reading matter than other Americans, another interesting statistical anomaly) or strolled along the riverbank, where they can sit in a café or board a boat for a river cruise.[4] At the northern end of the park, small crowds of people relaxed on grassy areas just across from Portland's Saturday Market, a crafts fair that has been held every week for almost as long as the park has existed. The booths of local craftspeople were set up under the Burnside Bridge, protection from the region's famously wet weather.

Demonstrations favoring parks and people over highways and the grand designs of urban planners were not uncommon elsewhere in the 1960s, of course. Jane Jacobs's *The Death and Life of Great American Cities*, published in 1961, tells the story of citizen activists in Manhattan who headed off plans to extend Fifth Avenue through Washington Square Park. Such protests, however, did not generally launch an era of civic engagement. But in Portland, the Riverfront for People group—and its success—signaled the start of growing activism and the beginning of an unusual push-and-pull between government and citizens that has helped shape the Portland metropolitan area and has made activism the norm here, part of how the city works, and an explicit, important part of decision-making processes.

"Process" is a word you hear frequently when Portlanders talk about life in their city. Sometimes it carries a certain tone of exasperation, because of the laborious, lengthy efforts required to get things done and the seemingly endless consultations with neighborhood associations and interest groups, including numerous "Friends of" organizations (Friends of Arnold Creek, Friends of Trees, Friends of the Performing Arts Center, and the 1000 Friends of Oregon are only a few examples). Michael Powell, owner of the famous Powell's Books downtown, has praised the process for creating, for instance, an attractive and efficient light-rail system for the region, but he expresses frustration that, because of the process, he had to go through a prolonged and ultimately futile struggle to make minor changes to the façade of his store. Occasionally, "process" has an edge of cynicism, a suggestion that it is sometimes mere window dressing, the appearance of citizen influence without the reality. (We will look at a couple of sources of that cynicism.) Often, though, the word is spoken with pride. "Process" here means participation, a collaborative endeavor to make (or keep) Portland a livable city. Carl Abbott, urban analyst and author of *Greater Portland,* says people here "trust government because they *are* government. Portland area politics is open to wide participation."[5]

The activist values and energy that surfaced in the Riverfront for People demonstration were reflected and reinforced by dramatic changes in Portland's government in the early 1970s. Citing historian E. Kimbark MacColl, Abbott notes that "there was only a 30 percent overlap between lists of the most powerful Portlanders as published in 1969 in the *Labor Press* and the most powerful Oregonians as published in 1975 in the *Oregon Times.* Between 1969 and 1973, the average age on Portland City Council dropped by fifteen years. . . ."[6]

Emblematic of change—and its local champion—was Neil Goldschmidt, Portland's mayor from 1973 to 1979. A relative newcomer to

Portland then (having moved to the city in 1967), he was elected to the city council in 1970. Two years later he was elected mayor, becoming the youngest mayor of a major U.S. city at age thirty-two.

Goldschmidt's administration focused on public transportation, neighborhoods, and a comprehensive approach to downtown revitalization and preservation. Notably, for our purposes, it also developed structures that not only supported citizen activism but embedded it in the government's decision-making processes. The most dramatic step in that direction was the creation of the Office of Neighborhood Associations, in 1974. The ordinance that established the office spelled out the direct, active role of the citizen groups in the process of planning and carrying out government policy:

> Any neighborhood association shall be eligible to recommend an action, a policy, or a comprehensive plan to the city and to any city agency on any matter affecting livability of the neighborhood, including, but not limited to, land use, zoning, housing, community facilities, human resources, social and recreational programs, traffic and transportation, environmental quality, open space and parks.[7]

The office provided technical training and expertise to members of neighborhood associations, along with modest funds for mailings and newsletters. Most important, it legitimized activism and built it into the official life of the city. Ethan Seltzer of Portland State University notes that neighborhood associations have existed in the Portland area since the 1940s and before. The first neighborhood groups, known as neighborhood councils, formed in the 1930s, local products of a national movement backed by Community Chests of America. So Goldschmidt's actions recognized rather than created the institution of the neighborhood association and perhaps in some sense made a virtue of necessity. In his doctoral thesis, "The Transformation of Civic Institutions and Practices in Portland, Oregon, 1960–1999," Steven Johnson points out that federal laws regarding the Economic Opportunities and Model Cities funding that Portland drew on in the 1970s required citizen participation.[8] But the city's unusual engagement with citizens' groups and the fact that citizen participation is a central feature of how government works have helped civic engagement flourish.

At its best, the civic life of Portland in the past three decades offers examples of the government genuinely responding to its citizens' calls for participation and that responsiveness encouraging further participation, especially in the form of flourishing citizen action groups. As in the case of the Dudley Street Neighborhood Initiative, the willingness of those in power to open the door to citizen influence rather than protect their "turf" is a critical element of the social-capital story.

As Johnson's work documents, the same waning in the activity and influence of traditional civic organizations (fraternal organizations, women's groups, and other long-established groups) occurred in Portland as in other parts of the country (as documented in *Bowling Alone*). But that falling off has not meant an overall decrease in civic engagement, as it has elsewhere, because of the dramatic growth of neighborhood associations and other local advocacy groups. Johnson notes an increase in advocacy groups from 31 in 1960 to 184 in the early 1970s; 65 of them were new neighborhood associations. The number of neighborhood associations and citizens' groups continued to grow through the decade and after. In 1985, Portland had 222 advocacy groups; in 1999, 402.

Especially in the 1970s and early 1980s, neighborhood associations and other activist groups worked with the government to realize a vision of a city enhanced by attractive public spaces and good public transportation, and by policies that would limit growth to preserve the environment and the quality of life of Portlanders. When Portland officials and residents defeated plans for the Mount Hood Freeway, which would have emasculated neighborhoods in East Portland as well as the eastern suburbs, the TriMet, Portland's regional transportation organization, put the money instead into a light-rail system, which now connects downtown with the parks and residential areas in the hills to the west and the city of Gresham and the airport to the east. Those years also saw the development of Pioneer Courthouse Square, a public meeting and performance space in the center of downtown.

The process of civic renewal was neither as linear nor as orderly and consensual as hindsight suggests. Throughout the 1970s and 1980s, civic activists intervened continually, mobilizing their neighbors behind an evolving agenda. Mayor Goldschmidt initially accepted the Mount Hood Freeway, and not a single local official opposed the proposed Western Bypass until STOP, led by Meeky Blizzard, and 1000 Friends of Oregon rallied citizen protest. Housing affordability and urban decay became a part of the regional planning discussion only through the strenuous efforts of 1000 Friends of Oregon and the Coalition for a Livable Future. Nor was this always a polite and gentle conversation. 1000 Friends of Oregon and its allies were pilloried when they pushed for antisnob zoning in the 1970s. In recent years a coalition of the Oregon League of Conservation Voters, 1000 Friends of Oregon, and labor unions has fought hard to defeat ballot challenges from champions of property rights. Politics in Portland isn't placid or cuddly.

The Role of Public Institutions

Two things stand out about the Portland experience: first, the skill, persistence, and reach of Portland's activist community, and second, the evolving capacity of public officials and government to respond and adapt. Where they might have viewed such citizen initiatives as challenges to their competence and authority, stonewalled attempts to make changes, and vilified and dismissed their critics, in Portland government officials have evolved a culture of adaptation and accommodation. Just as citizens honed their civic skills and vociferously pressed their views, government developed a culture of responding to and learning from, rather than rejecting, many grassroots initiatives. From this "call and response" evolved a pattern of citizen initiatives and government responses, with less of the acrimony, paralysis, and stasis that defeated change and discouraged activists in other cities.

Portland's regional metro government established an antisprawl "Urban Growth Boundary" (UGB), mandated for Oregon urban areas as part of a statewide environmental initiative spearheaded by Governor Tom McCall at the end of the 1970s, establishing an area outside which farms and open spaces would not be developed, with "infill" development of neighborhoods within the boundary instead. That type of increase in density brings with it an increase in economic diversity, since much of the infill in largely suburban neighborhoods would be in the form of apartments, mixing renters of various income levels with homeowners. Figures from the 2000 census indicate that the policy has in fact had this effect. In a recent article in the *Oregonian*, Betsy Hammond reports: "Poor families are less concentrated in the city of Portland and more likely to live in the suburbs—nearly all the suburbs—than a decade ago. Upper-income, middle-income and working-class people remain more likely to live near each other than in separate enclaves."[9] Here again, Portland bucks the national trend—in this case a trend toward greater economic segregation.

The unusual Portland story—and the powerful influence of the Urban Growth Boundary—should be seen in the context of an unusual state story. Oregon's Senate Bill 100, the land-use planning legislation that includes the Urban Growth Boundary provision, supports (in Carl Abbott's words) "a system of strong local planning carried on within enforceable state guidelines that express a vision of the public interest."[10] The state's backing for the idea of public good trumping private interest supports the city's.

In 1973, the state adopted its Statewide Planning Goals, beginning with a very strong commitment to citizen involvement. The legitimacy provided to citizen involvement has helped withstand multiple attempts to repeal the Goals over the past quarter century. Oregon's government system is distinguished as well by the extraordinary number of citizen advisory groups and commissions created by the state government.

Visitors to Portland see many of the results of what Abbott describes as "a political culture that treats land-use planning, with its restrictions on private actions, as a legitimate expression of the community inter-est."[11] Downtown is attractive and lively, with parks and public art and probably less automobile traffic than in any other thriving city, thanks in part to the free bus and light-rail service.

There is no single explanation for the openness of Portland's govern-ment and citizens to ideas of planned livability and stewardship of re-sources and its favoring of neighborhoods over economic development per se. Nor is there an easy way to account for the activism and power sharing that have characterized political life in the area since the early 1970s. Abbott and others talk about the modest size of the city and a his-tory of slow growth (as compared to booming Seattle, for instance) that made the city seem manageable and "imageable" as a whole. Commenta-tors also suggest that because the city was fairly homogeneous racially and economically, it was easier for many residents to think of themselves as members of one community and to avoid divisions along lines of race, in-come, and inner-city-versus-suburbs that have hindered efforts to unify other cities. (In 1990, only Minneapolis–St. Paul had proportionally fewer minorities than Portland among metropolitan areas with more than a million people.) Poverty in Portland is real, but it is a smaller problem than elsewhere, with less income disparity between city and suburbs than in most metropolitan areas of similar size. The 18 percent poverty rate among children in the city is no small problem, but it compares favorably with the 27 percent average rate of the fifty largest cities in the country.[12]

Nancy Biasi, former coordinator of citizen participation for the Office of Neighborhood Associations and currently working for the Bureau of Planning, agrees that manageable size and relative homogeneity are important factors.[13] She suggests that the business owners of Portland have never been as rich and powerful—or as showy—as the power elite in some cities. (Abbott talks about Portland's style of "conspicuous un-derconsumption.")[14] Biasi believes it is easier here to make connections "up and down as well as horizontally."

On the other hand, Portland was even smaller and more homoge-neous in the early 1970s, when (as we noted at the outset of this chapter) its level of civic engagement was much lower than it is now and no higher than in comparable cities elsewhere. Our puzzle is not why Portland has always been different from other cities—the evidence suggests that it *hasn't* always been different—but why it became so different in the 1970s and 1980s. Answering that question leads inevitably to the institutional innovations that began in the Goldschmidt era. The chronology of events strongly suggests that those institutions (epitomized by the Office of Neighborhood Associations) helped sustain and encourage the sort of civic activism that bubbled up from the grass roots in the 1960s in Portland (as elsewhere), but that flourished almost uniquely in Portland. Goldschmidt and his successors in local government seem to have been unusually effective at working with (and struggling with) activists to create innovative channels of access and a new spirit of openness that enabled the community to reach a new level of civic participation.

Something of a chicken-and-egg dilemma faces the analyst of civic engagement in Portland. Did Goldschmidt's innovations recognize a habit of activism or cultivate it? Was activism "homegrown," in part because the scale and homogeneity of the area gave people a sense of ownership and possibility, or did Portland attract activists from elsewhere, in part because of the real or imagined appeal of its liberalism and environmentalism? The answer is probably that the city's decades of activism grew from interlocking causes and effects.

David Bragdon, former head of the TriMet Council, member of the Metro Council, and, beginning in 2003, Metro Council president, believes that Portland's civic activism grew out of the ashes of failed liberal campaigns from the 1960s. Portlanders who supported Wayne Morse's Senate campaign, Eugene McCarthy's presidential bid, and the Robert F. Kennedy presidential campaign, cut short by Kennedy's assassination, essentially said, Bragdon argues, "The hell with national politics; we can make a difference locally." Partly as a result, he says, you find in Portland "a remarkable number of people who think it's possible to do things."

Ethan Seltzer says that some Portlanders were radicalized by the experience of urban renewal in the city in the 1960s. Here, as elsewhere, urban renewal destroyed a lively neighborhood to make way for a less crowded and more "rational" cityscape. Seltzer remarks that the new construction was more successful than most of what came out of urban renewal in that era, but the displacement of a vital Jewish and Italian neighborhood, and the spectacle of old synagogues damaged when engineers tried to move them, turned many people against the kind of large-scale urban "improvement" that saw dense, quirky neighborhoods as a problem, not a resource. Preserving rather than replacing Portland's other residential neighborhoods has been an aim of citizen and government activism since then.

Many people now engaged in Portland civic life also point to an influx of activists in the 1970s and 1980s as a contributing factor in the burgeoning civic involvement. Drawn by Portland's reputation as a progressive, livable city and by an image of Oregon as a relatively unspoiled, environmentally aware state, those newcomers were primed to protect the quality of life that they believed they would find here. In the early 1970s, Steve Johnson was an editor of *Rain*, an environmental journal. He remembers receiving letters from people in other parts of the country who were attracted by the idea of Oregon as an environmental paradise. Johnson says, "At first we told them, 'No, it sucks. They're clear-cutting the forests; the rivers are polluted.' Then we started thinking, If they get here and see it's not [what they thought], they're going to create it. So we started saying, 'It's great. Come on out.' "

Two of the powerful myths that have shaped American life are the promise of wealth ("The streets are paved with gold") and America as an unspoiled paradise. Unlike many who gravitated to cities that were booming, most of these newcomers to Portland were looking for a new Eden much more than for an opportunity to strike it rich. As Johnson suggests, they were primed for activism to preserve or create the quality of life they sought.

Ask newcomers to Portland how they got involved, and you hear a range of stories. Small-business owner and educational activist Mike Roach became involved in his daughter's preschool when she enrolled, a local and personal connection that has developed into an almost full-time commitment to education. Nancy Biasi was involved in her local neighborhood association before taking a related job with the city. Carl Flipper, who works for the Humboldt neighborhood association, had been active elsewhere before he moved to Portland and was determined to get involved here. But there are common themes. One is that connections happen readily in neighborhoods. Another is that neighborhood associations and other volunteer groups frequently serve as training grounds for more extensive involvement.

Biasi describes moving into her current neighborhood in 1982, already knowing one person on the block—the midwife who had delivered her child—and quickly coming to know other people. Connections were made through regular "blocktail parties," the local version of the block parties common in many Portland neighborhoods. (During Gold-schmidt's term as mayor, the city established a blanket insurance policy to cover block parties throughout the city so that neighborhood groups would not need to apply for permits or worry about liability.) Biasi also suggests that the density of neighborhoods close to downtown encourages connections among neighbors, saying, "If you live close to people, you have to know them." City dwellers elsewhere might disagree, but it is true that Portland's long-established neighborhoods, with their small lots, sidewalks, and, often, their own little downtown areas, make contact with neighbors easier and more likely than in suburban-sprawl suburbs with big houses on big lots and no town center. Virginia Breen, until recently with Oregon Public Broadcasting, says of her neighborhood, "Everybody has a dog; everybody walks. When we moved in, we immediately heard from ten neighbors."

Rick Seifert, who started a monthly community newspaper, the *Hillsdale Connection*, in 1994, identifies communication as an essential contributor both to a sense of community and to community involvement. "Communication defines community," he says. He believes that the *Connection* helped make this part of southwest Portland a real community: "When I started, there was no Hillsdale in fact, only in name."

Seifert reported on neighborhood and business association meetings in the paper, profiled people so readers could learn about their neighbors, and featured stories on the history of the area and planning for its future. All of this, he says, was a way to get people to focus on the community. He describes the unhappiness he felt walking to neighborhood association meetings past houses where the flicker and glow of light in the windows showed how many people were watching TV, distracted by stories and events that had little to do with their own lives or their own community. "Mass media are centrifugal," he comments. "They pull your attention away from the community. A local paper is centripetal, it draws you in." As a tangible example of the paper as a community-building tool, he describes the reaction to a brief piece inviting anyone interested in starting a farmers' market to meet at a local restaurant on a certain date. Thirty-five people showed up, and they launched several farmers' markets in the area.

A Positive Epidemic

However long the list of reasons for people's engagement with one another and with civic life—proximity, communication, the existence of neighborhood associations and other civic organizations—and however varied their stories of connecting through schools or local associations, or in other ways, it is clear that people participate because that is what many people do in Portland. A critical mass of citizens is involved, so involvement becomes the norm here, just as disengagement has become the norm elsewhere. Referring to *The Tipping Point*, Malcolm Gladwell's book about how ideas and behaviors cross a crucial threshold of occurrence or popularity to become much more prevalent, Mike Roach talks about what he calls "a positive epidemic of civic activism in Portland." He suggests that the prevalence of activism—activism as a social norm—breeds more activism. Roach says, "You see people being successful at it, you have visible proof that it can be done." The visible and active presence of a "remarkable number of people who think it's possible to do things" (in David Bragdon's words) convinces others that it is possible, desirable, and even expected that they, too, will participate and accomplish something.

Certainly, the signs of engagement—of something like a positive epidemic—are everywhere. The local papers are full of stories of citizen activism. The main focus of daylong activities at Pioneer Courthouse Square on the one-year anniversary of the September 11 terrorist attacks was volunteer opportunities. Kara Briggs, a reporter for *The Oregonian* who moved to Portland from Spokane, Washington, in the mid-1990s, says, "I'm amazed how often the people at the next table in ordinary restaurants, a deli or a coffee shop, are talking about city government or land use." Along with its numerous stories on community affairs, *The Oregonian* lists the times and places of neighborhood meetings—twenty-two meetings on September 10, 2002. In addition to providing information for participants, these listings signal to the community at large that neighborhood meetings are a part of daily life. Civic participation is in the air.

Nancy Biasi estimates that of the ninety neighborhood associations in the Portland metropolitan area, thirty of them are very active, thirty somewhat active, and thirty "moribund." Those numbers reflect the normal ebb and flow of galvanizing issues and the life cycles of organizations run by volunteers. To the extent that they show decreasing activity, they also signal a shift toward membership in special-interest groups that Steven Johnson documents in his thesis.[15] A change in the name of the city office that supports neighborhood groups from the Office of Neighborhood Associations to the Office of Neighborhood Involvement reflects the same trend.

Portland may be the only place where land-use legislation—the Urban Growth Boundary and related issues of density and infill—is a part of people's daily conversation, as Kara Briggs suggests, and a feature of the cultural as well as the political landscape. In 1999, local choreographer and performance artist Linda K. Johnson created an urban-boundary performance by camping out for thirty-six hours at six different urban-boundary sites, where the effect of the UGB was typically visible in the contrast between housing on one side of a road and farmland on the other. Mirroring the civic spirit of Portland, its emphasis on discussion and group participation, Johnson modified her work in midperformance, replacing the dances she had planned to perform at each site with conversations with area people to evoke their thoughts and feelings about the boundary.[16]

Contrasting Cases: Johnson Creek and the Annexation of Unincorporated Neighborhoods

Steve Johnson offers Johnson (no relation) Creek as an example of a successful government–civic activist partnership that capped a long history of failed attempts to impose solutions to the problems of a waterway that passes through Portland neighborhoods before emptying into the Willamette River. Johnson notes that over a period of fifty years forty-six reports or plans attempted—without success—to address environmental problems of flooding and poor water quality at Johnson Creek. Area residents attacked the research underlying the reports, the proposed fixes, the costs of plans.[17] A proposal developed by Metro in the late 1970s (when it "forgot" to engage with citizens) met with a storm of protest. Residents denounced a flood-control plan that they believed would benefit only a small percentage of property owners in the area but that all would have to fund. Voters defeated a measure designed to pay the $10 million cost of the plan and threatened the existence of the then-new regional government.

As Johnson points out, one reason for the long history of failure was the broad range of constituencies in the fifty-four-square-mile watershed. Johnson Creek flows through farmland, through suburban neighborhoods and higher-income urban neighborhoods, past shopping malls and parking lots.[18] Developing one plan that would satisfy residents of those varied areas was a major challenge; imposing a solution that would be widely acceptable proved impossible. The only way the residents and the city could arrive at a viable approach was to work together to reconcile their differences and discover or establish mutual interests. Johnson remarks, "It wasn't until the 1990s, when government agencies adopted a revised policy of co-producing studies and plans alongside citizens, as well as working hand-in-hand with over 175 nonprofit organizations to physically restore the watershed, that progress was finally achieved." He adds, "Urban watershed management is as much about mastering the art of civic participation as it is about the science of ecosystem management."[19] Citizens' groups that had organized to oppose earlier plans for the creek or to focus on the potential of the waterway formed the basis for later groups, notably the Johnson Creek Coordinating Committee, which worked with government in the 1990s. As part of its commitment to working with residents—an example of citizen-government partnership, not just "consultation" with citizens to get their support—Portland's Bureau of Environmental Services assigned an employee to work full-time with that committee. Civic participation was extensive, with more than 6,000 of the 175,000 citizens of the watershed actively participating in the process of finding solutions to the Johnson Creek problem.[20]

Ethan Seltzer, who was personally involved in the Johnson Creek effort and wrote his doctoral dissertation on the subject, says that one result of all of the consultation was a new environmental focus, one that attracted wider support. "The organizing principle changed from flood control to resource preservation," he says. "That became the basis for community commitment."[21] But arriving at that point, turning skeptical opponents into partners, required a long process of healing old wounds of suspicion and hostility.

Kara Briggs of The Oregonian describes city commissioner Eric Sten and his aides coming into meetings in small school cafeterias in the Johnson Creek area to find "100 people screaming mad." She says that Sten's aides spent a lot of time sitting down and talking with the most outspoken critics. Rich Rogers, one of those aides, remembers facing the skepticism and anger of area residents. He describes meeting Vern Stockwell early in the process, for instance. A forceful, imposing seventy-year-old with a rough demeanor, Stockwell was the kind of man who "poked you in the chest as he talked to you." He told Rogers, "Every year or so they send a new guy out here and I have to educate him."

But the city and the citizens gradually built a cooperative working relationship. "The key approach," Rogers says, "was to listen a lot." Here as elsewhere in these social-capital cases, listening to people's stories was essential. That included listening to local "folk science," which insisted that the floodplain had been drawn incorrectly on official maps. Residents maintained that a large area included in the designated floodplain would in fact never flood. "People believed it passionately, and we didn't feel confident that the city's science was a hundred percent accurate," Rogers says. When the city agreed to consider other possibilities, the citizens hired their own hydrologists and were proved right. As a result, the floodplain map was redrawn and people who had been inappropriately required to buy flood insurance received a rebate on their premiums. Equally important, residents began to believe that the government could be flexible and responsive and would not simply try to ram a plan down their throats this time. That confidence increased when the city promised that private land the government purchased to improve the creek would be acquired through a "willing seller" program; there would be no taking of property by eminent domain.

The Johnson Creek Restoration Plan that resulted from the long, cooperative process divides the creek into fifty-eight sections to ensure appropriate local restoration efforts within the overall commitment to environmental improvement and flood management. As of 2002, the work was still at an early stage, but Johnson points to valuable civic results of the process. One is the amount of civic participation itself. Johnson counts more than six thousand people involved in more than a thousand events connected with the watershed since 1990, including public meetings, regular citizens' meetings, restoration projects, tours, workshops, and cleanups.[22] A related gain is the education citizens received in the science of resource management and the art of political participation. Finally, Johnson observes the growth of a new "steward-ship ethic" among residents of the area, citing examples of people no longer dumping material in storm drains, as well as developing a new vig-ilance toward other threats to the creek.

After a long history of failure and false starts, the government learned (or learned again) that genuinely responding to citizens' demands that they be included in the process was the key. The story also illustrates the importance of developing a coalition among a rising number of interest groups to make concerted action possible.

Johnson Creek is a positive example of civic participation and city re-sponsiveness. However, the Portland story also includes instances of par-ticipation and partnership not functioning so well, when the mechanism of response to citizens' calls for participation seemed to break down. The best known, and a source of lasting bitterness and conflict, is the annex-ation by the city of Portland of "East Portland"—unincorporated areas east of Eighty-second Avenue and to the southwest during the 1980s. Carl Abbott draws a distinction between "progressive Portlanders" and the working-class immigrants and owners of small farms to the east, whom he describes as "people and neighborhoods of stubborn individu-als." He adds, "They don't much trust government and can't imagine getting good value for their tax dollars—the opposite of the progressive core."[23] Kara Briggs of *The Oregonian* confirms Abbott's account of dif-ferences between the large immigrant communities and the mainstream white community that include very different ideas about the role and re-liability of government.

Many residents of the area believe that the events of the 1980s justi-fied their distrust. Activist Bonnie McKnight, now cochair of the Russell Neighborhood Association and a resident of the unincorporated Park-rose neighborhood in the 1980s, says that back then eastern neigh-borhood associations joined in a committee to consider options for the area. They favored incorporating as an independent city, but then a fed-eral mandate to build a sewer system pushed residents toward annexa-tion by Portland. The largest concentration of population without sewers in the country, this area of more than a hundred thousand residents looked to the city to build the system and other infrastructure elements they needed. According to McKnight, city budgetary problems meant that residents of the annexed neighborhood, who had expected the city to finance the sewer system, ended up bearing most of the cost themselves and saw a decline in the quality of other services. Homeowners received sewer hookup bills of $8,000 to $10,000 soon after annexation, though a long fight eventually reduced those costs somewhat.[24]

Many residents of the annexed area still see themselves more as victims than as beneficiaries of Portland's vision of a livable city and a countryside protected from sprawl. They doubt their power to influence the government. Richard Bixby, who coordinates ten neighborhood associations in the area, says that many locals do not share downtown's enthusiasm for the Urban Growth Boundary, which has changed their neighborhoods dramatically:

> The majority in Portland say, "Protect forests and farmland from sprawl." People here say, "We want to protect space in our own neighborhoods." The look of inner neighborhoods hasn't changed much in 50 years. Here there has been massive change. Where there were farms there are now row houses and apartment buildings.

In fact, the area around Bixby's office on 106th Avenue has the look of a sprawling suburb: not the big new homes set in an acre of lawn you see elsewhere, but strip malls and cul-de-sacs with rows of new houses going up.

Many people in these neighborhoods believe that the government responds only to those who share its ideas and values. Bixby recognizes a vicious circle in which hostility toward government and an unwillingness to participate lead to effects that increase the hostility and decrease the likelihood of participation. When these neighborhoods were rezoned to allow for new construction and increased density, he says, "Organized neighborhoods that could get fifty people to City Hall got some of the rezoning rolled back," but neighborhoods that did not organize to confront the city "got hammered." Is City Hall accessible? From his vantage point in these eastern neighborhoods, Bixby's answer is yes, but. "If you want access to City Hall you can get it," he says. "You have to invest a little time. It's not always clear what the impact is. You can talk to a commissioner, tell him your idea, but whether it goes anywhere . . ."

In accounting for the uncommonly profuse and productive civic engagement of Portland in recent decades, we have emphasized the virtuous circle that we have termed "call and response." For the most part the civic dialectic in Portland has led to positive feedback: More grassroots activism has (often through conflict) led to more responsive public institutions, and more responsive institutions have in turn evoked more activism. Increased participation in Portland politics has been, from the start, highly contentious. Waves of raucous activism have been followed by periods of adaptation and relative quiet, until activists confronted public officials with a new set of challenges. Nevertheless, as political scientist Jeffrey Berry and his colleagues found in their 1993 study of Portland and three other cities, "increased participation and stronger neighborhood associations tend to reduce the gap between citizens and their government, not increase it."[25]

In most other metropolitan areas in America essentially the same chain of reciprocal causation has worked in reverse, creating a vicious circle of disengagement, unresponsive institutions, and further disengagement. Just as Bixby says, the annexation of East Portland provides a local intimation of that same negative cycle: Alienated citizens withdraw from participation, and that withdrawal itself produces less responsive government, which encourages further alienation and apathy.

Access and Influence

Longtime activists talk about how much like a small town Portland is, how "everyone knows everyone else." In her new job with the Bureau of Planning, where she is working to develop a coalition of parties to deal with problems of the Willamette River, Biasi says her approach involves calling people in her Rolodex. People who have been deeply involved in civic affairs know one another and are comfortable contacting one another to a greater degree here than in larger and more divided cities. Having lunch at an outdoor table of a Middle Eastern restaurant in East Portland, Mike Roach, the school activist (whom David Bragdon knows as the co-owner of a women's clothing store), runs into Pamela Echeverio, who in 1997 organized a thirty-thousand-person march through downtown Portland to protest underfunding of education. Echeverio recalls the parents and others concerned about the issue all in red T-shirts "flowing like a snake through the city." During that organizing effort (twelve hours a day for four months), she met and worked with Sho Dozono, the owner of Azumano Travel in Portland. In 2001, Sho organized the "Flight for Freedom," bringing a thousand Oregonians to New York City less than a month after the September 11 attack. Everyone in Portland knows Sho, who is also head of the Chamber of Commerce. And so it goes.

But "everyone" is a relative term. The people you do not know are likely to be invisible to you, so it is difficult to determine how many and what kinds of people and groups live outside the circle that includes your particular "everyone." However much residents of East Portland neighborhoods may bear or share responsibility for being outsiders, they are in fact not part of that community of mutual acquaintance. The same is true of other minority and outlying neighborhoods.

Carl Flipper coordinates block-grant funding for the Humboldt neighborhood association. Humboldt is a 50 percent African-American and 65 percent minority neighborhood north and east of downtown. Flipper describes his job as "trying to connect the dots in the neighborhood, especially for a low-income, ethnically diverse population not usually included in the process." African-American himself, he has, like Bixby, a mixed view on access and influence:

> I've found the community to be remarkably open to *me*, but I'm gregarious
> and I don't take no for an answer. You've got to show up and you've got to

have the persistence to find out who the decision makers are. For people who are less outgoing, community seems closed or actually is closed. Politicians are not knocking on *their* doors.

Flipper points to a number of regional issues that directly affect the Humboldt neighborhood—a new light-rail line; the expansion of an interstate highway—and the challenge of influencing those plans, which requires sustained community involvement in lengthy city processes. He suggests that access is a smaller problem for citizens than finding the stamina to stay engaged in multiple issues. Flipper mentions, too, the good and bad sides of the planned expansion of Portland Community College. The community needs the additional educational resources, but the college has alienated residents with its plan to use eminent domain to take property it wants to build on (in contrast to the "willing seller" approach to Johnson Creek improvements). On balance, though, Flipper's assessment is positive:

> I've not been to a single meeting where citizen input was stifled. That's why the damn meetings last three or four hours. Anyone can get an audience with the mayor, the school board, the commissioners. I don't know many examples of people in public office who don't want to do the right thing.

Bonnie McKnight is somewhat less positive about the ability of East Portland neighborhoods to influence events:

> We have been fighting to redefine what citizen participation means. We've had limited success in getting a required meeting with developers at the *beginning* of the process. We at the neighborhood level need to be more sophisticated. It's not good enough just to say, "Don't do it."

So she, too, divides the blame between a city government inclined toward pro forma consultation and residents who need to participate more energetically and constructively in the process. But she does see politicians failing to live up to earlier ideals of participation: "Goldschmidt wasn't afraid of the people. He knew if you explain what you want to do, people will allow you to do it. I don't think we've got leadership like that now."

As these varied viewpoints suggest, there is no way to sum up Portlanders' experiences of access and participation in a single formulation. During the last thirty years the city's governmental institutions and the value placed on involvement by both citizens and officials have created an unusual level of civic participation and an uncommonly open and responsive government. A look at civic life in the city bears out the statistics at the beginning of this chapter. A small plaque inside City Hall answers the question of how you get to City Hall: "By raising your hand." It is true that anyone can walk into City Hall and get a hearing, and that anyone determined to become involved in civic affairs can find a way to do so; the city does support its neighborhood associations and other activist groups. It is also true that many of the appealing things in Portland—the parks and open spaces downtown, the successful light-rail system, the thriving inner neighborhoods—are fruits of the cooperative work of government and citizen activists guided by a shared vision of a livable city in a healthy environment. At the same time, Portlanders who do not share in that vision tend to be marginalized (and sometimes marginalize themselves). The process of widening the circle of engagement beyond homogeneous, "small-town" Portland has a way to go. Also, Portland faces new challenges to its model of civic participation, including an influx of new immigrants who may not share the values of the 1970s and early 1980s and increasing neighborhood density as a consequence of the Urban Growth Boundary.

Portland Then and Now

Some tensions in Portland today spring in part from the successes of the last thirty years that have made it an attractive place to live. Although the city invests in affordable housing in most neighborhoods, the rising prices of housing, especially in newly vibrant inner neighborhoods, have made it difficult for low-income residents, and principally renters, to stay in their homes. So gentrification has meant some migration of lower-income Portlanders to the east and north. They have been joined there by new immigrants to the area, many Southeast Asian and, recently, Hispanic, sometimes with a limited grasp of English. At the same time, the Urban Growth Boundary has meant that many newcomers are moving to established neighborhoods whose density is being increased by infill housing—a change that many local residents oppose.

The strains that result have racial or ethnic overtones, although they probably have most to do with general resistance to change. In a November 2, 1999, story in *The Oregonian* called "Divisions Born of Diversity," Kara Briggs writes of an incident in Gresham, at one time an almost all-white small city on Portland's eastern border. A Mexican immigrant who had lived in Gresham for six years was walking her daughter home from school and stopped to rest on the curb outside the home of a thirty-two-year resident. When the resident asked them to move on and failed to understand the woman's reply in limited English, she turned her hose on: either to spray the pair or, as she stated, to spray nearby trees to make them leave. Briggs quotes the homeowner as saying, "I used to go for walks around here at night, but the whole neighborhood has changed. The kids are not the same. I don't even go out at night anymore." Though not representative of race relations in the Portland area, this story dramatizes broader issues: fear of change, the novelty of people who speak a different language, and (Briggs added in conversation) a homeowner's prejudice against renters. The argument, says Briggs, is that "they're not really residents; they don't pay taxes; they're not committed to the neighborhood."

Richard Bixby tells a more positive story about language and cultural barriers. In the area of East Portland where he works, Bixby set up a meeting with recent Russian immigrants and neighborhood leaders to begin to bridge language and cultural barriers before problems might arise. "The meeting was just so they could sit down and talk and get to know each other," Bixby says. "So when a problem comes up, they know who to call." But the city is still at an early stage of dealing with its relatively new diversity issues. The Urban Growth Boundary, which had a minor effect on neighborhoods within its borders in its early years, now means real change and, in some cases, real opposition that Portland must deal with.

Many longtime Portland activists contrast the civic-minded newcomers of the 1970s with what they judge to be the more self-interested ones of the 1990s. Mike Roach says that most newcomers to Portland in the 1970s came for the "right reasons." That is, they were environmentalists and believed that the public good could outweigh private interests. Beginning in the mid-1980s, however, Portland has attracted people more focused on their own quality of life who want to "circle the wagons around their house." Nancy Biasi makes a similar point, saying, "Neighborhood organizing used to be around change; now it's more about maintaining the status quo." Roach describes these later arrivals as "fodder for the antitax, antigovernment people." Probably allowance should be made for a certain amount of "golden age" nostalgia that remembers past cooperation more vividly than past conflict.

The distinction between selfless past activism and narrow, self-interested, not-in-my-backyard obstructionism now may not be as clear as it seems. Early victories over highway development and hospital expansion may have benefited Portland as a whole and fit into its broad vision of a livable city, but they were driven by the people most directly affected, who did not want a highway running through their neighborhoods or new hospital facilities displacing their homes. The Johnson Creek story is partly about stewardship of a shared resource but also about taking into account what people do and do not want in their own backyards.

But evidence of a real shift in Portland neighborhood politics does exist. Through analysis of 1985 and 1999 news stories about local issues, Steve Johnson finds:

> In 1985, 75% of the news about neighborhood action was positive. Neighborhood associations were described as saving neighborhoods, hosting block parties, and involved in positive encounters with government

through sanctioned planning processes. In the 1999 news, the opposite was true. Two-thirds of the news about neighborhood action was negative. Headlines referred to neighborhoods as battle zones: "Battle of Boise," "Long Dispute over Fire Station Resolved," "North Portland Opposes Jail," "Two of Portland's Victories for NIMBY Movement," "Southeast Neighborhoods Unsatisfied with City Services."[26]

Without mentioning the 1990s newcomers per se, Carl Abbott talks about the danger their supposed attitude represents, saying, "The community consensus in Portland is continually under challenge—not from machine politics as in Boston or Chicago, but from the values of privatism."[27] The greatest danger for Portland may be a new "tipping point," where privatism and skepticism about the responsiveness of government become the norm and positive reinforcement of the habits of participation and cooperation begins to diminish.

If Portland is to maintain its uncommon level of citizen engagement, its officials and civic-minded activists cannot simply decry the forces of privatism; they need to find a way to bring into "the process" more of the people who are antitax and antigovernment but are nevertheless citizens of Portland. Whatever the outcome, the future of civic engagement in Portland, like that of its past thirty years, will be well worth watching.

Conclusion
Making Social Capital Work

As we said at the outset of this voyage across America, virtually no one sets out to "build social capital." Protagonists in our stories set out to raise farm incomes in Mississippi or help poor kids in Philadelphia or build parks in Portland or save souls in Los Angeles. However, they saw that achieving their substantive objectives would be easier (or perhaps would only be possible) if they strengthened and then exploited social networks. Thus, building social capital was an essential part of their strategy. Indeed, what distinguishes our cases from other efforts to organize unions, run large companies, build churches, or improve reading skills is that the protagonists here understand and emphasize the centrality of relationships and interpersonal connections.

The benefits of social capital spill beyond the people immediately involved in the network and can be used for many other purposes. The more neighbors who know one another by name, the fewer crimes a neighborhood as a whole will suffer. A child born in a state whose residents volunteer, vote, and spend time with friends is less likely to be born underweight, less likely to drop out of school, and less likely to kill or be killed than the same child—no richer or poorer—born in another state whose residents do not. Society as a whole benefits enormously from the social ties forged by those who choose connective strategies in pursuit of their particular goals.[1] We know from many studies that social capital can have what economists call "positive externalities." That is, quite apart from their utility in solving the immediate problem (improving wages at Harvard or test scores in Philly), interpersonal ties are useful for many other purposes.

In each case presented in this book, there were other possible strategies for achieving the immediate objectives—say, increasing farm subsidies to help poor farmers or adding homework to improve test scores—and some of those strategies might have been quicker and even cheaper, at least in terms of people's time, than the social-capital strategies pursued. However, we believe that strategies that ignore the value of social networks would have been less effective in the immediate task, less sustainable over the long term, and less fruitful in a broader sense.

Building redundant contacts into an organization's routines might seem inefficient. Having a coffee room where Philadelphia tutors can schmooze might seem extravagant if the purpose of the exercise is only to teach reading. UPS's insistence on maintaining biweekly meetings of its Greensboro health-and-safety committee even after serious accidents have dropped to almost nil might seem an irrational use of valuable time. Letting kids in Waupun learn about government access by trial and error might seem an inefficient approach to civics education. HUCTW's preference for face-to-face encounters rather than memos or newsletters does seem bizarrely inefficient to some national union officials. One-on-ones and house parties might seem an awfully slow, indirect, and apolitical way to organize a political movement in the Rio Grande Valley. Relying on neighborhood groups to solve the problems of the Johnson Creek watershed in Portland was much more protracted than adopting a solution designed by hydraulic engineers in City Hall would have been, but the final outcome was better. Moreover, the relationships built (almost inadvertently) in that process can be reused to resolve other local issues that were not even visible to the initial watershed activists.

Using the social-capital lens allows us to see that in each of these cases the supposed inefficiency actually is essential for creating the virtuous circles of human connectivity that are basic to the organization's effectiveness and that have valuable spillover effects beyond the group itself. As civic reformers in Portland correctly understand, the "process" is crucial to the product.

This is not a book about how to organize evangelical churches or re-build blighted neighborhoods or tutor poor kids. There are other books devoted to those aims. Rather, we focus specifically on the connective strategies that are the shared feature of all our cases. In that sense, our hope is that these stories will offer encouragement and insights for any-one contemplating a "social-capital strategy" for his or her substantive problem, be it cleaning up a polluted river, improving the lot of undocu-mented immigrants, or attacking public corruption.

Agents and Structural Conditions

The success of a voyager depends in part on his or her navigational skills and in part on the wind and weather and tides. Building social capital depends both on the actions of protagonists and on key enabling structural conditions in the broader environment, many of which are immutable in the short run (though not in the long run). For the most part, however, our case studies focus on the actions in the foreground, not the structural conditions in the background. For example, the tax code, by allowing deductions for some activities of voluntary organiza-tions and disallowing deductions for other activities (such as political action), has a powerful indirect effect on the structure of philanthropy in America. But the tax code does not appear in our stories.

Similarly, the uniquely American role of large private foundations in funding nonprofit activities plays an important role in many of our stud-ies. Ernie Cortés, marching in the Rio Grande Valley, and Liz Lerman, dancing in Portsmouth, both depend on foundation funding, and one can suppose that other would-be Ernies and Lizzes are not dancing or marching because they did not win foundation funding. But foundations are almost invisible in our stories.

To take another example of structural conditions that shape the possibilities for participation and connection, social-capital building is

demonstrably hampered by urban sprawl and by the increasingly complex schedules of two-career families.[2] Connective approaches to problem solving could be substantially enhanced by antisprawl metropolitan
planning and by greater flexibility in work hours. But neither public policies on transportation and housing nor private firms' policies on release
time for community service appear anywhere in our stories.

Education itself is often the most powerful predictor of high levels of
social capital. Educated people and educated communities have skills
and resources that enable them to form and exploit social networks more
readily, whereas less educated communities have to struggle harder to do
so. But investment in education as a condition for social-capital building
rarely appears in our stories.

Of course, tax codes, highway building, and educational investment
are all determined by public policy choices. Thus, the preceding discussion underlines the fact that only a few of the many different ways that
government policies impact community participation and civic engagement take center stage in the stories we have told. Certainly, in the preceding pages we have seen community activists targeting local and
state-level institutions, as when the Do Something sixth-graders lobbied
the Waupun City Council and the commissioner of railroads to demand
that their railroad crossing be made safer, or when Valley Interfaith demanded commitments from political candidates at public accountability
sessions.

Several other cases showed state actors taking a central role in initi-
ating connective projects. Mayor Richard M. Daley supported Chicago's
community-library innovation as a fundamental "community anchor,"
part of his broader program of investment in neighborhoods. Without his
support, Mary Dempsey could not have pursued her strategy (and probably would not have been Chicago's head librarian in the first place).
Mayor Neil Goldschmidt in Portland introduced a new, more responsive,
decentralized structure of government, and as we have seen, Portland
politics from the 1970s to today have evinced an often acrimonious but
eventually productive "call and response" pattern between grassroots

groups and government officials. The creation of the Office of Neighborhood Associations, the effort to involve such groups in decision making, and the training of the groups' members had a major role in their proliferation. By opening up to local organizations and giving them responsibility, government created an incentive for local organization. On the other hand, the fact that activists pressured the city government to give them a voice was integral to that development.

Meanwhile, more pervasively—often almost invisible in the background—government policies were crucial to the substantive results achieved in many cases. Indeed, in some cases specific government actions were prerequisites for the creation of social capital. It was the state power of eminent domain, "loaned" to DSNI, that enabled community redevelopment of the urban triangle at the core of Dudley Street. Philadelphia's Experience Corps's tutoring program depended on state and federal educational funding. In Tupelo, George McLean's Rural Community Development Councils were in part conduits for government agricultural technical assistance. The jobs program and new sewers in Texas were funded by the state. Even the mayor's Rolodex in Portsmouth served as the starting point for Liz Lerman's networking.

To be sure, misguided public policies can also weaken or destroy social capital. If the urban village of Dudley Street was encouraged in important ways by public policy in Boston in the 1990s, only a few decades earlier and a few miles away "urban renewal" helped destroy the urban village of Boston's West End, as Herbert Gans chronicled. Government power can be used in destructive as well as constructive ways. Nevertheless, public power is often a necessary ingredient in the building of community.

So the argument sometimes heard that civil society alone can solve public issues if only the state would get out of the way is simply silly. In the examples above, government support of participatory strategies was crucial to the projects' success. In an ideological environment that demands short-term returns on public investment, such support may require real courage from the politicians involved. Social-capital strategies for solving collective problems may demand redundancies and apparent inefficiencies; require local participation, which can derail top-down planning; but in the long run bring benefits that spill over far beyond any "target" population.

Political actors (or potential funders) who demand streamlined processes and wholly predictable results may short-circuit or undercut the process. In contrast, Mayor Goldschmidt in Portland and the foundations supporting the Dudley Street Neighborhood Initiative in Boston were committed to local participation, even when it meant that their own plans were waylaid by locals' concerns and priorities. Mayor Daley's neighborhood-development strategy required a commitment to the public value of vibrant libraries, without demanding a constant accounting of short-term results to justify the continued investment. Likewise, the Lila Wallace–Reader's Digest Arts Partners Program—the origin of Liz Lerman's Portsmouth dance—is committed to community arts participation as an end in itself, requiring no further justification.

Thus, if the goal you are working toward requires major investment or political access, it helps to be blessed with "true believers" in positions of power: individuals committed to grassroots participation who will follow the social-capital route through all its apparent meanderings. On the other hand, in all the cases studied, interpersonal connections and civic engagement among ordinary citizens were essential to making participatory democracy work. Lupita Torres and her neighbors needed roads paved in their barrio. Their conviction that they had the right and the duty to speak out in order to make sure elected officials administered public money—"our money"—wisely forced their mayor to act as if he believed that were so. Mobilizing voters by the scores of thousands, Valley Interfaith is able to demand access and accountability even in a state whose formal structures are far less geared to citizen involvement than those of Portland, Oregon.

Our cases, in sum, "hold constant" many powerful background factors. The risk of this approach is that it may falsely obscure the importance of large-scale structural constraints that affect the ability of community actors to build social capital. The obverse advantage is that our approach more closely focuses on the strategic choices that actually confront those actors. Elsewhere we have offered some "macro-level" ideas about how public and corporate policy should be reformed to encourage more social-capital building in America.[3] In this book we focus instead on local choices and grassroots strategies. Our hope is that community activists and would-be social capitalists (and those who would support them, like foundation executives and local officials) will be able to glean useful lessons for action from these cases.

The preceding chapters offer a travelogue of sorts: a set of portraits of the places we visited and the people who have made those places the way they are. In this chapter we step back and ask what we learned from the journey. Much of the success in each "success story" depended on particular circumstances of time, place, culture, and personality. We have discovered no simple rules for social-capital building. But we have discovered that common challenges were faced in many different instances. Not all good things go together in social-capital formation (if it were easy, everyone would choose this route—and stick with it). Often several strategic objectives exist in tension with one another, demanding difficult trade-offs or creative balancing acts. Here we discuss several common dilemmas in detail.

Dilemmas of Size and Scope

Many of the projects we have described were initiated by people with vast ambitions: to bring social justice and political power to the impoverished Rio Grande Valley, to revolutionize youth civic education across the nation, to "transform the aging of America," to save every soul for Christ. These are no small aims. Yet to pursue these goals through connective strategies, organizers had somehow to reconcile them with the basic fact that smaller is better for social-capital creation.

Researchers have repeatedly found that social capital is higher in smaller settings—smaller schools, smaller towns, smaller countries, and so on.[4] Listening and trusting are easier in smaller settings. One-on-one, face-to-face communication is more effective at building relationships and creating empathy and understanding than remote, impersonal communication. Smaller groups enable members to get to know one another more easily. Smaller groups work better in part because they can be more homogeneous than large gatherings; participants have more shared assumptions and easier tacit communication. Beyond that, the more extensive interchange that is possible in smaller groups makes it possible to discover unexpected mutuality even in the face of difference. Small size also makes individual responsibility for maintaining the group intensely clear, pushing members to, as Saddleback ministers say, "discern your gifts for the church."

Smaller groups also offer easier footholds for initial steps. This is probably the most universal feature of the connective strategies pursued in our cases. One-on-one home visits and school-based "house meetings" where participants sit and talk in groups of six to ten are *the* fundamental building blocks of Texas Industrial Areas Foundation organizing. Within Valley Interfaith, face-to-face conversations between teachers and parents gradually built a shared sense of goodwill and efficacy. Similarly, Saddleback Church and All Saints Church rely on a dense array of small groups to avoid the problems of anonymity and alienation inherent in massive size. Face-to-face encounters are an essential part of Saddleback's strategy, beginning with "greeters" but not ending there. The union organizers at HUCTW make one-on-one conversation their defining principle. As Gladys McKenzie says, "We don't want to be pen pals. We want to connect with a face." "They knew my shoe size," Joyce Guarnieri jokes.

It is perhaps surprising to find the same dedication to face-to-face conversation undergirding the operations of UPS, a vast corporation in an industry where speed and efficiency are the essence of competitiveness. At UPS hubs, formal practices like the prework communication meeting are accompanied by a very strong norm of daily conversation between managers and employees. Managers travel personally to sites and get together monthly for face-to-face meetings. As participants recognize, this is not "a memo kind of company," and the social capital built through redundant personal contacts has brought measurable advances in areas such as accident reduction and worker retention. In contrast, it seems that the relative absence of face-to-face contact associated with the craigslist Web site limits the amount of real and sustainable social capital it can create. Clearly, learning about other people's lives through the site gives users a "sense of community," but can this "sense" spill over into material support or helpful interventions in the same way that lunchtime parking lot conversations between UPS workers do? The evidence is debatable.

The need for redundancy of contact to foster virtuous circles of mutual responsibility means that not only size but density matters. Experience Corps is built around ongoing one-on-one relationships between tutors and students, but the program could never work as it does if these tutor-student pairs were scattered across the city. Instead, organizers carefully "cluster" volunteers in a limited number of schools in order to increase the density of contact and support. Similarly, Do Something works in multiple schools within particular sites (Waupun, Milwaukee, Greendale, Shawano) rather than dispersing its efforts across the state of Wisconsin.

In sum, smaller is better for forging and sustaining connections. On the other hand, bigger is better for critical mass, power, and diversity. Protagonists in all our stories want to grow and expand. Most of their objectives require power, and power is enhanced by size. Furthermore, community building benefits from a sense on the part of participants that they are a part of something important and growing. There is also a need to economize on effective leadership (a scarce resource), which means that really effective leaders should be working on a big scale.

Furthermore, for achieving diversity and "bridging social capital" (discussed in more detail below), size is necessary. Smaller can easily mean more parochial, and smaller groups risk a not-in-my-backyard orientation. If there's somebody else nearby who is not part of "us," there is a constant temptation to redefine borderline problems as Somebody Else's problems. This pattern seems to be an emerging problem in Portland, where observers report, "Neighborhood organizing used to be around change; now it's more about maintaining the status quo." Similar problems have shadowed efforts at urban neighborhood government, for instance in places like in Minneapolis, where NIMBY rivalries between adjacent communities are said sometimes to have sapped the vitality of local institutions. Therefore, even at the outset organizers need to consider how to combine the advantages of small scale with the offsetting advantages of large scope.

One clear solution is federation: nesting small groups within larger groups.[5] Small groups within larger organizations can foster the personal relationships that would not be so easily formed within the larger organization alone. Tupelo's Rural Community Development Councils are built out of neighborhood groups of ten to twelve families. Saddleback Church and All Saints Church follow the same approach: the Class 101 membership groups at Saddleback and the Covenant One groups at All Saints make it possible to combine the resources only large churches can offer with the personal support and kindred connections that people seek in small religious communities. In a parallel way, on a larger scale yet, Valley Interfaith and its umbrella, the TIAF, are organizations of organizations. Their ability to mobilize tens of thousands draws on ties of trust and solidarity formed within the far smaller religious congregations at their base.

This "nested," federal strategy is especially effective when (as in Saddleback and All Saints) members can participate in more than one small group, thus weaving personal ties among the small groups and reinforcing a sense of identity with the larger whole. Do Something is a national organization comprising many local groups, and thus has the potential to pursue this strategy on a nationwide scale, but so far, except for a nascent support network for Do Something coaches, building horizontal ties among local groups (even within single states) remains a task for the future.

The bottom-line advice for managing dilemmas of size and scope is one familiar to guerrilla *comandantes* and Rotarians alike: create a cellular structure with smaller groups linked to form a larger, more encompassing one. Organizational choices that facilitate "mixing" and "bridging" among small groups can harness the benefits of both intimacy and breadth. If training or travels are designed to bring local leaders together, the cellular structure can also help particular success stories spread and so speed institutional learning.

Dilemmas of Cohesion and Diversity

Building social ties among people who already share a reservoir of cultural referents, family history, or personal experience is qualitatively different from building ties among those who do not—different in how it gets done, how often it gets done, and what happens as a result. For this reason analysts find it helpful to distinguish between "bonding social capital" (ties that link individuals or groups with much in common) and "bridging social capital" (ties that link individuals or groups across a greater social distance). Both kinds of connections are valuable to us as individuals, but bridging is especially important for reconciling democracy and diversity.[6] A society that has only bonding social capital risks looking like Bosnia or Belfast. Yet bridging social capital is intrinsically less likely to develop automatically than bonding social capital—birds of a feather flock together. Social-capital strategists need to pay special attention to the tougher task of fostering social ties that reach across social divisions.

Bridging is not about "Kumbaya" cuddling. It is about coming together to argue, as much as to share. This was precisely Harold Washington's dream for Chicago: that it might be a place where "black and white, Asian and Hispanic, male and female, the young, the old, the disabled, gays and lesbians, Moslems, Christians and Jews, business leaders and neighborhood activists, bankers and trade unionists—all have come together to mix and contend, to argue and to reason, to confront our problems and not merely to contain them."

Several of the cases presented here confirm that homogeneity makes connective strategies easier. Saddleback's small groups form tight and lasting relationships in part because they are designed to bring together people with similar interests or circumstances in addition to the vivid evangelical belief system all Saddleback congregants share. All Saints' small groups, diverse by design, likewise foster communication and contact but create fewer lasting interpersonal ties. Similarly, many observers have suggested that Portland's relative homogeneity in terms of race, ethnicity, and wealth made instituting and maintaining participatory structures easier in the 1970s. More recently the movement of new immigrants into outlying neighborhoods seems to have exacerbated conflicts between these and the old-line "progressive" downtown and made the articulation of citywide collective needs—and the search for citywide solutions—more difficult.

Such cases bear out the general pattern that bridging ties are harder to build than bonding ones. Thus it is particularly enlightening to observe the careful strategies that some projects have put in place to initiate and sustain bridging ties.[7] For instance, the values and organizational principles guiding Valley Interfaith are explicitly designed to bridge ethnic and religious differences. Nevertheless, it has been a continuing struggle for the Texas Industrial Areas Foundation to weave Latino Catholics, black evangelicals, and suburban whites into a single fabric.[8]

Dudley Street's residents are similarly diverse in terms of their cultural origins, but their shared economic straits and greater physical proximity, with its attendant common frustrations (if your curb is my curb, your eyesore is my eyesore), might seem to have made collaboration an obvious choice there. In this light, the lengths to which organizers have had to go to counter ethnic tensions are striking. The DSNI built proportional representation into its formal bylaws and instituted an informal practice of rotating leadership positions among the three major ethnic groups. Both practical and symbolic elements are inclusive by design: the brochure, newsletter, and meeting announcements are published in English, Spanish, and Cape Verdean Portuguese, while on neighborhood playgrounds, maps and murals celebrate residents' disparate origins.

Chicago's Near North Branch Library was carefully located and designed to bridge the Gold Coast and Cabrini Green, and in this it has been partially successful. Shared space may be a necessary condition for bridging, but it is not sufficient, as any observer of dining halls in formally integrated U.S. high schools and colleges knows. However the library system's active book groups do bridge ethnic, gender, class, and age distinctions, as does the Bezazian Branch's Neighborhood Writing Alliance, whose members gather weekly for workshops and readings. This fact mirrors evidence from other sources that, in general, the creative and performing arts bring together more ethnically diverse participants than any other type of association.[9]

Liz Lerman's professional life is dedicated to building on this particular strength, using participatory dance to create connection across social divides. The Portsmouth dance project aimed to bridge shipyard and town, which were divided both by social class (working class versus professionals) and by ideology (national defense versus "green" peaceniks). The process brought people from the two communities together, establishing intimacy and trust. Although the connection was symbolized by the ribbons joined on the Memorial Bridge in the grand finale, bridging social capital was actually built over the two long years of development and rehearsal, rather than in the performance itself.

Experience Corps aims to build intergenerational bonds, aware that "old heads" have disappeared from many inner-city neighborhoods.[10] The program turns out to be creating interethnic bridges as well, since within Philadelphia's program mostly African-American seniors are teaching many Latino kids. In a similar way, demographic change had created compound differences between UPS managers and their potential workers a generation earlier. Company leaders' proactive response was to send their managers—largely white, Irish Catholic, and ex-military—to work in inner cities, to build connections in the communities on which the company's future would depend. Three decades later, minorities hold more than a quarter of managerial positions, women make up one fifth of the company's U.S. workforce, and UPS is consistently ranked among *Fortune* magazine's "50 Best Companies for Minorities."

Birds of a feather flock together, folk wisdom tells us, but you don't need to be an ornithologist to know there's more to birds than feathers. In public debate these days, "diversity" is sometimes a code word referring to racial identity and nothing else. But of course as the above cases remind us, there are multiple, cross-cutting dimensions of differentiation in modern North American society. The corollary is that there are therefore multiple potential dimensions of similarity. Groups that bond along some axes can bridge along others. Many of Saddleback Church's small groups are organized around commonalities in family structure or life-cycle stage: singles groups, single-parents-of-teenage-children groups, mothers-of-preschoolers groups. Philadelphia's Experience Corps volunteers share the experience of living as elders in a society often blind to the abilities of its older citizens, a commonality that is emphasized by the program's rhetoric and that binds volunteers together regardless of race or creed.

Crafting cross-cutting identities is a powerful way to enable connection across perceived diversity. That is, bridging may depend on finding, emphasizing, or creating a new dimension of similarity within which bonding can occur. One often underestimated technique for creating new identities and bridging social distance, as well as for helping to create social capital in other ways, is telling stories.

Using Stories to Build Connections

Organizing is about transforming private aches and pains into a shared vision of collective action. Sometimes a single leader provides a compelling vision that links immediate issues to a broader project: George McLean played that role in Tupelo. But more often in our cases the process of "interest articulation" and "interest aggregation" (to use jargon from political science) emerged from carefully nurtured conversations among ordinary folks. Kris Rondeau stresses the need for HUCTW members to "find their own voice" within the union. The same insight pushes Do Something coaches to let kids "own" their projects. This means backing off—sometimes difficult for a conscientious teacher. So Do Something organizers repeat the mantra "Let young people lead."

Civic idealism can be an asset in community building, but creating social capital means recognizing people's interests and needs (including their need for fun and fellowship), not just their ideals. Social capital is not just about broccoli, but about chocolates, too. Craigslist works because it attracts people looking for apartments and jobs, dates and friends, not true believers in "virtual community." Modern dance worked to build community between lawyers and welders in Portsmouth because it was fun. Community builders need to start with what the participants really care about, not some external agenda. That is why storytelling turned out to be a crucial technique for building social capital in many of our stories.

Stories help people to construct and reconstruct their interests. For HUCTW and Valley Interfaith, personal storytelling is the very foundation of collective action. The key to organizing, Ernie Cortés and Kris Rondeau believe, is getting potential recruits to acknowledge and recognize their interests. Because the collective agenda grows out of overlapping personal stories, that agenda has far more staying power than it would were it imposed from without or formulated in advance.

Personal narratives are a uniquely powerful medium for expressing needs and building bonds. People like to tell their own stories; most like to listen to others' as well. The pleasures of narrative are addictive, as anyone who has found himself bleary-eyed with a great novel at three in the morning can attest. Craig Newmark reports that some people read his Web site's lists "just for the personal stories." Telling and listening to stories creates empathy and helps people find the things they have in common, which then eases the formation of enduring groups and networks. Reflecting on the unexpectedly prominent role of storytelling in our case studies, we find that three different sorts of narratives play roles in building and sustaining connection: "I" stories, "we" stories, and "they" stories.

Eliciting personal narratives can be an "easy-on ramp" for recruiting or integrating new members into an organization. By revealing vulnerabilities and creating empathy, "I" stories build trust. Recall how Mr. Ortiz's account of his grandson's death broke down barriers between him and the other parents at Palmer Elementary School. Liz Lerman elicited personal stories from potential dancers as a way to begin communicating across Portsmouth's great divide. She turned gestures from those stories into a meaning-laden vocabulary of movement and then retold the stories through dance to an audience that included the participating communities and spread beyond them. At every stage of the Shipyard Project storytelling was used to bridge gaps of understanding between the different communities.

Finding commonalities among "I" stories is a powerful technique. Reframing individual trajectories as a collective tale can create the crosscutting identities that turn bridging distance into bonding ties. We tell our own stories, and through our stories we redefine who "we" are. At both Saddleback and All Saints, members of small groups are encouraged to share their "spiritual autobiographies" as a key tool for transcending differences. When Dudley Street Community Center coordinator Pat Riddick put up a time line at a "unity meeting" and asked residents of different origins to tell the story of their involvement with the site, those present began to focus on their shared story of arrival and engagement, rather than the individual stories of entitlement they had brought into the room.

If "I" stories are essential to building new connections, "we" stories are equally valuable in sustaining those connections. Recounting how "we" overcame past obstacles and achieved unexpected successes reinforces shared identity and frames strategic choices for the future. The annual recalling of Jim Casey stories among UPS managers helps to burnish a particular corporate identity; hub workers spontaneously do the same when recalling the heroic exertions of Christmases past. Moreover, stories of collective triumph can be used to spread the gospel, as exemplified by Vaughn Grisham's ongoing effort to publicize the Tupelo story.

Sometimes it is argued that collective identity necessarily implies exclusion, that every "we" requires a "they." What is the role played in social-capital building by stories about the "target" of the organizing, about "the enemy"?

Having an enemy can help to create social capital. Social historian Theda Skocpol has shown that the successive waves of association building in America have been closely associated with major wars.[11] In *Bowling Alone,* Putnam reported that World War II played an important role in creating the "long civic generation." In the aftermath of the September 11 attacks, trust among Americans of all races and ethnicities shot upward.[12] Community organizers from Saul Alinsky on the left to Ralph Reed on the right have recognized the usefulness of identifying an enemy. As Reed once noted, "It's no accident that it's called 'Mothers Against Drunk Driving,' not 'Mothers for Sober Driving.' "

Moreover, substantive progress on an organization's agenda often genuinely does require conflict, not merely as a technique for "consciousness raising" but in order to solve the problem at hand. If Dudley Street was to be cleaned up, the organizers understood, they would have to take on both City Hall and the trash dumpers. "Don't Dump on Us" was not just a rallying cry, it was a substantive policy. Social capitalists cannot shun conflict.

We are struck, however, that many of our success stories involve organizations that work hard to avoid demonizing "the enemy," even in tense and conflict-ridden situations. The TIAF strategically pairs its hard-nosed accountability sessions with the commitment to maintain working relations with politicians who oppose it. Kris Rondeau sought to build a cooperative relationship with Harvard even while fighting Harvard for recognition. Recall the HUCTW slogan, "It's not anti-Harvard to be pro-union." HUCTW's contract is unusually short, and not a single grievance has yet been filed under it. Even the fervently evangelical Saddleback ministers do not demonize the unchurched. Rick Warren is not Cotton Mather. Saddleback was built less by brimstone and fire than by the promise of sociability.

In fact, given the role that "enemies" play in many theoretical accounts of community building, we were surprised to notice that in many of our cases—the Shipyard Project, Do Something, Experience Corps, the Chicago libraries, craigslist, Tupelo—it is virtually impossible to discern any enemy at all against whom the organizers sought to rally support. We cannot aspire to the close-knit community of Salem, it is sometimes said, without finding witches to shun. No witches, no Salem. Yet in many of our stories, participants have forged strong bonds of connection without demonizing anyone.

Slow Boring of Hard Boards

Real social change takes time—lots of it. In the tumultuous winter of 1919, as young German democrats grappled with issues of fundamental political and social reform in the aftermath of World War I, a group of students sought counsel from Max Weber, the distinguished social theorist. His response, "Politics as Vocation," is a classic statement of the practical ethics of public life.[13] Wary of the easy lure of quick fixes, Weber used a humble, craftsmanlike metaphor to convey the importance of patient, steady persistence. Social and political change, he explained, requires "a strong and slow boring of hard boards."

Successful community builders in our cases, too, recognize that crafting lasting relationships and mutual trust takes time. The heart of the Portsmouth Shipyard Project was the nearly two years of preparation rather than the week of performance, as satisfying as that proved to be. As Paula Rais observed, "You need time to meet, to get to know one another and trust each other, to let common issues bubble to the surface." Building trust among the various factions in the Dudley Street neighborhood required five years of hard work; success in Tupelo took decades and is still ongoing.

Building social capital is neither all-or-nothing nor once-and-for-all. It is incremental and cumulative. Rick Warren has built the Saddleback congregation one family at a time, working each newcomer through a gradual process of affiliation, moving steadily from casual visitor to

Crowd (regular attenders) to Congregation (baptized members), to Committed (tithing activists), and finally to Core (those dedicated to ministering to others). Years of patient work, building relationships that could be formed only over time, were essential to the HUCTW organizing success, an approach to organizing that is criticized by conventional union organizers precisely because it is so time-intensive.

The path to success through connective strategies can be long. This means it is all the more important to take aim at concrete, discrete, and feasible targets along the way. In the cases above we saw small victories—the end of illegal dumping in Dudley, a railroad sign in Waupun, a sales tax increase in the Rio Grande Valley—build a crucial sense of efficacy. Importantly, these modest initial forays were framed in terms of a larger purpose of collective action, not as onetime events. Each small victory must be seen as a bite-size version of the larger vision.

Like the proverbial New England farmer asked for directions by a passer-by, social scientists and historians recently have called our attention to "path dependence," that is, where you can go and how to get there depend on which path brought you here. Some places you just can't get to from here, whereas others are easier to reach (depending on how you got here). Because building social capital and trust is cumulative, social life is replete with vicious circles. Weak social capital fosters the symptoms of social disintegration, such as crime and poverty, and those symptoms in turn further undermine social connections. Dudley Street, like many other central city neighborhoods in America in the 1980s and 1990s, was caught in just such a vicious circle, as was Tupelo in the 1930s. Within every vicious circle, however, are the seeds of a virtuous circle, for if you can make progress on building social capital, that progress will improve the conditions for further advance. Precisely that dynamic is visible in the Valley Interfaith and Tupelo cases, and others as well, interrupting the inimical "them as has, gits, and them as don't, don't" syndrome.

Awareness of the difficulty of building social capital where it is most needed leads naturally to the strategy, visible in many of our cases, of "recycling" whatever shards of social connectivity are available, that is, reusing existing social networks by directing them to new purposes. As Saul Alinsky, the renowned community organizer and godfather of the Industrial Areas Foundation, put it succinctly, "All organizing is re-organizing."

By working through existing church communities, for example, Valley Interfaith used preexisting ties of trust and reciprocity as the basis for a new, more socially activist movement. The national organizers of Do Something learned the same lesson when their initial strategy of creating local chapters failed, and they turned to a school-based strategy that drew on existing relationships, rather than having to recruit youngsters one by one. To reach beyond habitual readers, the Chicago Public Library works closely with schools as well, reaching parents through their children. To identify potential tutors, Experience Corps recycled the faint network embodied in the AARP mailing list, and Liz Lerman recycled the Portsmouth mayor's phone tree. Studies of social movements that range from the democracy movement that overturned the communist regime in East Germany to the antinuclear movement after the Three Mile Island disaster to the civil rights movement of the 1960s have shown that ideological commitment and objective self-interest are less powerful predictors of who gets involved than are preexisting friendship networks.[14]

"Find existing networks that can be recycled" is thus one important lesson for social capitalists. Movements that rely on that approach, however, need a complementary strategy for encouraging "walk-ins" and for reaching out to the socially disconnected. The Texas Industrial Areas Foundation uses house meetings and community marches to reach the disengaged. Mary Dempsey explains that the library must reach beyond existing reading groups to connect with, for example, immigrant groups. Dudley Street's cold-call door-knocking campaigns and Saddleback's smiling greeters represent comparable strategies for reaching beyond existing networks.

The path-dependent character of social-capital building means that in many ways success breeds success. In Dudley Street, the "Don't Dump on Us" campaign showed residents what they could accomplish by working together and laid the groundwork for bolder efforts. As people develop habits and skills of civic engagement, they can apply those resources in new domains. In Portland each successive wave of civic mobilization created new pools of activists that could be drawn on in subsequent efforts. Trust is a sociological breeder reactor.

But our cases also illustrate that success brings its own challenges to social capitalists. The success of the Near North Branch Library in helping to revitalize the neighborhood around Cabrini Green seems to have contributed to a process of gentrification that is undermining the capacity of that library to create bridges across lines of race and class. Dudley Street activists, too, have been conscious of the risks of gentrification, though so far they have been unusually successful in fostering "development without displacement." Tupelo, as we have seen, now grapples with the challenges posed not by poverty but by economic development. When people are no longer poor, the idea of shared fate (and shared solutions) is less persuasive. Mutual dependency is less visible and less urgent. To Portland's civic activists today, we discovered, the unparalleled successes of the 1970s and 1980s are less salient than the new challenges posed precisely by those successes.

A special challenge for social movements is how to sustain momentum through the inevitable periods of leadership transition. This is, of course, a classic organizational dilemma, what Max Weber termed the "routinization of charisma." One key is to develop grassroots leaders with autonomy—not just a single general and a mass of foot soldiers. Valley Interfaith and the other Texas Industrial Areas Foundation groups will probably survive the departure of Ernie Cortés precisely because TIAF consciously focuses on identifying and developing leaders from the community as a central organizational task.

In Portland, Mayor Goldschmidt and other officials created neighborhood government structures in the 1970s that supported citizen activism, not only providing opportunities for participation but embedding them in the government's decision-making process. Portland's trend toward civic reengagement was not halted by the exit of Goldschmidt and his cohort. Likewise, although Tupelo misses George McLean, the consultation and collaboration among local employers, educators, and elites has survived his passing. Community involvement in Tupelo has come to be embodied in multiple overlapping associations, which, just like participatory government structures in Portland, demand activism, channel it, and reward it. In each city sustainability resulted from structural changes that permanently affected the "return" on organizing.

It is less clear in other cases whether the connective strategies will survive the departure of founding leaders and activists. Will HUCTW still prefer a capella rehearsals to leafleting when Kris Rondeau and her cohort are no longer around? Will union organizers still take the time to follow members' personal lives and respond to their family crises? Part of the challenge comes from organizational fatigue and entropy—the difficulty of maintaining momentum once the excitement of early achievements is past. Part of the challenge comes from expansion and turnover, as people originally fired up by a unique vision are succeeded by people who have joined an ongoing enterprise. From Tupelo to UPS, those who have been nurtured by particular social-capital-rich environments speak of the struggle to "keep the spirit alive," of trying to craft an awareness of history that inspires rather than stultifies.

It is also worth noting that continuing social-capital formation may not mean continuing a particular project or group. Liz Lerman's Shipyard Project did not aim to be enduring; it aimed to be transformative, and there is evidence that it was. Jane Hirshberg left venue-based arts administration for community-based projects after the Shipyard Project gave her a taste of participatory art. Shipyard commander Peter Bowman joined the Portsmouth Music Hall board; Nancy Hill and other participants founded a new local arts group; veteran shipyard worker Charlie Lawrence continued performing in community theater. Clearly the skills, interests, and personal ties they developed through their involvement with Lerman's group have flourished even after the dance troupe moved on.

Creating Common Spaces:
Urban Planning, Local Media, and Technology

Again and again, we find that one key to creating social capital is to build in redundancy of contact. A single pitch is not enough, whether you are pitching unionization or Christian salvation. Common spaces for commonplace encounters are prerequisites for common conversations and common debate. Furthermore, networks that intersect and circles that overlap reinforce a sense of reciprocal obligation and extend the boundaries of empathy.

Sociologists refer to this aspect of social networks as "multistrandedness": how many different layers of connection do they unite? When you frequently encounter the same person at the market and the ball field and a political rally, your ties with her are multistranded. We saw in the pages above that particular practices can facilitate the forging of multistranded ties. Thus, Saddleback's lawn flags make visible the overlap among networks of religious community, neighborhood residence, and national identity. Like the "Are You Reading *Mockingbird*?" buttons in Chicago, they allow participants to recognize affiliations they share with folks they see every day, opening the door to the conversations that can turn shared interests or common membership into personal connection.

Urban planning, architecture, and technology can each foster redundancy and multistrandedness by creating opportunities for encounters that knit together existing ties. Because local arrays of built space and communications technology act as "background structural factors" in most of our cases, their true importance is not always manifest. But in certain of our cases, activists have made crafting spatial infrastructure a conscious priority. The Chicago library system altered its fundamental mission (and changed its physical planning) precisely because leaders recognized the importance of shared space for building community. Experience Corps organizers create places and occasions for their volunteers to meet up—mailboxes in the school office, a classroom with coffee and doughnuts to start the day—and human support networks flourish within them. "If this room wasn't here," says one volunteer, "we'd be in bad shape."

Urban design can facilitate the same dynamics on a larger scale. Tom McCall Waterfront Park was an important victory for social capitalists in Portland precisely because it replaced a superhighway (designed to speed commuters out of the city) with a public park (designed to foster common conversations and repeated encounters). Dudley Street activists struggled six years for a community center that could bring their weight-lifting benches, computer lab, and after-school programs under a single roof. Local post offices around the country used to provide sites for redundant, multistranded encounters, but that role as a site for social-capital creation was not part of the intended purpose of the U.S. Postal Service. Saving "inefficient" local post offices would have made more sense if their contribution to community building had been part of the cost-benefit equation.

Local newspapers that provide a forum for exchange among editors, reporters, readers, and residents (categories that themselves overlap) play a comparable role. In their pages, interviewers and interviewees explain innovations, rally support, display successes, tell personal stories that crystallize collective aims, and hold local leaders and organizations accountable to the community. Above all, they provide a common space for common arguments. It is no coincidence that Portland and Tupelo— the two cases in which social-capital building seems to have become fully embedded in the public life and governance processes of an entire city— both have unusually active and enduring local newspapers.

As we searched out case studies of social-capital formation for this book, we found new communications technologies to be most important as support and stimulus for long-standing forms of community, rather than as instigators of radically new "virtual communities" (despite the expectations of some optimistic pundits and despite our best efforts to find examples of the latter). The Do Something Web site turned out to be one of the least dynamic parts of the project, much to the founders' surprise. Yet in the same years the need to access resources available only online was drawing Chicagoans back into libraries, providing the public demand that has helped turn the new local libraries into crossroads and clearinghouses for the neighborhoods that surround them.

Craigslist, too, is both a crossroads and a clearinghouse for a physical community: the greater Bay Area. As is the case with the Chicago libraries, individuals turn to craigslist with a specific query. Again like the libraries, the richness of craigslist as a social site is the way disparate resources and myriad social networks overlap in a single space, so that one query leads to multiple encounters, which can deepen into ongoing relationships. In this sense craigslist is the very opposite of a narrowband listserv, where the only thing that links participants is their interest in one topic (be it 1964 T-birds or Italian politics) and the ties created online never overlap with participants' offline social worlds. Renting apartments and finding backgammon companions for trips to the Laundromat are not normally handled on the same channel. That they are in craigslist is the reason the Web site has become a true connective tissue for Bay Area lives.

Of course, it is still early in the life cycle of the Internet as a social force; the future may hold important innovations. We venture to suggest that those innovations that allow us to link virtual to other kinds of connections will be the most powerful in their effects. Computer-based technology matters not because it can create some new and separate form of virtual community, but because it can broaden and deepen and strengthen our physical communities. Just as an alloy is a mixture of several metals that has different and more advantageous properties than those of any of its constituents, so we should be aiming to craft alloys of electronic and face-to-face networks that are more powerful and useful than either kind alone.

Like plazas and parks, local newspapers, and neighborhood libraries, Internet technology could create social spaces within which we see how our numerous networks of interest and interaction overlap and intersect. In constructing any such spaces, we have a vital collective stake in fostering local input and ensuring public access. Claims about the economic benefits of privatization or consolidation in all these realms (urban spaces, municipal services, media, and communications) need to be evaluated in the light of social-capital "externalities," or we risk signing away vital community resources before we fully recognize their worth.

Over the past generation, America's communities have undergone profound social and cultural changes, which meant that as the new millennium dawned, we were no longer building the dense webs of encounter and participation so vital to the health of ourselves, our families, and our polities. These changes included the privatization of leisure time that accompanied the explosion of electronic entertainment; the labor market changes that drew ever greater numbers of adults out of home-based unpaid work and into long hours of paid employment; and the suburban sprawl that bifurcates our communities of residence from our communities of work.[15] Reweaving social webs will depend in part on the efforts of dedicated local leaders who choose to pursue their goals (whether teaching phonics, unionizing workers, or reducing on-the-job injuries) through the sometimes slow, frequently fractious, and profoundly transformative route of social-capital building. But reweaving will also depend on our ability to create new spaces for recognition, reconnection, conversation, and debate. Creating these spaces will require innovative uses of technology, creative urban and regional planning, and political will.

Notes

INTRODUCTION

1. In one respect we did not seek diversity: All our cases are United States—based because of practical limits on our ability to identify and evaluate potential cases of innovative social-capital building in other countries. Nevertheless, we believe that Americans have much to learn from cross-national comparison, as illustrated in part in the international case studies reported in *Democracies in Flux: The Evolution of Social Capital in Contemporary Society*, Robert D. Putnam, ed. (New York: Oxford University Press, 2002).

CHAPTER 1: VALLEY INTERFAITH

1. Dennis Shirley, *Valley Interfaith and School Reform* (Austin: University of Texas Press, 2002), p. 27.
2. Ibid.
3. Our thanks to Sister Judy Donovan for this story.
4. Catalina Mendiola, conversation with Feldstein, November 11, 2002.
5. Much of the background information about the IAF and the development of the Texas IAF comes from Dennis Shirley, *Community Organizing for Urban School Reform* (Austin: University of Texas Press, 1997) and Mark R. Warren, *Dry Bones Rattling: Community Building to Revitalize American Democracy* (Princeton: Princeton University Press, 2001).
6. Ernesto Cortés, Jr., "Reweaving the Social Fabric," in *The Southwest IAF Network: 25 Years of Organizing*, Alicia Hernandez-Sánchez, ed. (Austin: Interfaith Education Fund, 1999), p. 58.

7. Shirley, *Community Organizing for Urban School Reform*, pp. 39–41.
8. Cortés, "Reweaving the Social Fabric."
9. Ernesto Cortés, Jr., "Reclaiming Our Birthright," in *The Southwest IAF Network*, p. 4.
10. Ernesto Cortés, Jr., quoted in Cheryl Dahle, "Social Justice: Ernesto Cortés Jr.," *Fast Company*, no. 30 (December 1999), p. 294.
11. Joe Hinosa, conversation with Feldstein.
12. Hinosa, conversation with Feldstein.
13. Shirley, *Community Organizing for Urban School Reform* and *Valley Interfaith and School Reform*.
14. See Warren, *Dry Bones Rattling*, p. 84.
15. Geoff Rips, *Changing the Political Culture of the Texas Border: The Industrial Areas Foundation and Texas Colonias* (Austin: Texas Center for Policy Studies, September 2000), p. 27.
16. Texas Health and Human Services Commission, Health and Human Services Commission data on the Web (taken from "Lower Rio Grande Fact Sheet, Valley Interfaith").
17. State and Valley numbers are 1999 data from Texas Department of Human Services; U.S. 1996 data come from "Health Insurance Status of the Civilian Non-institutionalized Population" (from fact sheet).
18. Idaleica Valdez, conversation with Feldstein, November 11, 2002.
19. Cortés, "Reclaiming Our Birthright," p. 7.
20. From Ed Chambers, *Organizing for Family and Congregation*, quoted in Warren, *Dry Bones Rattling*, p. 213.
21. Warren, *Dry Bones Rattling*, p. 95.
22. Marshall Ganz, "Making Democracy Work?" *Contexts*, vol. 1 (Fall 2002), pp. 62–63. For an insightful description and evaluation of Valley Interfaith and the Texas Industrial Areas Foundation, see Paul Osterman, *Gathering Power: The Future of Progressive Politics in America* (Boston: Beacon Press, 2002).

CHAPTER 2: BRANCH LIBRARIES

1. Geoffrey Nunberg, "Will Libraries Survive?" *American Prospect*, vol. 9, no. 41 (November/December 1998).
2. Cited by Commissioner of Libraries Mary Dempsey in an interview by Evan St. Lifer, *Library Journal*, May 15, 2001, p. 41.
3. Mayor Richard M. Daley, quoted in Eleanor Jo Rodger, "Helping Cities Work," *Library Journal*, May 15, 2001, p. 42.

4. Ray Oldenburg, *The Great Good Place: Cafés, Coffee Shops, Community Centers, Beauty Parlors, General Stores, Bars, Hangouts, and How They Get You Through the Day,* 2d ed. (New York: Marlowe, 1997).

CHAPTER 3: THE SHIPYARD PROJECT

1. Most of the information in this chapter is taken from interviews with Jane Hirshberg, Liz Lerman, Nancy Hill, Paula Rais, Charlie Lawrence, Peter Bowman, and Genevieve Aichele by Don Cohen in April 2002.
2. Interview in the video *The Shipyard Dance: Art Meets the Military* (Acadia Pictures, Kittery, Maine, 1998).
3. *The Shipyard Dance.*

CHAPTER 4: THE DUDLEY STREET NEIGHBORHOOD INITIATIVE

1. Quotations from Julio Henriquez, Egidio Teixeira, Catherine Flannery, Ruth Grant, and Joe Susi, and some quotes from John Barros, are from conversations with Lois Shea, September 2002.
2. This and other quotations from Bob Holmes are from a phone interview by Cohen, July 3, 2002.
3. Charles Finn, quoted in Peter Medoff and Holly Sklar, *Streets of Hope: The Rise and Fall of an Urban Neighborhood* (Boston: South End Press, 1994), p. 25.
4. Medoff and Sklar, *Streets of Hope,* p. 12.
5. See "Dudley Neighborhood Profile," report prepared for Urban Village Working Group, Dudley Street Neighborhood Initiative, by the Local Learning Partnership, Abt Associates Inc., and MAPC (2003) and Holly Sklar, "Dudley Street Neighborhood Initiative: Building on Success, 1984–2002" (Dudley Street Neighborhood Initiative document, 2002).
6. Bob Holmes, quoted in Medoff and Sklar, *Streets of Hope,* p. 42.
7. Holmes interview by Cohen.
8. Bill Slotnik, quoted in Medoff and Sklar, *Streets of Hope,* p. 53.
9. Tito Fuster, interview by Cohen, June 11, 2002.
10. Medoff and Sklar, *Streets of Hope,* p. 57.
11. The history of DSNI's early activities is taken mainly from Medoff and Sklar, *Streets of Hope.*
12. Medoff and Sklar, *Streets of Hope,* p. 69.
13. Holmes interview by Cohen.

14. Mayor Ray Flynn, quoted in Medoff and Sklar, *Streets of Hope*, p. 142.

15. Herbert J. Gans, *The Urban Villagers: Group and Class in the Life of Italian-Americans* (New York: Free Press, 1962).

16. Discussion of the development process is from Pat Riddick interview by Cohen, June 11, 2002.

17. "Rebuilding Communities Initiative Resident Survey," 1996.

18. John Barros, interview by Cohen, June 16, 2002.

CHAPTER 5: THE TUPELO MODEL

1. Laura Nan Fairley, "George A. McLean and the *Tupelo Journal*," *The Press and Race*, David R. Davies, ed. (Jackson: University of Mississippi Press, 2001), p. 142. Much of the Tupelo story presented here is derived from the work of Vaughn L. Grisham, Jr., especially his *Tupelo: The Evolution of a Community* (Dayton, Ohio: Kettering Foundation Press, 1999) and his conversations with Cohen in March 2002.

2. Vaughn Grisham and Rob Gurwitt, *Hand in Hand: Community and Economic Development in Tupelo* (Washington, D.C.: Aspen Institute, Rural Economic Policy Program, 1999), p. 12; www.census.gov/hhes/www/income/cphls/cphl123p.html, "Counties Ranked by Per Capita Income Within the United States and Within the State: 1989," pp. 81, 82; Putnam interview with Stuart A. Rosenfeld, April 9, 2003; Helene Cooper, "Tupelo, Miss., Concocts an Effective Recipe for Economic Health: Education, Racial Harmony Lure Firms, Which Then Are Expected to Pitch In," *Wall Street Journal*, March 3, 1994, A1.

3. George McLean, "Rural Community Development," 1946, quoted in Grisham, *Tupelo*, p. 94.

4. Hodding Carter, "Tupelo, Miss.," *Saturday Evening Post*, February 17, 1951.

5. Grisham, *Tupelo*, p. 94.

6. Grisham and Gurwitt, *Hand in Hand*, p. 35; Grisham, *Tupelo*, pp. 14, 16.

7. Grisham and Gurwitt, *Hand in Hand*, pp. 53–54.

8. Ibid., pp. 51–52.

9. Lewis Whitfield, former president, Deposit Guarantee Bank, and chair, CREATE, interview by Feldstein, November 9, 2002.

10. Whitfield, conversation with Feldstein.

11. Lloyd Gray, conversation with Feldstein, November 18, 2002.

12. Gray, conversation with Feldstein, November 9, 2002.

13. Cooper, *Wall Street Journal*, A6.

14. Hodding Carter III, e-mail to Feldstein, October 24, 2002; Cooper, *Wall Street Journal*, A6.
15. Grisham and Gurwitt, *Hand in Hand*, p. 63.
16. Bo Beaulieu, director, Southern Rural Development Center, Mississippi State University, correspondence with Feldstein, October 21, 2002.

CHAPTER 6: SADDLEBACK CHURCH

1. For a detailed overview of trends in religious participation in America, see Robert D. Putnam, *Bowling Alone: The Collapse of American Community* (New York: Simon & Schuster, 2000), pp. 65–79. Our account of Saddleback and All Saints congregations in this chapter comes in part from interviews with congregants and leaders, as named in the text, by Cohen, May 2002.
2. Patricia Leigh Brown, "Megachurches as Minitowns," *New York Times*, May 9, 2002, D1.
3. Rick Warren, *The Purpose-Driven Church: Growth Without Compromising Your Message & Mission* (Grand Rapids, Michigan: Zondervan, 1995), pp. 169–171, 290.
4. Ibid., p. 290.
5. Lyle E. Schaller, *The Very Large Church: New Rules for Leaders* (Nashville: Abingdon Press, 2000), p. 214.
6. Charles Trueheart, "Welcome to the Next Church," *Atlantic Monthly*, August 1996, p. 54.
7. Warren, *Purpose-Driven Church*, p. 312.
8. Ibid., p. 324.
9. Ibid., p. 173.
10. Schaller, *Very Large Church*, p. 50.
11. Ibid., p. 42.
12. Ibid., p. 30.
13. Ibid., pp. 50, 97.

CHAPTER 7: DO SOMETHING

1. Quotations from program participants come from interviews by Don Cohen and Sara Hallman, April 2002.
2. For overviews of the evidence on youth civic engagement and the long-run effects on adult participation, see Constance A. Flanagan and Nakesha

Faison, "Youth Civic Development: Implications of Research for Social Policy and Programs," *Social Policy Report,* vol. 15, 2001, pp. 3–16; William A. Galston, "Political Knowledge, Political Engagement, and Civic Education," *Annual Review of Political Science,* vol. 4 (2001), pp. 217–234; Cynthia Gibson, *From Inspiration to Participation: A Review of Perspectives on Youth Civic Engagement* (report to the Grantmaker Forum on Community and National Service, 2001), at www.gfcns.org/pubs/Moving%20Youth%20report%20REV3.pdf; M. Kent Jennings and Laura Stoker, "Generations and Civic Engagement: A Longitudinal Multiple-Generation Analysis" (paper presented at the annual meeting of the American Political Science Association, San Francisco, August 30–September 2, 2001); Mary K. Kirlin, "The Role of Adolescent Extracurricular Activities in Adult Political Engagement," working paper 02, University of Maryland Center for Information and Research on Civic Learning and Engagement, March 2003, at www.civicyouth.org/PopUps/WP02%20Kirlin%20no%20cover.pdf; and Robert D. Putnam, *Bowling Alone.* For the Stanford conference conclusions, see Judith Torney-Purta et al., "Creating Citizenship: Youth Development for a Free and Democratic Society," Executive Summary: Conference Consensus Document, Stanford Center on Adolescence, 1999, at www.stanford.edu/group/adolescent.ctr/Conference/confindex.html, p. 1.
3. Some of this information is taken from a May 2000 interview with Andrew Shue by Sarah M. and Whitney S., published online at www.teenink.com.
4. Anthony Welch, phone interview by Cohen, May 6, 2002.

CHAPTER 8: THE HARVARD UNION OF CLERICAL AND TECHNICAL WORKERS

1. John P. Hoerr, *We Can't Eat Prestige: The Women Who Organized Harvard* (Philadelphia: Temple University Press, 1997).
2. Arnold Zack, interview by Feldstein, October 13, 2002.
3. Kate Bronfenbrenner, Sheldon Friedman, Richard W. Hurd, Rudolph A. Oswald, and Ronald L. Seeber, *Organizing to Win: New Research on Union Strategies* (Ithaca, N.Y.: Cornell University Press, 1998), pp. 1, 6. Bronfenbrenner and her colleagues offer evidence that bottom-up, person-to-person organizing is more effective than the traditional approach, and they present case studies of several unions, such as the Service Employees International Union (SEIU) and the Union of Needle Trades, Industrial, and Textile Employees (UNITE), that have experimented with the grassroots approach.
4. Ted Barrett, Quoted in Hoerr, *We Can't Eat Prestige,* p. 177.

5. A fuller account of the failed campaigns appears in Hoerr's *We Can't Eat Prestige*, from which, again, much of this information is taken.

6. See Hoerr, *We Can't Eat Prestige*, p. 103.

7. Ibid., p. 95.

8. Kris Rondeau, interview by Cohen, March 8, 2002.

9. Joyce Guarnieri, Ken Tivey, Evan Keely, Shauna Cagan, and Margot Chamberlain were interviewed by Lois Shea.

10. Rondeau interview, March 8, 2002.

11. Anne Taylor, interview by Cohen, March 11, 2002.

12. Kris Rondeau, in "Women's Ways of Organizing," interview by Lisa Oppenheim, no. 1991; *Labor Research Review*, 18, no. 1991; Center for Labor and Community Research, 1991, p. 50.

13. Gladys McKenzie, in "Women's Ways of Organizing," pp. 50–51.

14. Taylor interview.

15. See Ellen O'Conner, "The Union Kind," *Worcester Magazine*, August 27–September 2, 1997, p. 14.

16. Hoerr, *We Can't Eat Prestige*, p. 122.

17. Marie Manna, interview by Cohen, March 26, 2002.

18. Rondeau interview, March 8, 2002.

19. Hoerr, *We Can't Eat Prestige*, pp. 186–189.

20. This and other Rondeau comments from an interview by Feldstein, January 3, 2003.

21. Hoerr, *We Can't Eat Prestige*, pp. 225–226.

22. Ibid., p. 226.

23. Ibid., p. 240.

24. Rondeau interview, March 8, 2002.

25. Elisabeth Szanto, quoted in O'Conner, "The Union Kind," p. 12.

26. O'Connor, "The Union Kind," p. 10.

27. Rondeau interview, March 8, 2002.

28. Taylor interview.

CHAPTER 9: EXPERIENCE CORPS

1. Harris Wofford interview with Feldstein, March 3, 2003.

2. "Lesson for Life: Experience Corps," *Civic Ventures Innovations* 2 (Fall 2001) (published by Civic Ventures, San Francisco).

3. Marc Freedman, interview by Cohen, February 9, 2002. The brief history of Experience Corps told here is derived from Marc Freedman, *Prime Time: How Baby Boomers Will Revolutionize Retirement and Transform America*

(New York: Public Affairs, 1999), and from the interview with Freedman by Cohen.

4. Sargent Shriver, quoted in Freedman, *Prime Time*, p. 86.

5. See Freedman, *Prime Time*, pp. 175–179.

6. Robert Tietze, interview by Cohen, Philadelphia, February 20, 2002.

7. Elijah Anderson, *Streetwise: Race, Class, and Change in an Urban Community* (Chicago: University of Chicago Press, 1990), p. 3.

8. Marc Freedman and Linda Fried, *Launching Experience Corps* (San Francisco: Civic Ventures, January 1999), p. 60.

9. Freedman, *Prime Time*, p. 16.

CHAPTER 10: UPS

1. Details of Walter Hooke's involvement with the internship come from a conversation Don Cohen had on June 27, 2002, with Ed Cahill, current director of the program in Chattanooga, and from a 1997 UPS videotaped interview with Hooke, Cahill, and Aileen Hernandez.

2. For evidence on the links between social capital and work, see Putnam, *Bowling Alone*, chapters 5 and 11, and the many works cited there.

3. Some material for this chapter comes from Don Cohen's research on UPS for *In Good Company*, written with Laurence Prusak. For a discussion of driver lunchtime conversations, see Cohen and Prusak, *In Good Company: How Social Capital Makes Organizations Work* (Boston: Harvard Business School Press, 2001), p. 95.

4. Jim Kelly, quoted in Cohen and Prusak, *In Good Company*, p. 22.

5. George D. Smith, *Our Partnership Legacy* (Greenwich, Conn.: UPS, 1970), pp. 44–45.

6. Linda Kaboolian, conversation with Putnam, September 2002.

7. Cost of lost business is from Barbara Durr and Ien Cheng, "How UPS Delivered a New Deal," *Financial Times*, August 1, 2002.

8. Lea Soupata is quoted in Durr and Cheng, "How UPS Delivered a New Deal."

9. Durr and Cheng, "How UPS Delivered a New Deal."

10. "Checking Up on CHSP," *Inside UPS*, April 1999, p. 4.

CHAPTER 11: CRAIGSLIST.ORG

1. UCLA Internet report, "Surveying the Digital Future: Year Three" (Los Angeles: UCLA Center for Communication Policy, January 2003), pp. 19, 54.

Of course, another important use of the Internet for most people is information processing and retrieval. That, too, is having powerful effects on our lives—this book, for example, could hardly have been completed without our ability to retrieve information from the Web easily. However, information processing and retrieval in itself does not build social capital, so we disregard that function here.

2. Ibid., p. 55.

3. Unless otherwise noted, quotations from Craig Newmark are from a phone interview with Cohen, August 29, 2002.

4. Craig Newmark, interview with Katharine Mieszkowski, *Net Company*, Winter 2000, p. 26.

5. Andrew Cohill and Andrea Kavanaugh, *Community Networks: Lessons from Blacksburg, Virginia* (Norwood, Mass.: Artech House, 2000).

6. Bill Werde, "A Web Site as 18-Ring Circus of Supply and Demand," *New York Times*, January 23, 2003; Anita Hamilton, "Find It on Craig's List," *Time*, March 3, 2003.

7. Howard Rheingold, *The Virtual Community: Homesteading on the Electronic Frontier* (Reading, Mass.: Addison-Wesley, 1993).

8. Ibid., p. 2.

9. Ibid., pp. 2, 32.

10. William A. Galston, "(How) Does the Internet Affect Community? Some Speculation in Search of Evidence," in Elaine Ciulla Kamarck and Joseph S. Nye Jr., eds., *democracy.com? Governance in a Networked World* (Hollis, N.H.: Hollis Publishing, 1999), p. 53.

CHAPTER 12: PORTLAND

1. On Portland's neighborhood government, see Ken Thomson, *From Neighborhood to Nation: The Democratic Foundations of Civil Society* (Lebanon, N.H.: University Press of New England, 2001), pp. 137–138; Jeffrey M. Berry, Kent E. Portney, and Ken Thomson, *The Rebirth of Urban Democracy* (Washington, D.C.: Brookings Institution Press, 1993).

2. The survey evidence presented here is drawn from the Roper Social and Political Trends archive, 1973–1994, as described in Putnam, *Bowling Alone*, p. 420, and available at www.ropercenter.uconn.edu/dataacq/roper_trends.html. Unfortunately, the archive ends in 1994. For the present analysis we isolated all respondents from Oregon from a city with a population between 250,000 and 1 million or a suburb of such a city. (Portland was the only such city.) We then compared the metropolitan Portland responses to

responses from all other comparably sized cities in America. For these two decades the archive includes 4,086 respondents from Portland and approximately 103,300 respondents from other comparably sized metropolitan areas. Although we present here only the simplest results, year by year, we also confirmed that the patterns reported in the text hold true even when controlling for the variables of age, education, gender, race, and income. We also explored the differences between central cities and suburbs; both Portland and its suburbs experienced the civic boom, although the effects were somewhat greater in the city itself. We found no evidence of any comparable civic boom in Oregon outside of the Portland metropolitan area, nor in Seattle, Washington, another northwest metropolis to which Portland is sometimes compared.

3. Carl Abbott, *Greater Portland: Urban Life and Landscape in the Pacific Northwest* (Philadelphia: University of Pennsylvania Press, 2001), pp. 136–138.

4. Figure on reading expenditures cited in Abbott, *Greater Portland,* p. 23.

5. Abbott, *Greater Portland,* pp. 81–82.

6. Ibid., p. 140.

7. Steven Johnson, "The Transformation of Civic Institutions and Practices in Portland, Oregon, 1960–1999" (doctoral dissertation, 2002), p. 29.

8. Ibid., p. 14. The authors thank Johnson for his generosity in sharing his fascinating dissertation and his time.

9. Betsy Hammond, "Rules Mingle Income Groups," *Oregonian,* May 15, 2002.

10. Abbott, *Greater Portland,* p. 161.

11. Ibid., p. 6.

12. Ibid., pp. 76, 77.

13. Except when other sources are indicated, the comments of Portlanders are derived from interviews with Cohen in September 2002.

14. Abbott, *Greater Portland,* p. 84.

15. Johnson, "Transformation of Civic Institutions and Practices."

16. Abbott, *Greater Portland,* pp. 167–168.

17. Johnson, "Transformation of Civic Institutions and Practices," p. 1.

18. Ibid., p. 4.

19. Ibid., pp. 1–3.

20. Ibid., pp. 36–37.

21. Ethan Seltzer, interview by Cohen, September 11, 2002.

22. Johnson, "Transformation of Civic Institutions and Practices," p. 35.

23. Abbott, *Greater Portland,* p. 125.

24. Ibid.

25. Berry et al., *The Rebirth of Urban Democracy*, as summarized in Thomson, *From Neighborhood to Nation*, p. 106.
26. Johnson, "Transformation of Civic Institutions and Practices," p. 11.
27. Abbott, *Greater Portland*, p. 205.

CONCLUSION: MAKING SOCIAL CAPITAL WORK

1. For evidence, see Putnam, *Bowling Alone*, section 4.
2. For evidence, see Putnam, *Bowling Alone*, section 3.
3. See "Better Together: Report of the Saguaro Seminar on Civic Engagement in America" (Cambridge, Mass.: John F. Kennedy School of Government, Harvard University, 2000) at www.bettertogether.org.
4. For evidence, see Putnam, *Bowling Alone*.
5. On the role of federated groups in American history, see Theda Skocpol, *Diminished Democracy: From Membership to Management in American Civic Life* (Norman: University of Oklahoma Press, 2003).
6. For one vivid example, see Ashutosh Varshney, *Ethnic Conflict and Civic Life: Hindus and Muslims in India* (New Haven: Yale University Press, 2002), in which Varshney found that murderous violence between Hindus and Muslims in India is substantially inhibited by what we term "bridging social capital" in Indian communities.
7. Even though the Tupelo innovations took place during the civil rights movement in Mississippi, racial bridging is not a major part of that story. On the other hand, George McLean and his colleagues were much less committed to segregation than their counterparts elsewhere in the South in that era, and race relations in Tupelo may be better than elsewhere in the area.
8. On the efforts of the Texas Industrial Areas Foundation to manage ethnic and religious diversity, see Warren, *Dry Bones Rattling: Community Building to Revitalize American Democracy* (Princeton: Princeton University Press, 2001).
9. This finding appears, for example, in the Social Capital Community Benchmark Survey, which we conducted in 2000. For more details on this survey, see www.ksg.harvard.edu/saguaro/communitysurvey/.
10. See Elijah Anderson, *Code of the Street: Decency, Violence, and the Moral Life of the Inner City* (New York: W. W. Norton, 1999).
11. Theda Skocpol, "United States," in *Democracies in Flux: The Evolution of Social Capital in Contemporary Society*, ed. Robert D. Putnam (New York: Oxford University Press, 2002).

12. Putnam, *Bowling Alone*, chapter 14; Robert D. Putnam, "Bowling Together: The United State of America," *American Prospect*, vol. 13 (February 11, 2002), pp. 20–22.

13. Max Weber, "Politics as a Vocation," in *From Max Weber: Essays in Sociology*, eds. H. H. Gerth and C. Wright Mills (New York: Oxford University Press, 1946), pp. 77–128 (quotation at p. 128).

14. For evidence, see Putnam, *Bowling Alone*, chapter 9.

15. For evidence, see Putnam, *Bowling Alone*, section 3.

Index